Introduction to Counselling Skills

Praise for the book

'This text is a welcome addition to the literature available to both student and lecturer; professional and interested member of the public; novice and expert. The careful exploration of terms and the identification of skills enable the reader to relate the contents to their own particular situation. Each chapter has clearly identified outcomes, facilitating the reader to assess their progress. The numerous examples are practical and relevant. Inclusion of activities throughout the book facilitates the reader's engagement with, and learning through, the process. Using clear and readily accessible language, the RUC model is shown to be applicable across a wide range of contexts.'

Dorothy Ferguson, Medical Social Worker and grief therapist

'This book is a superb reference for counselling skills trainers and students. It presents practical key skills that are described and discussed clearly and concisely. Each chapter is completed by imaginative and helpful exercises that facilitate the reader to fully experience and integrate the focus of learning.'

Dr Margaret E. Smith, Programme Leader/Senior Lecturer, University of Derby

'This book is now in its third edition and interestingly adds two relevant sub-themes to its impressive range of subject matter as well as an updated reference list. The text (and accompanying exercises) offers a sound, practical and accessible introduction that serves to ground the purpose, application and practice of counselling skills, underpinned by apposite and judicious author observations. It will appeal to a cross section of professional, educational and training contexts including health, care, social work and counselling disciplines.'

Gerry Skelton, social work and counselling educator, trainer and practitioner

'A useful update to the previous edition, particularly with the addition of the two new chapters on relaxation intervention and managing crises. These issues are often overlooked in counselling training. The book is useful even for the novice practitioner.'

Debbie Thackray, Senior Lecturer in Social Work, Manchester Metropolitan University

Introduction to Counselling Skills

Text and Activities

Third Edition

Richard Nelson-Jones

Los Angeles • London • New Delhi • Singapore • Washington DC

First edition published 2000
Reprinted 2001, 2003, 2004
Second edition published 2005
Reprinted 2006

This third edition published 2009

SAGE Publications Ltd
1 Oliver's Yard
55 City Road
London EC1Y 1SP

SAGE Publications Inc.
2455 Teller Road
Thousand Oaks, California 91320

SAGE Publications India Pvt Ltd
B 1/I 1 Mohan Cooperative Industrial Area
Mathura Road
New Delhi 110 044

SAGE Publications Asia-Pacific Pte Ltd
33 Pekin Street #02-01
Far East Square
Singapore 048763

Library of Congress Control Number: 2007937134

British Library Cataloguing in Publication data

A catalogue record for this book is available from the British
Library

ISBN 978-1-84787-338-5
ISBN 978-1-84787-339-2 (pbk)

Typeset by CEPHA Imaging Pvt. Ltd., Bangalore, India
Printed in Great Britain by The Cromwell Press Ltd, Trowbridge,
Wiltshire
Printed on paper from sustainable resources

Contents

List of activities

Preface

Welcome to the third edition of *Introduction to Counselling Skills: Text and Activities*. The following are answers to some questions that you may have about the book.

What is the book's purpose?

This is an introductory book not just for those wishing to become counsellors and psychotherapists, but also for those wanting to help others in professional and voluntary settings. This breadth of readership is made possible with an introductory book, since the basic skills of counselling, psychotherapy and helping are essentially the same. However, those wishing for a briefer book on helping are referred to the latest edition of my *Basic Counselling Skills: A Manual for Helpers*, whereas those wanting a more advanced book are referred to the latest edition of my *Practical Counselling and Helping Skills*.

Who is this book intended for?

I intend the book to be for the following audiences:

- lecturers teaching practical classes in counselling skills in colleges, universities, adult education centres and voluntary settings;
- students in educational settings who are training for counselling and helping services: for instance as counsellors, psychologists, nurses, health care workers, social workers, youth workers, community workers, welfare advisers, personnel officers, human relations consultants, pastoral care workers, and teachers;
- students developing counselling and helping skills in voluntary agencies: for instance agencies focused on marital and relationship work, the bereaved, lesbian and gay people, those in crisis, and the mentally ill; and
- interested readers who are not on training courses.

What are the book's contents?

Part One consists of five introductory chapters. Chapter 1 answers the question of who are counsellors, psychotherapists and helpers. Chapters 2 and 3 introduce the notion that people possess communication skills and mind skills that can be used for good or ill. In addition, time is spent describing feelings and physical reactions and stating why they are not skills. Chapters 4 and 5 focus on the three stages of the Relating–Understanding–Changing (RUC) counselling and helping process and on the importance of creating strong relationships with clients.

Part Two covers the relating stage of the RUC model. Chapter 6 shows readers how to respond to clients from the internal – as contrasted with the external – frame of reference. Chapter 7 focuses on body messages for showing attention and interest. Chapter 8 trains readers in reflecting both feelings and the reasons for them. Chapter 9 describes how to start the counselling and helping process and Chapter 10 deals with problems like managing resistant clients and making referrals.

Part Three covers the understanding stage of the RUC model. Chapters 11, 12 and 13 focus on assessing how clients feel and physically react, think, and communicate and act. Chapter 14 covers some additional skills, such as challenging clients, giving them feedback and self-disclosing to them. Chapter 15 looks at how to monitor clients' behaviour, make summaries as appropriate and identify some mind skills and communication/action skills to improve.

Part Four covers the RUC model's changing stage. Chapter 16 deals 'with the how to solve problems' approach, in which counsellors or helpers facilitate change for clients. Chapter 17 describes the coaching skills of speaking, demonstrating and rehearsing clients in changed ways of thinking and communicating. Chapters 18 and 19 present a series of interventions for improving how clients communicate and act and also for improving their mind skills, for instance creating rules, perceptions and self-talk. Chapter 20 on negotiating homework, Chapter 21 on conducting middle sessions and Chapter 22 on terminating counselling and helping each provide you with practical information on how to perform these tasks.

Part Five presents some further considerations. Chapter 23 focuses on relaxation and meditation, while Chapter 26 discusses ways of helping clients to manage crises. Chapter 25 looks at different characteristics that counsellors or helpers and clients may possess, for instance culture and race. Chapter 26 examines some ethical issues and dilemmas, both of counselling and helping and of being a student. Chapter 27 makes some suggestions for running and participating in training groups and supervision. Chapter 28 looks at the main theoretical schools and approaches to counselling and then reviews some research issues. Finally Chapter 29 gives you some ideas about where to go next in developing your counselling and helping skills and in becoming more human.

Apart from Chapter 1, each chapter contains some activities to help you develop your knowledge and skills. Though I assume that you are learning introductory counselling and helping skills in a group, this may not always be the case. Nevertheless, you may still want to perform the activities either on your own or, if possible, with a partner. When doing the activities, all concerned should ensure that no one feels under pressure to reveal any personal information she or he does not want to. In addition, the book contains a glossary of counselling and helping terms.

Acknowledgements

I warmly thank the following people at Sage who have helped to bring this book to published light: Alison Poyner and the editorial staff and also the manuscript production and design staff whose efforts contributed to the quality of the final product.

A final word

I wish you every success in attaining your objective of improving your counselling skills so that you can help clients to lead more effective lives.

Richard Nelson-Jones

'Guided tour' of pedagogical features

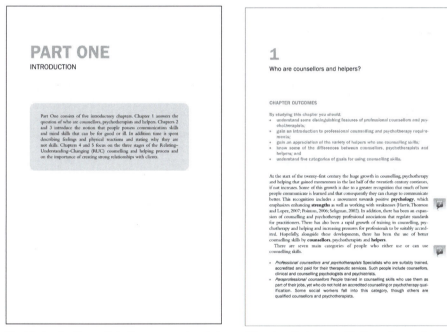

PART ONE

INTRODUCTION

Part One consists of five introductory chapters. Chapter 1 answers the question of who are counsellors, psychotherapists and helpers. Chapters 2 and 3 introduce the notion that people possess communication skills and mind skills that can be for good or ill. In addition time is spent describing feelings and physical reactions and stating why they are not skills. Chapters 4 and 5 focus on the three stages of the Relating–Understanding–Changing (RUC) counselling and helping process and on the importance of creating strong relationships with clients.

1

Who are counsellors and helpers?

CHAPTER OUTCOMES

By studying this chapter you should:
- understand some distinguishing features of professional counsellors and psychotherapists;
- gain an introduction to professional counselling and psychotherapy requirements;
- gain an appreciation of the variety of helpers who use counselling skills;
- know some of the differences between counsellors, psychotherapists and helpers; and
- understand five categories of goals for using counselling skills.

At the start of the twenty-first century the huge growth in counselling, psychotherapy and helping that gained momentum in the last half of the twentieth century continues, if not increases. Some of this growth is due to a greater recognition that much of how people communicate is learned and that consequently they can change to communicate better. This recognition includes a movement towards positive **psychology**, which emphasizes enhancing **strengths** as well as working with weaknesses (Harris, Thoreson and Lopez, 2007; Pointon, 2006; Seligman, 2002). In addition, there has been an expansion of counselling and psychotherapy professional associations that regulate standards for practitioners. There has also been a rapid growth of training in counselling, psychotherapy and helping and increasing pressures for professionals to be suitably accredited. Hopefully, alongside these developments, there has been the use of better counselling skills by **counsellors**, psychotherapists and **helpers**.

There are seven main categories of people who either use or can use counselling skills.

- *Professional counsellors and psychotherapists* Specialists who are suitably trained, accredited and paid for their therapeutic services. Such people include counsellors, clinical and counselling psychologists and psychiatrists.
- *Paraprofessional counsellors* People trained in counselling skills who use them as part of their jobs, yet who do not hold an accredited counselling or psychotherapy qualification. Some social workers fall into this category, though others are qualified counsellors and psychotherapists.

Part Introductions: Sets the scene as to what will be discussed and reviewed in the forthcoming chapter.

Chapter Outcomes: Bullet points at the beginning of each chapter indicate the key learning outcomes and benefits that you will achieve from that section, pulling together all the main issues and points raised and discussed.

- *Voluntary counsellors* People trained in counselling skills who work on a voluntary basis in settings such as Relate in the UK or Relationships Australia, youth counselling services, church-related agencies and numerous other voluntary agencies.
- *Helpers using counselling skills as part of their jobs* Here the main focus of the job may be nursing, teaching, preaching, supervising or managing and providing services such as finance, law, funerals, trade union work and so on. These jobs require people to use counselling skills some of the time if they are to be maximally effective.
- *Peer helpers* People who use counselling skills as part of peer helping or **support networks** of varying degrees of formality. Such peer support networks frequently cover areas of **diversity** such as culture, race, sexual orientation and support for women and for men.
- *Informal helpers* All of us have the opportunity to assist others, be it in roles such as partner, parent, relative, friend or work colleague.
- *Counselling, psychotherapy and helping students* Students using counselling skills on supervised placements as part of counselling, psychotherapy and helping courses.

Throughout this book the terms counsellor and helper and **counselling skills** are mainly used rather than psychotherapist or psychotherapy or therapeutic skills. Throughout the book the term **client** is used for the recipients of counselling skills.

Who are counsellors and psychotherapists?

Psychotherapy is derived from the Greek word *therapeia* meaning healing. Though there has been a lessening of this distinction, some years ago counsellors and psychotherapists were often perceived differently. Increasingly, counselling has come to be viewed as either the same or similar to psychotherapy. However, because counselling and psychotherapy represent diverse rather than uniform knowledge and activities, it is more helpful to think that the terms mean counselling and psychotherapy approaches rather than a single entity.

Possibly, the terms psychotherapy and psychotherapist are more used than counselling and counsellor in medical settings. However, there is a blurring of this distinction, though most psychiatrists probably still view themselves as conducting psychotherapy rather than counselling. Psychotherapy is still a term used to discuss longer-term and deeper work with mental disorders, though this is not always the case. However, many psychologists and counsellors work in medical settings, have clients with recognized medical disorders and do longer-term and deep work. Furthermore, the distinction between people who have mental disorders as contrasted with problems of living is not clear-cut. Consequently, even in medical settings the term counselling may be just as appropriate as psychotherapy.

In Britain there has been a recent development emphasizing the similarities between counselling and psychotherapy. In 2000, the British Association for Counselling changed its name to become the British Association for Counselling and Psychotherapy (BACP). A prime reason for this was because many of its members already considered themselves as psychotherapists. In 1998 the Psychotherapy and Counselling Federation of Australia (PACFA) was established. Here, as well as commonalities, some differences between psychotherapists and counsellors are still acknowledged, though it remains to be seen how long PACFA continues to make such distinctions.

Many British and Australian counsellors and psychotherapists are neither members of BACP or PACFA. Some receive their qualifications in other professional associations such as those in counselling psychology, clinical psychology and **psychiatry** and consider this sufficient. Furthermore, in Britain, in addition to BACP there is the United Kingdom Council for Psychotherapy (UKCP), which has organizational members training people in psychotherapy. Example 1.1 illustrates different kinds of professional counsellors and psychotherapists.

What constitutes professional training as a counsellor or psychotherapist? Though subject to change, the following provides some idea of requirements. Courses recognized by BACP have a minimum of 400 hours staff/student contact time with, in addition, students undertaking a minimum of 100 hours of supervised counselling practice. Such courses can be of one year full-time or spread over two, three or four

Example 1.1 Professional counsellors and psychotherapists

Evan, 56, is an accredited counsellor who works for a health care organization with patients with problems such as excessive **stress**, managing pain and recovering from and preventing further heart attacks. Though much of his work is individual, when necessary Evan works with couples and families. In addition, Evan also conducts a small private practice.

Gillian, 29, is a psychologist in a large pharmaceutical company. Much of the time she is helping individuals to perform better and to manage setbacks and disappointments in their work and outside lives. Some of Gillian's time is spent in training staff groups in work-related skills, such as customer relations and job interviewing. In addition, Gillian advises management on personnel policies and procedures.

Paul, 47, is a counselling psychologist in a university counselling centre. Though most clients are undergraduate and postgraduate students, he also has a few who are academic and non-academic staff members. Much of Paul's caseload consists of working for no more than three or four sessions with clients presenting with work-connected problems. Paul also leads groups for students in such areas as assertion skills, **study skills** and relationship skills. In addition, Paul conducts a small private practice consisting of members of the general public.

Vicki, 38, is an accredited psychotherapist in private practice. Her caseload is a mixture of children and adults who visit her in her consulting rooms. Vicki does a mixture of individual, couples, family and group work.

Julie, 46, is a trained and accredited marriage and family counsellor. She works mainly for the local branch of a national relationship counselling agency where she counsels individual partners, couples and, where appropriate, other family members. In addition, Julie conducts a private practice specializing in relationship concerns.

Glossary: An easy source of information about commonly-used terms. This is a useful, accessible and easy to find definition of a concept or theory that has been mentioned in the main text. Glossary terms in the text are indicated by a symbol in the margin.

Examples: Concepts and theories are given context through the inclusion of practical 'real-life' illustrations that will assist in the understanding of concepts and theories.

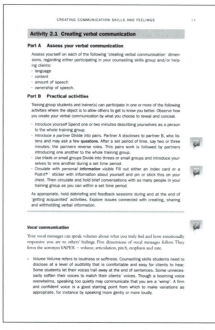

Activity 2.1 Creating verbal communication

Part A   Assess your verbal communication

Assess yourself on each of the following 'creating verbal communication' dimensions, regarding either participating in your counselling skills group and/or helping clients:
- language
- content
- amount of speech
- ownership of speech.

Part B   Practical activities

Training group students and trainer(s) can participate in one or more of the following activities where the object is to allow others to get to know you better. Observe how you create your verbal communication by what you choose to reveal and conceal.

- *Introduce yourself* Spend one or two minutes describing yourselves as a person to the whole training group.
- *Introduce a partner* Divide into pairs. Partner A discloses to partner B, who listens and may ask a few **questions**. After a set period of time, say two or three minutes, the partners reverse roles. This pairs work is followed by partners introducing one another to the whole training group.
- *Use triads or small groups* Divide into threes or small groups and introduce yourselves to one another during a set time period.
- *Circulate with personal information* visible Fill out either an index card or a Post-it®* sticker with information about yourself and pin or stick this on your chest. Then circulate and hold brief conversations with as many people in your training group as you can within a set time period.

As appropriate, hold debriefing and feedback sessions during and at the end of 'getting acquainted' activities. Explore issues connected with creating, sharing and withholding verbal information.

Vocal communication

Your vocal messages can speak volumes about what you truly feel and how emotionally responsive you are to others' feelings. Five dimensions of vocal messages follow. They form the acronym VAPER – volume, articulation, pitch, emphasis and rate.

- *Volume* Volume refers to loudness or softness. Counselling skills students need to disclose at a level of audibility that is comfortable and easy for clients to hear. Some students let their voices trail away at the end of sentences. Some unnecessarily soften their voices to match their clients' voices. Though a booming voice overwhelms, speaking too quietly may communicate that you are a 'wimp'. A firm and confident voice is a good starting point from which to make variations as appropriate, for instance by speaking more gently or more loudly.

Activities: Interactive exercises that assist in the focusing and application of the various theories and concepts that have been discussed. These activities will support your understanding and contemplation of important points and issues raised in the text.

PART ONE

INTRODUCTION

Part One consists of five introductory chapters. Chapter 1 answers the question of who are counsellors, psychotherapists and helpers. Chapters 2 and 3 introduce the notion that people possess communication skills and mind skills that can be for good or ill. In addition, time is spent describing feelings and physical reactions and stating why they are not skills. Chapters 4 and 5 focus on the three stages of the Relating–Understanding–Changing (RUC) counselling and helping process and on the importance of creating strong relationships with clients.

1

Who are counsellors and helpers?

CHAPTER OUTCOMES

By studying this chapter you should:
- understand some distinguishing features of professional counsellors and psychotherapists;
- gain an introduction to professional counselling and psychotherapy requirements;
- gain an appreciation of the variety of helpers who use counselling skills;
- know some of the differences between counsellors, psychotherapists and helpers; and
- understand five categories of goals for using counselling skills.

At the start of the twenty-first century the huge growth in counselling, psychotherapy and helping that gained momentum in the last half of the twentieth century continues, if not increases. Some of this growth is due to a greater recognition that much of how people communicate is learned and that consequently they can change to communicate better. This recognition includes a movement towards positive **psychology**, which emphasizes enhancing **strengths** as well as working with weaknesses (Harris, Thoreson and Lopez, 2007; Pointon, 2006; Seligman, 2002). In addition, there has been an expansion of counselling and psychotherapy professional associations that regulate standards for practitioners. There has also been a rapid growth of training in counselling, psychotherapy and helping and increasing pressures for professionals to be suitably accredited. Hopefully, alongside these developments, there has been the use of better counselling skills by **counsellors**, psychotherapists and **helpers**.

There are seven main categories of people who either use or can use counselling skills.

- *Professional counsellors and psychotherapists* Specialists who are suitably trained, accredited and paid for their therapeutic services. Such people include counsellors, clinical and counselling psychologists and psychiatrists.
- *Paraprofessional counsellors* People trained in counselling skills who use them as part of their jobs, yet who do not hold an accredited counselling or psychotherapy qualification. Some social workers fall into this category, though others are qualified counsellors and psychotherapists.

- *Voluntary counsellors* People trained in counselling skills who work on a voluntary basis in settings such as Relate in the UK or Relationships Australia, youth counselling services, church-related agencies and numerous other voluntary agencies.
- *Helpers using counselling skills as part of their jobs* Here the main focus of the job may be nursing, teaching, preaching, supervising or managing and providing services such as finance, law, funerals, trade union work and so on. These jobs require people to use counselling skills some of the time if they are to be maximally effective.

- *Peer helpers* People who use counselling skills as part of peer helping or **support networks** of varying degrees of formality. Such peer support networks frequently cover areas of **diversity** such as culture, race, sexual orientation and support for women and for men.
- *Informal helpers* All of us have the opportunity to assist others, be it in roles such as partner, parent, relative, friend or work colleague.
- *Counselling, psychotherapy and helping students* Students using counselling skills on supervised placements as part of counselling, psychotherapy and helping courses.

Throughout this book the terms counsellor and helper and **counselling skills** are mainly used rather than psychotherapist and psychotherapy or therapeutic skills. Throughout the book the term **client** is used for the recipients of counselling skills.

Who are counsellors and psychotherapists?

Psychotherapy is derived from the Greek word *therapeia* meaning healing. Though there has been a lessening of this distinction, some years ago counsellors and psychotherapists were often perceived differently. Increasingly, counselling has come to be viewed as either the same or similar to psychotherapy. However, because counselling and psychotherapy represent diverse rather than uniform knowledge and activities, it is more helpful to think that the terms mean counselling and psychotherapy approaches rather than a single entity.

Possibly, the terms psychotherapy and psychotherapist are more used than counselling and counsellor in medical settings. However, there is a blurring of this distinction, though most psychiatrists probably still view themselves as conducting psychotherapy rather than counselling. Psychotherapy is still a term used to discuss longer-term and deeper work with mental disorders, though this is not always the case. However, many psychologists and counsellors work in medical settings, have clients with recognized medical disorders and do longer-term and deep work. Furthermore, the distinction between people who have mental disorders as contrasted with problems of living is not clear-cut. Consequently, even in medical settings the term counselling may be just as appropriate as psychotherapy.

In Britain there has been a recent development emphasizing the similarities between counselling and psychotherapy. In 2000, the British Association for Counselling changed its name to become the British Association for Counselling and Psychotherapy (BACP). A prime reason for this was because many of its members already considered themselves as psychotherapists. In 1998 the Psychotherapy and Counselling Federation of Australia (PACFA) was established. Here, as well as commonalities, some differences between psychotherapists and counsellors are still acknowledged, though it remains to be seen how long PACFA continues to make such distinctions.

Many British and Australian counsellors and psychotherapists are neither members of BACP or PACFA. Some receive their qualifications in other professional associations such as those in counselling psychology, clinical psychology and **psychiatry** and consider this sufficient. Furthermore, in Britain, in addition to BACP there is the United Kingdom Council for Psychotherapy (UKCP), which has organizational members training people in psychotherapy. Example 1.1 illustrates different kinds of professional counsellors and psychotherapists.

What constitutes professional training as a counsellor or psychotherapist? Though subject to change, the following provides some idea of requirements. Courses recognized by BACP have a minimum of 400 hours staff/student contact time with, in addition, students undertaking a minimum of 100 hours of supervised counselling practice. Such courses can be of one year full-time or spread over two, three or four years part-time. Training offered by organizational members of UKCP is not normally

---

Example 1.1 Professional counsellors and psychotherapists

Evan, 56, is an accredited counsellor who works for a health care organization with patients with problems such as excessive **stress**, managing pain and recovering from and preventing further heart attacks. Though much of his work is individual, when necessary Evan works with couples and families. In addition, Evan also conducts a small private practice.

Gillian, 29, is a psychologist in a large pharmaceutical company. Much of the time she is helping individuals to perform better and to manage setbacks and disappointments in their work and outside lives. Some of Gillian's time is spent in training staff groups in work-related skills, such as customer relations and job interviewing. In addition, Gillian advises management on personnel policies and procedures.

Paul, 47, is a counselling psychologist in a university counselling centre. Though most clients are undergraduate and postgraduate students, he also has a few who are academic and non-academic staff members. Much of Paul's caseload consists of working for no more than three or four sessions with clients presenting with work-connected problems. Paul also leads groups for students in such areas as assertion skills, **study skills** and relationship skills. In addition, Paul conducts a small private practice consisting of members of the general public.

Vicki, 38, is an accredited psychotherapist in private practice. Her caseload is a mixture of children and adults who visit her in her consulting rooms. Vicki does a mixture of individual, couples, family and group work.

Julie, 46, is a trained and accredited marriage and family counsellor. She works mainly for the local branch of a national relationship counselling agency where she counsels individual partners, couples and, where appropriate, other family members. In addition, Julie conducts a private practice specializing in relationship concerns.

shorter than four years part-time duration. Such training involves supervised clinical work and usually personal therapy in the model being taught. In Australia, PACFA requires courses run by its member associations to have 200 hours of training and 50 hours of **supervision** relating to 200 hours of client contact. From 2009, PACFA will require new members to have courses offering 400 hours of training followed by 750 hours of client contact and 75 hours of supervision (PACFA, 2006).

Regarding professional counsellors and therapists, two further points are worthy of mention. First, a number of people, such as some social workers and nurses, combine professional qualifications in their primary role with professional qualifications in counselling and psychotherapy. Second, completion of an approved course of counselling and psychotherapy training can no longer be equated with accreditation, since increasingly professional counsellors and psychotherapists are required to undertake mandatory continuing professional development (CPD) requirements by their professional associations.

Who are helpers?

Sometimes, the term helper is used as a generic term to cover all those engaged in using counselling and helping skills, be they counselling and psychotherapy professionals or otherwise. However, increasingly the professionalization of counselling and psychotherapy makes such usage inaccurate. Here the term 'helper' is used in a more restricted sense to include all those people who offer counselling skills to other people, yet who are not qualified and accredited counsellors, psychotherapists or their equivalent. This introductory book is highly relevant to all such people in addition to those training to become professional counsellors and therapists.

Paraprofessional counsellors are trained in counselling skills, but at a level that falls short of professional counselling or psychotherapy accreditation. For example, some nurses have attended a number of counselling courses and may be skilled at dealing with the problems of specific categories of patients. People with such backgrounds might be called counsellors in their work settings, for example nurse counsellors. Alternatively, they might remain being called nurses. However, if the term 'counsellor' in a given context is limited only to those with recognized specialist professional qualifications and accreditation in the area, nurses doing paraprofessional counselling should be categorized as helpers, despite the quality of their skills.

Example 1.2 illustrates helpers who are using counselling skills either as paraprofessionals, in voluntary settings, as part of their jobs or on a peer support basis.

Example 1.2 Helpers using counselling skills

Paraprofessional counselling
Lesley, 27, is a social worker, who has taken a number of courses relevant to and on counselling and who works with distressed individuals and families to improve how they communicate and to make them more economically self-reliant.

Example 1.2 Helpers using counselling skills – cont'd

Melissa, 35, works as a counsellor in a pregnancy advisory service where individuals and couples consult her about birth control **information** and decisions. Melissa finds it important to use counselling skills since contraception is a very sensitive topic for some clients to discuss.

Voluntary counselling

Chris, 24, works as a volunteer in a programme designed to support people with HIV/AIDS and their partners. After some initial training in counselling and caring skills, Chris regularly visits the homes of those to whom he has been assigned as a helper.

Catherine, 47, has taken a number of courses in counselling and now works as a volunteer for an agency supporting schizophrenic clients and their families.

Helpers using counselling skills as part of their jobs

Sanjay, 38, is a community and youth worker in an inner city area. His duties involve liaising with the Asian migrant community in his local council's jurisdiction and helping them and their children with their practical and emotional problems, including **coping** with racist incidents.

Frank, 55, is a priest who has undergone considerable training in counselling, though not enough to be professionally qualified. In his church role, Frank uses his counselling skills with clients ranging from those who wish to explore their spiritual concerns to those who have family, work and other problems.

Peer helping

Terry, 31, meets regularly with Ian, 34, as part of a men's support network. Terry and Ian engage in co-helping in which whenever they meet they share the time between them so that each has a turn to be in the client and helper roles.

Nicola, 26, and Heather, 23, engage in co-counselling as part of a group of women who are learning to become more confident and assertive. In addition, Nicola and Heather also attend a training group about the role of women in society.

The demonstrations in Example 1.2 are only illustrative of the vast range of people who use counselling skills when performing helping roles.

Let's take a further look at some ways in which helpers can be distinguished from professional counsellors and psychotherapists. So far, two main distinguishing areas have been identified. Helpers perform different *roles* to those of counsellors and psychotherapists. Counsellors have as their primary role conducting counselling, whether this be individual, couples, group or **family counselling**. Helpers often either have their primary role in another area or are using helping skills in voluntary and peer support capacities. Related to different roles, helpers differ from counsellors in their *training*. Counsellors are primarily trained to counsel, whereas helpers may be primarily trained to be social workers, nurses, probation officers, priests, welfare workers, managers and in a host of other occupations. Furthermore, voluntary workers usually have primary work roles in non-counselling occupations, for which they have likely received the bulk of their training.

The *goals* of helpers can both overlap with, yet differ, from those of counsellors. The primary purpose of counselling and psychotherapy is to help clients address psychological issues in their lives, for example, becoming less depressed or anxious, and to work through decisions and **crises** that have a distinct psychological dimension to them. Sometimes such psychological issues are central to helping. On other occasions, helpers use counselling skills to assist people to deal with goals where the overt psychological dimensions may appear secondary, if not irrelevant, to the recipients of the services. Some illustrations of this phenomenon exist in Example 1.2: for instance, receiving pregnancy advice or spiritual assistance.

The *settings* or contexts for helping can differ from those for counselling. Most often counselling takes place in offices, be they private or institutional, set aside specially for that activity. The decor of such offices is designed to support the purpose of counselling, for instance functional easy chairs with a coffee table between them. Often, counselling services are located in specially designated areas, for instance student counselling services. Helpers may sometimes use counselling skills in areas designed for counselling, for instance in some voluntary agencies. However, frequently helpers use counselling skills in locations that represent their primary work role. Such locations include personnel offices, classrooms, tutorial rooms, hospital wards, outplacement clinics, churches, banks, law offices and community centres. Furthermore, while counsellors rarely go outside formal locations, helpers such as priests, nurses, social workers and members of peer support networks may use counselling skills in people's home settings.

A further distinction is that often the *relationship* in which helpers use counselling skills often differs from the more formal counselling relationship, which is likely to have clear boundaries structured around the respective tasks of counsellor and client. Sometimes **helping relationships** may have similarly clear helper–client boundaries, though the prime agenda may or may not be psychological counselling. Frequently, however, helping relationships take place in the context of other relationships, such as teacher–student, priest–parishioner, line manager–worker, social worker–client, nurse or doctor–patient. Whereas dual relationships, in which counsellors perform more than one role in relation to clients, are frowned upon in counselling, they may be built into the fabric of many helping relationships. Furthermore, as mentioned above, sometimes helping relationships include home visits.

Why use counselling skills?

In a nutshell, the main purpose or goal of using counselling skills is that of assisting clients to develop personal skills and **inner strength** so that they can create happiness in their own and others' lives (Nelson-Jones, 2003). Counsellors and helpers assist clients to help themselves. As such, they use counselling skills to develop clients' capacity to use their human potential both now and in future. The following discussion is mainly focused on working with ordinary people rather than with severely disturbed clients.

Counsellors and helpers' use of counselling skills can be broken down into five different goals. Some of these goals may seem more modest than the nutshell suggestion, but nevertheless these goals may be appropriate in the circumstances.

The first or *supportive listening* goal is to provide clients with a sense of being understood and affirmed. Attaining this goal requires counsellors and helpers to be skilled at **listening** to clients, taking their perspectives, and sensitively showing them that they have been heard accurately. The primary purpose of introductory counselling skills training is to help students become better at listening and showing understanding to clients. Counsellors and helpers with good listening skills can comfort, ease suffering, heal psychological wounds, and act as sounding boards for moving forward. For instance, an employee just made redundant, a patient recently given a diagnosis of a life-threatening illness, or a school child who has been bullied may, above all, need counsellors and helpers able to listen deeply.

Second, there is the *managing a problem situation* goal. Clients may want help dealing with specific situations that are problematic for them. In addition, counselling and helping may best proceed if a specific situation within a larger problem is addressed rather than trying to deal with the whole problem. With a shy college student client, rather than focus on the broader problem of shyness, counsellor and client might focus on a particular shyness situation of importance to the client, such as being able to start a conversation with a classmate. Supportive listening and managing problem situation goals are perhaps the easiest goals for beginning students and informal helpers to focus on.

Third, there is the *problem management* goal. Though some problems are limited, many other problems can be larger and more complex than specific situations within them. For example, George's problem was that he felt depressed. Together, the counsellor and George identified the following dimensions to his problem: obtaining or creating employment for himself, being more assertive with his wife, participating in recreational outlets, reactivating his friendship network, and learning to sleep better. Another example is that of clients with children going through a divorce. Here, dimensions of the problem might include obtaining a just divorce settlement, maintaining self-esteem, relationships with children, a possible move of home, and learning to live as a single adult again. Egan's book *The Skilled Helper* (2007) is a prime example of a book that has its major focus on problem management.

Fourth, there is the *altering poor skills that create problems* goal. Other terms for poor skills include problematic, deficient or insufficiently effective skills. Here the assumption is that problems tend to repeat themselves. In the past, clients may have been repeating underlying **mind skills** and **communication** or **action skills** deficiencies and are at risk of continuing to do so again. For instance, workers who keep moving jobs may again and again set themselves up to become unhappy or to get fired. Another example is that of clients poor at public speaking who require skills both for now and in future. Thus the problem is not just the presenting problem, but the poor skills that create, sustain or worsen the problem (Nelson-Jones, 2005).

Fifth, there is the *bringing about a changed philosophy of life* goal. Here, clients can competently manage **problem situations**, manage problems and alter **problematic** **skills** as a way of life. Such people might be termed self-actualizing, fully functioning or even enlightened when they are able to achieve a changed philosophy of life. However, this fifth or elegant goal is largely beyond the scope of this beginning counselling and helping skills book.

2

Creating communication skills and feelings

CHAPTER OUTCOMES

By studying and doing the activities in this chapter you should:
- understand what is a counselling skill;
- understand how counselling skills students and clients create verbal communication;
- understand how counselling skills students and clients create vocal communication;
- understand how counselling skills students and clients create bodily communication; and
- understand the role of feelings and physical reactions.

What is a counselling skill? One meaning of '**skills**' pertains to *areas* of skill: for instance, **listening** skills or **disclosing skills**. Another meaning refers to *level of competence*, for instance, skilled or unskilled in an area of skill. However, **competence** in a skill is best viewed not as an either/or matter in which **counsellors**, **helpers** and counselling skills students either possess or do not possess a skill. Rather, within a skills area, it is preferable to think of yourself as possessing *good skills* or *poor skills* or a mixture of the two. In all skills areas you are likely to possess mixtures of **strengths** and deficiencies. For instance, in the skills area of listening, you may be good at understanding clients, but poor at showing understanding. Similarly, in just about all areas of their functioning, clients will possess a mixture of poor and good skills. A third meaning of skill relates to the *knowledge and sequence of choices* entailed in implementing the skill. The essential element of any skill is the ability to implement sequences of choices to achieve objectives. For instance, if counsellors and helpers are to be good at listening deeply and accurately to clients, you have to make and implement effective choices in this counselling skills area.

In counselling and helping there are two main categories of skills. First, there are communication and action skills, or skills that entail external behaviour. Second, there are **mind skills**, or skills that entail internal behaviour. Readers may wonder why feelings skills and physical reactions are not mentioned as skills. The reason for this is that feelings and physical reactions are essentially part of your instinctual or animal nature and are not skills in themselves. However, counselling skills students and clients can influence how you feel and physically react by how you communicate/act and think.

Creating communication and action

There are five main ways counselling skills students and clients can send messages by creating communication and taking action. *Verbal* communication consists of messages sent with your words: for example, saying 'I understand what you are saying' or 'I don't understand.' *Vocal* communication consists of messages sent through your voice: for instance, through volume, articulation, pitch, emphasis and speech rate. *Bodily* communication consists of messages sent by your body: for example, through gaze, eye contact, facial expression, posture, gestures, physical proximity and clothes and grooming. ***Touch* communication** is a special category of bodily communication. Messages sent by touch include: what part of the body you use, what part of another's body gets touched, and how gentle or firm is the touching. ***Taking action* communication** consists of messages you send when not face-to-face with others: for example, sending a follow up note to a **client** who has missed an appointment.

Verbal communication

Let's look at some dimensions of verbal communication or talk.

- *Language* Language consists of many elements other than whether people are English-speaking or not. For instance, there may be a formal language, words that either BBC or ABC news readers might use, as well as an informal or colloquial language, such as words you might use with mates in the pub.
- *Content* Content may refer to topic area, problem area or the task being undertaken, such as learning counselling skills. In addition, content refers to the focus of talk, whether it be about yourself, others or the environment. Furthermore, content can refer to the evaluative dimension of talk, for example, depressed clients may say many negative things about themselves such as 'I'm worthless' and 'I just don't seem to care any more'.
- *Amount of speech* Shyness is a common term attached to people who experience difficulty when it is to their turn to talk. In some, but not all counselling approaches, clients talk more than helpers. However, some clients may be talkative from the start, others warm up as helping progresses, and yet others talk haltingly throughout even though the helping may be successful. Counselling skills students can also talk too much or too little.
- *Ownership of speech* A useful distinction exists between 'You' messages and 'I' messages. 'You' messages focus on the other person and can be judgmental: for example, 'You don't appreciate what I'm doing for you' or 'You're not listening to me properly'. 'I' messages use the word 'I' and are centred in a person as the sender: for instance, 'I feel unappreciated' or 'I'm experiencing not being heard correctly'.

Activity 2.1 Creating verbal communication

Part A   Assess your verbal communication

Assess yourself on each of the following 'creating verbal communication' dimensions, regarding either participating in your counselling skills group and/or helping clients:
- language
- content
- amount of speech
- ownership of speech.

Part B   Practical activities

Training group students and trainer(s) can participate in one or more of the following activities where the object is to allow others to get to know you better. Observe how you create your verbal communication by what you choose to reveal and conceal.

- *Introduce yourself* Spend one or two minutes describing yourselves as a person to the whole training group.
- *Introduce a partner* Divide into pairs. Partner A discloses to partner B, who listens and may ask a few **questions**. After a set period of time, say two or three minutes, the partners reverse roles. This pairs work is followed by partners introducing one another to the whole training group.
- *Use triads or small groups* Divide into threes or small groups and introduce yourselves to one another during a set time period.
- *Circulate with personal **information** visible* Fill out either an index card or a Post-it® sticker with information about yourself and pin or stick this on your chest. Then circulate and hold brief conversations with as many people in your training group as you can within a set time period.

As appropriate, hold debriefing and feedback sessions during and at the end of 'getting acquainted' activities. Explore issues connected with creating, sharing and withholding verbal information.

Vocal communication

Your vocal messages can speak volumes about what you truly feel and how emotionally responsive you are to others' feelings. Five dimensions of vocal messages follow. They form the acronym VAPER – volume, articulation, pitch, emphasis and rate.

- *Volume* Volume refers to loudness or softness. Counselling skills students need to disclose at a level of audibility that is comfortable and easy for clients to hear. Some students let their voices trail away at the end of sentences. Some unnecessarily soften their voices to match their clients' voices. Though a booming voice overwhelms, speaking too quietly may communicate that you are a 'wimp'. A firm and confident voice is a good starting point from which to make variations as appropriate, for instance by speaking more gently or more loudly.

- *Articulation* Articulation refers to the clarity of speech. Counselling skills students and clients who enunciate words well are easier to understand than those who don't.
- *Pitch* Pitch refers to the height or depth of your voice. An optimum pitch range includes all the levels at which a pleasing voice can be produced without strain. Errors of pitch include either being too high pitched or too low pitched.
- *Emphasis* A counselling skills student's voice uses emphasis when responding to clients' feelings and nuances and when sharing feelings. Students may use either too much emphasis and seem melodramatic or too little emphasis and come across as wooden. In addition, you may use emphasis in the wrong places.
- *Rate* Often speech rate is measured by words per minute. Speech rate depends not only on how quickly words are spoken, but on the frequency and duration of pauses between them. If speaking very quickly, counselling skills students may appear anxious and clients can have difficulty understanding you. On the other hand, too ponderous a speech rate can be boring. However, pausing and being silent at the right times is another important aspect of speech rate.

Activity 2.2 Creating vocal communication

Part A   Assess your vocal communication

1 Self-assessment

Assess yourself on each of the following 'creating vocal communication' dimensions regarding either participating in your counselling skills group and/or helping clients:
- volume
- articulation
- pitch
- emphasis
- speech rate
- use of pauses and silences
- other important areas not listed above.

2 Obtain feedback

Obtain feedback from the other students in your training group and from your trainer(s) on your good and poor vocal **communication skills.**

Part B   Change a specific dimension of vocal communication

Pick a specific dimension of vocal communication that you think you might improve, for instance you may have a tendency to talk too softly. Then hold a conversation with a partner in which you work on improving the specific dimension of vocal communication you have targeted. Either during or at the end of your conversation ask for feedback on how you are doing.

If appropriate, afterwards you and your partner reverse roles.

Bodily communication

Both when speaking and listening, counselling skills students and clients disclose yourselves through how you communicate bodily. Some of the main forms of bodily communication follow.

- *Facial expressions* Facial expressions are perhaps the main vehicle for sending
  body messages. Ekman, Friesen and Ellsworth (1972) have found that there are
  seven main facial expressions of emotion: happiness, interest, surprise, fear, sadness, anger, and disgust or contempt. Your mouth and eyebrows can convey much
  information: for instance, 'down in the mouth' and 'raised eyebrows'.
- *Gaze* Gaze, or looking at other people in the area of their faces, is both a way of
  showing interest and also a way of collecting facial information. Speakers look at
  listeners about 40 per cent of the time and listeners look at speakers about
  70–75 per cent of the time. Gaze is useful for coordinating speech: for example,
  speakers look just before the end of utterances to collect feedback about their
  listener's reactions. Women are more visually attentive than men in all measures
  of gaze (Argyle, 1999).
- *Eye contact* Eye contact is a more direct way than gaze of sending messages, be
  they of interest, anger or sexual attraction.
- *Gestures* Gestures are physical movements that can frame or illustrate words coming
  before, during or after what is being said. An example of using a gesture to display
  and emphasize an emotion is clenching your fist to show aggression. Gestures may
  also illustrate shapes, sizes or movements, particularly when these are difficult to
  describe in words. How you gesture can vary according to your sex. Sometimes men's
  gestures are larger, more sweeping and forceful, while women's gestures are smaller
  and more inhibited. Gestures can also take the place of words: for example, nodding
  your head either up-and-down or sideways for saying 'yes' or 'no', respectively.
- *Posture* A counselling skills student's posture may convey various messages.
  Turning your body towards the client is more encouraging than turning away from
  them. In addition, whether you lean forwards or backwards may indicate interest or
  disinterest. Height tends to be associated with status: for instance, you 'talk down
  to' or 'talk up to' someone. Women may be at a disadvantage unless a man's body
  posture is changed: for instance, by sitting down.

  Posture may also communicate how anxious you are: for instance, sitting with arms
  and legs tightly crossed suggests being emotionally as well as literally uptight.
  However, if a woman, it is possible to appear too relaxed: some men may mistakenly
  perceive uncrossed and open legs as a sign of sexual availability whether a skirt,
  trousers or jeans is worn. Such **perceptions** manifest a double standard in how people
  decode body messages.
- *Physical closeness* The degree of physical closeness that is comfortable
  for Britons and Antipodeans is generally the same. The zones vary according
  to the nature of the relationship. In the *intimate zone* (between 6 to 18 inches)
  it is easy to touch and be touched. This zone is reserved for spouses, lovers, close
  friends and relatives. The *personal zone* (between 18 and 48 inches)
  is appropriate for less close friends and for parties and other social gatherings. The *social zone* (between 4 to 12 feet) is comfortable for people not known

at all well. The *public zone* (over 12 feet) is the distance for addressing public gatherings.

- *Clothes* If clothes do not make the counsellor or helper, they certainly send many messages that can influence how much and in which areas clients reveal themselves. These messages include social and occupational standing, sex-role identity, ethnicity, conformity to peer group norms, rebelliousness and how outgoing they are. While maintaining your individuality, counselling skills students need to dress appropriately for your clientele: for example, delinquent teenagers probably respond better to informally dressed helpers than do stressed business executives.

- *Grooming* Personal grooming also provides important information about how well you take care of yourself; for instance, clean or dirty, neat or tidy. In addition, the length and styling of your hair sends messages about what sort of person you are.

Activity 2.3 Creating bodily communication

Part A   Assess your bodily communication

1 Self-assessment

Assess yourself on each of the following 'creating bodily communication' dimensions regarding either participating in your counselling skills group and/or working with clients:
- facial expression
- gaze
- eye contact
- gestures
- posture
- physical proximity
- clothing
- grooming
- other important areas not listed above.

2 Obtain feedback

Obtain feedback from the other students in your training group and from your trainer(s) on your good and poor bodily communication skills.

Part B   Change a specific dimension of bodily communication

Pick a specific dimension of bodily communication that you think you might improve, for instance you may have a tendency to sit with too rigid a posture. Then hold a conversation with a partner in which you work on improving the specific dimension of bodily communication you have targeted. Either during or at the end of your conversation ask for feedback on how you are doing.

If appropriate, afterwards you and your partner reverse roles.

Feelings and physical reactions

To a large extent, you are what you feel. Important feelings include happiness, interest, surprise, fear, sadness, anger, and disgust or contempt. Dictionary definitions of feelings tend to use words like 'physical sensation', 'emotions' and '**awareness**'. All three of these words illustrate a dimension of feelings. Feelings as *physical sensations* or as *physical reactions* represent your underlying animal nature. People are animals first, persons second. As such you need to learn to value and live with your underlying animal nature. The word *emotion* implies movement. Feelings are processes. You are subject to a continuous flow of biological experiencing. *Awareness* implies that you can be conscious of your feelings. However, at varying levels and in different ways, you may also be out of touch with them.

Physical reactions both represent and accompany feelings and, in a sense, are indistinguishable. For example, bodily changes associated with **anxiety** can include galvanic skin response – detectable electrical changes taking place in the skin, raised blood pressure, a pounding heart and a rapid pulse, shallow and rapid breathing, mus- cular **tension**, drying of the mouth, stomach problems such as ulcers, speech difficulties such as stammering, sleep difficulties, and sexual problems such as complete or partial loss of desire. Other physical reactions include a slowing down of body movements when depressed and dilated eye pupils in moments of anger or sexual attraction. Sometimes people respond to their physical reactions. For example, during anxiety and panic attacks, they may first feel tense and anxious and then become even more tense and anxious because of this initial feeling.

Feelings and physical reactions are central to the counselling and helping process. Counselling skills students require the capacity to experience and understand both your own and your clients' feelings. However, just because feelings represent your animal nature, this does not mean that you and your clients can do nothing about them. In counselling and helping, three somewhat overlapping areas where feelings and accompanying physical reactions are important include experiencing feelings, expressing feelings and managing feelings. In each of these three areas, counselling skills students can work with clients' communications/actions and thoughts and mental processes to influence how they feel and physically react.

3

Creating mind skills

CHAPTER OUTCOMES

By studying and doing the activities in this chapter you should:
- understand what mind skills are;
- be introduced to creating rules and creating perceptions;
- be introduced to creating self-talk and creating visual images; and
- be introduced to creating explanations and creating expectations.

What are mind skills?

You can learn **counselling skills** and assist **clients** much more effectively if you harness your **mind**'s potential. How can you control your thoughts so that you can beneficially influence how you communicate? First, you can understand that you have a mind with a capacity for super-conscious thinking – or thinking about thinking – that you can develop. Second, you can become much more efficient in thinking about your thinking if you view your mental processes in terms of **skills** that you can train yourself to exercise and control. Third, in daily life as well as in your counselling skills training, you can assiduously practise using your mind skills to influence your **communication**. Below are descriptions of six central mental processes, or **mind skills**. I illustrate this chapter more by the mind skills of students of counselling skills rather than by those of clients. Later in the book this balance gets redressed.

Creating rules

Rules are the 'dos' and 'don'ts' by which you lead your life. All counsellors, helpers, counselling skills students and clients have inner rule-books that guide how you live and work. Who sets the rules? Influences from the past and present have helped to create and to sustain everyone's rules: for example, family, religion, gender, culture, race, peer group, age, exposure to the media and so on.

You may have rational and altruistic reasons for creating and sustaining your rules. In addition, you may sustain some rules through less rational factors. **Habit**, or persisting communicating in the same old unexamined way, is one such factor. Fear is another important factor. You may be afraid that you will lose out in some significant way if you examine and change your rules.

Example 3.1 Creating demanding and preferential rules

Demanding rules
- 'I must be the perfect student.'
- 'I must be liked by everyone.'
- 'I must always be in control of the training group.'

Preferential rules
- 'I'd prefer to be a highly competent student, but I'm learning and am bound to make some mistakes.'
- 'I'd prefer to be liked, but its also even more important to be true to myself.'
- 'I'd prefer to influence the training group to attain its **goals,** but total control is both undesirable and unrealistic.'

Wanting immediate gratification is a third factor keeping you in unproductive rules. Like a child you may demand that you must have what you want NOW, rather than balance longer-term with shorter-term considerations. Ellis, the founder of **rational–emotive behaviour therapy**, considers that people create and maintain much of their distress and unhappiness through demanding and absolutist thinking, making demands, rather than through preferential thinking, having preferences (Ellis, 2003; 2008).

Example 3.1 emphasizes the distinction between demanding and preferring. Notice that each of the demanding or unrealistic rules has been reworded to become a preferential or realistic rule.

Activity 3.1 Creating rules

Demanding rules about yourself as a learner

1. Look at Example 3.1 and then list at least three demanding rules you either do or might possess concerning how you should learn introductory counselling skills.
2. What are likely to be the consequences of possessing the above demanding rules on your **feelings, physical reactions** and communication?

Preferential rules about yourself as a learner

3. Again look at Example 3.1 and restate the demanding rules you listed above into more **preferential rules** about learning introductory counselling skills.
4. What are likely to be the consequences of possessing the above preferential rules on your feelings, physical reactions and communication?

Creating perceptions

One of the most influential approaches to cognitive **psychotherapy** is that of American psychiatrist Aaron Beck (Beck, 1976; Beck and Weishaar, 2008). Whereas Ellis emphasizes preferential thinking, based on realistic rules, Beck emphasizes propositional thinking, based on testing the reality of perceptions about yourself, others and the environment. Both preferential and propositional thinking are useful mind skills. This section focuses on how accurately you perceive yourself rather than on how accurately you perceive others.

The **self-concept** is your picture of yourself, what you think of as 'I' or 'Me'. It consists of a series of different perceptions of varying degrees of accuracy. Areas of your self-concept concern perceptions regarding family of origin, current relationships, body image, age, gender, sexual orientation, culture, race, social class, religious beliefs, health, work, study activities, leisure pursuits, tastes and preferences, among others.

Centrality is one dimension of self-concept: 'What is really important to me?' For instance, if you are a committed Christian, your faith is fundamental to your self-concept. Another dimension of self-concept is that of positive and negative evaluations of personal characteristics: 'What do I like and dislike about myself?' A further important dimension of self-concept is that of how confident you are. You may accurately perceive your level of confidence or over- or underestimate it.

The self-concepts of all counselling skills students contain perceptions of varying degrees of accuracy about your skills: for example, perceptions of your **listening** skills and questioning skills. You may accurately perceive your skill level in a particular area or inaccurately perceive that you are either more or less skilled than you really are.

Some counselling skills students possess a tendency to underestimate skill levels. The term pathological critic is sometimes used to describe the pathological inner voice that attacks and judges a person. While all students have areas on which you need to work, when in pathological critic mode you perceive your skills far too negatively. For example, negative perceptions that you may hold about your listening skills include that they are hopeless, unchangeable and worse than those of fellow students.

Conversely, counselling skills students can perceive your skill levels too positively, even to the extent of becoming instant experts. Sometimes you may use self-protective habits that defend your current estimation of your ability. You may deny certain aspects of the feedback that you receive from your trainers and fellow students: for instance, that you are too inclined to give advice rather than listen. Alternatively you may distort and selectively filter out incoming **information**: for example, only partly acknowledging the full extent of a piece of positive or negative feedback.

A principal skill of learning to perceive more accurately is being able to distinguish fact from inference. Take the statement 'All Aborigines walk in single file, at least the one I saw did'. That you saw one Aborigine is fact, that all Aborigines walk in single file is inference or factually unsupported supposition. Counselling skills students need to guard against tendencies to jump to unwarranted conclusions. Furthermore, you need to be prepared to change or modify your conclusions in light of emerging information.

Example 3.2 Reality-testing a perception

Situation
A student assesses her/his performance just after the half-way stage of a 60-hour introductory counselling skills course.

Initial unrealistic perception
'I'm doing poorly on my counselling skills course.'

Reality-testing the initial perception
'I know that I have a tendency to put myself down. Where is the evidence that I'm doing poorly? I started off the course listening poorly. I'd never had any training in listening skills and thought the best way to help people was to give good advice. Also, I felt intimidated because the other students are older and more experienced than me. However, the feedback I've received both from the trainer and from my fellow students is that they think I'm improving. In fact, on my middle of course **assessment** cassette, I received an above-average grade. The trainer gave me some feedback about how I might improve, but that does not mean that I am doing poorly. What is a realistic skills level for this stage of the course? I think I expect too much of myself too soon. So far I have had limited opportunity to practise my skills and they still do not feel natural to me. I'm very aware of thinking about what I do all the time. Furthermore, along with learning new skills I'm having to unlearn some bad old habits.'

Revised realistic perception
'While I wish I were doing better, my progress is satisfactory for this stage of the course.'

Example 3.2 depicts a counselling skills student, who initially jumps to an unduly negative conclusion about her/his level of performance, and then reality tests the perception to see how accurately it fits the available facts.

Activity 3.2 Creating perceptions

Think of a situation in regard to either learning introductory counselling skills or in your workplace, where you may be jumping to a conclusion based on inference rather than on fact. Taking the Example 3.2 illustration of testing the reality of an initial perception, engage in a process of questioning the adequacy of your initial perception and replacing it with a more realistic perception.

Creating self-talk

Self-talk goes by numerous other names, including inner monologue, inner dialogue, inner speech, self-verbalizing, self-instructing and talking to yourself. In any counselling relationship, there are at least three conversations going on: the public conversation plus the counsellor's and the client's private self-talk.

All verbal thinking can be regarded as self-talk. However, here the focus is on a specific area of self-talk, namely instructing yourself in order to cope with specific learning counselling skills and helping situations better. Some self-talk is preconscious or automatic, which is not necessarily bad. For instance, when learning to drive a car, you first receive instructions, which you then consciously repeat to yourself to the point where these self-instructions became automatic. In some instances, however, automatic self-talk may be unhelpful.

Negative self-talk can be contrasted with **coping self-talk**. A distinction can be made between coping, 'Doing as well as I can', and mastery, 'I have to be perfect'. Coping emphasizes **competence** rather than perfection. In reality, most people use a mixture of negative and coping self-talk. Negative self-talk refers to anything that you say or fail to say to yourself before, during or after specific situations that contributes to potentially avoidable negative feelings, physical reactions and communications. If you create negative self-statements, such as 'I can't cope' or 'Will I make it?', you risk weakening yourself internally through unskillful thinking. Consequently, you may become less in control of your feelings as well as your thoughts. You also put yourself at risk of communicating externally in inappropriate ways: for example, by excessive approval seeking.

Example 3.3 illustrates two possibilities for a student's self-talk before attending the first session of a counselling skills training group where she or he does not know anyone else. Usually people mix negative with coping self-talk, but here the differences are highlighted.

Example 3.3 Creating negative and coping self-talk

Situation
Thinking of attending the first session of a counselling skills training group.

Negative self-talk
'I don't know anyone. I am sure that all the other students will be much more experienced than me and know much more about counselling skills than I do. I'm worried what they and the trainer are going to think of me. I may start blushing and stammering. I can feel my heart pounding just at the thought of it. I so want to be liked and to get an excellent grade.'

Coping self-talk
'I'm looking forward to going to the first session. I've been wanting to learn more about counselling skills for some time and its just great to be getting started. I know I may be a little nervous at the first session, but that's life. I'll just tell myself to calm down and take it easy. If I start talking too quickly, I can slow my speech. In the past I've always been a good student and I am optimistic about doing well again this time.'

With coping self-talk you calm yourself down, become clear as to your goals, and coach yourself in appropriate communications. Furthermore, you increase your confidence by acknowledging **strengths**, support factors and previous experience of success. If anything, coping self-talk should be regarded as a necessary part of – rather than as a sufficient whole for – dealing with specific situations in counselling skills training and helping work.

Activity 3.3 Creating self-talk

1 Think of a particular situation in relation to introductory counselling skills training that you might experience as stressful.

Negative self-talk

2.1 Using Example 3.3 as a guide, develop negative self-talk in regard to the situation.
2.2 What would be the consequences of your negative self-talk on how you feel and communicate?

Coping self-talk

3.1 Again using Example 3.3 as a guide, develop coping self-talk, focused on calming and coaching yourself, in regard to the situation.
3.2 What would be the consequences of your coping self-talk on how you feel and communicate?

Creating visual images

When experiencing any significant feeling or sensation, you are likely to think in pictures as well as words. Relationships with fellow counselling skills students, colleagues and clients also take place on a pictorial level. Not only are others seen face-to-face, but you store pictures about them in your mind.

Counselling skills students can differ not only in how much you visualize but also in how vividly. Vividness incorporates the degree to which all relevant senses – sight, smell, sound, taste and touch – are conjured up by the visual image. Another possible aspect of vividness is the extent to which visual images elicit or are accompanied by feelings, for instance hope and sadness.

Some of you either possess well-developed powers of imagery or can develop the skills of visualizing vividly. Others may experience difficulty in visualizing vividly and need to emphasize other ways of controlling your thinking. In general, the more you can experience the senses and feelings attached to your images, the better you can use visualizing as a **self–helping** skill. As with self-talk, the visual images that you create can be negative, coping or a mixture of both.

Example 3.4 illustrates how counselling skills students can create either helpful or harmful visual images to accompany your self-talk. The example here is that of a mature student holding down a job who is on the way to a counselling skills evening class after a stormy workplace staff meeting lasting all afternoon. Though life is not always this simple, frequently by using good visualizing skills it can be made much less difficult.

Example 3.4 Creating harmful and helpful visual images

Situation
A student on the way to a counselling skills evening class after a stormy workplace staff meeting in the late afternoon.

Negative self-talk and visual images
'I'm absolutely furious that my so-called colleagues did not support me. I can just see them sitting there smugly looking after their own interests. They don't really seem to care for the clients. I'm picturing myself at the meeting getting attacked and outvoted. In particular, I can see Andrea and Shaun coming on strong and ganging up on me. They look so aggressive and as if they are enjoying putting me down. I just can't get their faces out of my mind.'

Coping self-talk and visual images
'Let's leave office politics at the office. You can't win them all. I'm on my own time now. Calm down and breathe slowly and regularly. Imagine that peaceful place on the beach I like to mentally visit when I'm feeling stressed ... [conjures up the sights, sounds, smell, taste and touch sensations of the scene]. Enjoy the calm peaceful sensations attached to lying there and relaxing without a care in the world ... [stays in the scene]. Now I'm on my way to my counselling skills class that I enjoy. I can see the friendly faces of my trainer and fellow students and of the fun we have together learning counselling skills with all its ups and downs. I'm starting to feel better already.'

Activity 3.4 Creating visual images

1. Think of a particular situation in relation to introductory counselling skills training that you might experience as stressful (it may be the same situation as in Activity 3.3 above).

Negative self-talk and visual images

    2.1 Using Example 3.4 as a guide, develop negative self-talk and visual images in regard to the situation.

    2.2 What would be the consequences of your negative self-talk and visual images on how you feel, physically react and communicate?

Coping self-talk and visual images

    3.1 Again using Example 3.4 as a guide, develop coping self-talk and visual images, focused on calming and coaching yourself, in regard to the situation.

    3.2 What would be the consequences of your coping self-talk and visual images on how you feel, physically react and communicate?

Creating explanations

Explanations of cause are the reasons that you and others give for what happens. These explanations can influence how you think about your past, present and future. Also, explanations of cause influence how you feel, physically react and act. Frequently, people make explanatory errors that interfere with their motivation and effectiveness. Let's take the example of the women's movement. When women explained their lack of status as being due to male dominance, they were relatively powerless. However, when women also attributed their lack of status to their own insufficient assertion, they empowered themselves.

Counselling skills students can stay stuck in personal problems through wholly or partially explaining their causes inaccurately. Your unresolved personal problems may negatively intrude into your counselling skills training and helping work. Possible faulty explanations for the causes of problems include: 'It's my genes', 'It's my unfortunate past', 'It's my bad luck', 'It's my poor environment', 'It's all their fault', or 'It's all my fault'. Sometimes counselling skills students succumb to the temptation of externalizing problems: you are the victim of others' inconsiderate and aggressive behaviours. Such students explain cause from outside to inside. However, change usually requires explaining cause from inside to outside.

As counselling skills students you can strengthen or weaken your motivation to attain higher skills levels by how you explain the causes of your successes and failures. For instance, you may rightly or wrongly assign the causes for your good or poor counselling skills performance to such factors as prior experience, ability, effort, **anxiety**, task difficulty, trainer competence, adequacy of training environment, opportunities to practise skills, competing demands from other course subjects, financial worries,

---

Example 3.5 Creating harmful and helpful explanations

Harmful explanations

In regard to counselling skills training, it would mean believing that it is up to the trainer and the other group members to make sure that you do well. Being quick to complain when difficulties occur in the training group – for instance, a handout is not forthcoming or the video malfunctions – whether or not these are beyond the control of the trainer. Bringing to skills training an underlying 'Ain't it awful' attitude to life and looking for allies to turn the training group into a students versus trainer 'us–them' combative environment.

Helpful explanations

In regard to counselling skills training, accepting responsibility for making the most of the opportunities that are either provided or that you can create. Working hard to keep your side of the skills training contract. If difficulties occur in the training group, not being a doormat. Accepting what cannot be immediately changed, for example the photocopier breaking down, and assertively collaborating with the trainer and fellow students to improve matters that can be changed.

external work pressures, external relationship pressures, supportive home environment, supportive work environment, or luck, to mention a few. Unfortunately some students are adept at making excuses that mask an inability to assume genuine **personal responsibility** for becoming more skilled. Assuming personal responsibility for counselling skills involves the ability to explain cause accurately and, where possible, to address relevant considerations constructively.

Example 3.5 illustrates how students can create either harmful or helpful explanations for what happens inside your counselling skills training groups.

Activity 3.5 Creating explanations

1 Using the rating scale below, rate the importance you attach to each of the listed factors to explain how successful you will be in learning introductory counselling skills:

4 Extremely important
3 Very important
2 Moderately important
1 Slightly important
0 Of no importance

Your rating   *Factors*

_____   my prior experience at helping
_____   how able I am
_____   the amount of effort I will make
_____   how anxious I will get
_____   the difficulty of the learning tasks
_____   how competent the trainer(s) is
_____   how good the training facilities are
_____   the opportunities I will get to practise my skills
_____   competing demands from other elements of the course, if relevant
_____   financial worries
_____   the degree of support from my work environment
_____   the degree of support from my home environment
_____   my physical health
_____   luck
_____   other factors not mentioned above (please specify and rate each)

2 Summarize your main explanations for how successful you will be in learning introductory counselling skills.
3 Can you alter any of your explanations to increase your chances of success? If so, what revised explanations might you have?

Creating expectations

Humans seek to predict their futures so that they can influence and control them. Consequential thinking entails creating expectations about the consequences of

Example 3.6 Creating harmful and helpful expectations

Situation

Michelle, a counselling skills student, was required to hand in an end of first semester counselling skills course assessment videotape of a full single interview.

Harmful expectations

Michelle's final assessment videotape was poor in that she was far too controlling and did not listen properly to her client. Michelle's skills trainer, Mandy, was aware that she was strong in the academic components of the course and related to her fellow students well. However, she considered Michelle's anxiety level to be too high in her practical skills work. Consequently, rather than fail her videotape, Mandy had a chat with Michelle to explore what was going on. Michelle admitted to being highly anxious over making the assessment videotape.

As the conversation continued, it transpired that Michelle had tremendously high expectations for herself. Michelle related how, when growing up, she felt she always had to strive to prove herself to her mother who had continuously favoured her older sister and who regarded Michelle as an 'also ran'. Now Michelle was making herself anxious again trying to meet inner expectations that had outlived any purposes they may have served in her past and were positively counter-productive now. Michelle thought her new insight very useful to understanding and moving beyond her present impasse.

Helpful expectations

Mandy and Michelle agreed that she could re-submit her final assessment videotape in three weeks' time. During the intervening period Mandy gave Michelle three extra individual supervisions, which focused on helping her become more relaxed both mentally and in her external communication. Michelle increasingly learned a more realistic set of expectations about interviewing competently for this stage of the course and not having to prove her worth as a person to an external authority figure. She gained a level of anxiety that was sufficient to help her to strive for interviewing competence, but not so high that her mind created incompetence. Michelle re-submitted her videotape and passed comfortably.

communication and actions. For good or ill, you can create and influence your consequences, including your own and others' feelings, physical reactions, thoughts and communications.

Consequential thinking can be overdone. Harmful anxiety is a feeling generated by excessive preoccupation with dangerous consequences. In addition, you can become frozen with indecision if too much time is spent trying to predict consequences. Furthermore, in both counselling contacts and daily life, all spontaneity may be lost if you are continually preoccupied with the consequences of communication. You create expectations about the positive and negative consequences of your own and others' communication. Sometimes you make accurate inferences concerning consequences. On other occasions you may overestimate or underestimate the probability of loss or gain.

In counselling skills training and in helping, you create expectations of varying degrees of accuracy about your competence and coping ability. Such expectations influence how confident you feel and how you communicate. Communicating counselling skills competently is not simply a matter of knowing what to do. You need the confidence to use your skills. Expectations about competence differ from expectations about outcomes. Expectations about competence involve predictions about your ability to accomplish a certain level of performance, for instance listening. Outcome expectations involve predictions about the likely consequences of your performance, for instance if a counselling student listens skilfully then clients will probably experience and explore their feelings more fully.

Expectations about your level of competence also influence how much effort to expend and how long to persist in the face of setbacks and difficulties. Unlike self-doubt, strong expectations of competence strengthen resilience when engaging in difficult tasks. In addition, expectations about level of competence influence how you think and feel. Members of counselling skills groups who judge yourselves to be insufficiently competent in dealing with the demands of your skills group may tend to exaggerate your personal deficiencies, become disheartened more easily, and give up in the face of difficulties. On the other hand, members with a strong sense of personal competence, though possibly temporarily demoralized by setbacks, are more likely to stay task-oriented and to intensify your efforts when your performance in skills training falls short of your goals.

Related to expectations about your level of competence are expectations about your ability to cope with difficult situations and people. In counselling skills training and helping work, your lack of confidence about your ability to cope with difficulties, **crises** and critical incidents can worsen how you handle them, if and when they occur. Ironically, at the times when you need to be most realistic and rational, your emotional brain can take over and strong feelings can overcome reason.

Example 3.6 illustrates how a student started out on an introductory skills training course by having unrealistic expectations about her counselling skills, which interfered with and undermined how she interviewed. Then, as the course progressed, she learned more realistic expectations that supported her interviewing.

Activity 3.6 Creating expectations

Part A   Expectations about counselling skills training

1 What are your expectations about the goals and outcomes of your introductory counselling skills training group and how realistic are they?
2 What are your expectations about the processes of your introductory skills training group and how realistic are they likely to be?

Part B   Expectations about yourself

1 What are your expectations about how you will perform during the training group and how realistic are they?
2 What are your expectations about the outcomes you will personally obtain from your training group and how realistic are they?

4

The counselling and helping process

CHAPTER OUTCOMES

By studying and doing the activity in this chapter you should be able to:
- **understand what is meant by a counselling and helping process model;**
- **understand some of the advantages and disadvantages of counselling and helping process models;**
- **gain an overview of the three stage Relating–Understanding–Changing counselling and helping process model; and**
- **gain knowledge of some counsellor skills and client processes involved in each stage of the model.**

Counsellors and **helpers** see **clients** in a wide variety of contexts and with many different primary and secondary agendas. Furthermore, your contact with clients may be brief and intermittent rather than on a regular basis. To assume that there is a single counselling and helping process that covers all these situations is inaccurate. Nevertheless, many counsellors, helpers, trainers and students find it useful to think of your use of **counselling skills** with clients as constituting a process (Egan, 2007; Nelson-Jones, 2005).

When thinking of counselling and helping, the word 'process' has at least two main meanings. One meaning is that of movement, the fact of something happening. Such processes can take place within counsellors and clients and between them. Furthermore, counselling and helping processes can take place outside as well as inside **counselling relationships** and after as well as during counselling relationships. Another meaning of the word 'process' is that of progression over time, especially a progression that involves a series of stages. The two meanings of the word 'process' overlap in that the processes within and between counsellors, helpers and clients change as counselling progresses through various stages.

Counselling and helping process models are simplified step-by-step represen- tations of different **goals** and activities at progressive stages. They are structured frameworks for viewing the counselling process that provide ways of assisting coun- selling skills students and practitioners to think and work more systematically. Counselling process models work on the assumption that the use of counselling skills is cumulative, and that insufficient application of skills in the earlier stage or stages negatively influences the ability to help in later stages.

In this chapter a basic three-stage model of the counselling and helping process gets presented. The underlying idea is that many clients come with fairly specific problems. Sometimes, the problems may have a large psychological component, like learning to set limits assertively on unwanted sexual advances. On other occasions, clients may bring problems that, on the surface at least, do not contain complex psychological components, such as needing financial, legal or retirement planning advice.

When applying counselling and helping models, a useful distinction to bear in mind is that between an overall problem, for instance examination **anxiety**, and specific situations within an overall problem, such as addressing a specific upcoming exam. In general it is best to start learning how to apply a counselling and helping process model by working with specific situations within overall problems rather than with overall problems in their totality. However, in some kinds of counselling and helping, for instance financial or careers advice, an approach to training based on such a distinction may not be valid.

With counselling and helping models a further issue is that of how much to focus on identifying and changing clients' poor **mind skills** and poor **communication/action skills** that may not only contribute to their current problems but place them at risk of repeating mistakes. In very brief counselling and helping, practitioners may consider that there is neither sufficient opportunity nor enough client motivation for addressing such underlying issues, but this is not always the case.

The Relating–Understanding–Changing (RUC) counselling and helping process model

A **Relating-Understanding-Changing (RUC)** counselling and helping process model is presented (see Box 4.1). Each of the three stages is named after the main task for counsellor and client. The fact that the model is presented in three stages may imply a degree of tidiness inappropriate to the actual practice of counselling and helping.

Box 4.1 The Relating–Understanding–Changing (RUC) counselling and helping process model

Stage 1: Relating
Main task: To start establishing a collaborative working relationship

Stage 2: Understanding
Main task: To assess and agree on a shared definition of the client's problem(s)

Stage 3: Changing
Main task: To assist the client to change so that the problems and **problem situations** are addressed more effectively than in the past

---

Often the stages overlap, and sometimes practitioners find it necessary to move backwards and forwards between stages. Maintaining flexibility can be important.

Stage 1: the Relating stage

The counsellor/helper in the process
Counselling and **helping relationships** start at, if not before, the first meeting between counsellors and clients. For instance, how as a counsellor you handle telephone calls can decide whether clients want to proceed with having an appointment. You also need to calm yourself down and get your helping space ready before you open the door of your offices to meet clients. A preliminary phase of the relating stage is the introductions phase, the purpose of which can be described as meeting, greeting and seating. The session starts with the moment of first contact with the client. When meeting clients in a waiting area, they may perceive it as more friendly if, as well as saying their names, you go over to them and show them into your office rather than just stand at the door. Clients should politely be shown to their seats and helped to feel safe. At an appropriate moment, possibly even in the waiting area, the counsellor may greet them along the lines of: 'Hello, I'm ... a counsellor here.' The issue of what counsellors and helpers and your clients call each other can be handled according to the formal or informal **rules** of the context in which you help.

How the session gets started may vary according to the counselling or helping context as well as according to the counsellor's and the client's wishes. For example, some contexts require some basic **information** gathering at the start of sessions. Apart from this, the main choice in starting a session is whether first to allow clients to tell their stories and then do some **structuring** about the nature of the contact or the reverse. My preference is for letting clients talk first and 'get their problem(s) off their chest'. Sometimes, clients come with one clearly identified **problem situation**, for example how to handle anxiety concerning an important job interview in a week's time. On other occasions, they may have many or more complex problems. In any event, counsellors and helpers should create an emotionally comfortable relationship and use active **listening** skills to help clients to overview their main reasons for coming to see you. If there is more than one problem area, you can summarize and identify the different problem areas and ask clients which one they want to address. Then, assuming the counselling contact is brief, you can ask them to identify a particular situation within the problem to work on together.

The client in the process
Clients wonder whether they can trust their counsellors and helpers, what is going to happen, whether their secrets will be divulged elsewhere and whether they will be treated with sympathy and respect. They want to be assisted to feel comfortable and safe. They may not find it particularly easy to talk about certain aspects of their problems and they want to be able to go at their own pace. They appreciate counsellors with calm and reassuring presences, who do not overpower them, and who are prepared to hold back and let them say why they have come. Clients can feel overwhelmed by problems. Given limited time for counselling or helping, many clients may think it better to try to make progress on just one of them.

Stage 2: the Understanding stage

The counsellor/helper in the process
Both counsellor or helper and client require a fuller understanding of the specific problem situation the client has selected. Often, clients feel at an impasse in problem situations. Getting them to describe the situation more fully in a supportive emotional climate can loosen their thinking, enlighten them and encourage them to think that they may be able to manage it better. Based on the foundation of good active listening skills, counsellors and helpers use questioning skills that elicit information about clients in relation to their problem situations in such areas as: thoughts, **feelings** and **physical reactions**; attempts to cope in the past, including interactive patterns established with significant others; the situation's context; **perceptions** of personal **strengths**, resources and support factors; and any other considerations that either counsellors or clients consider pertinent. Sometimes, counsellors engage clients in mini role plays that can go some way to eliciting the actual verbal, **vocal** and **bodily communications** employed in situations.

Counsellors and helpers seek to enlarge as well as to clarify the clients' understanding of situations, including their contribution to sustaining negative aspects of them. You may ask **questions** that elicit information relevant to the clients' mental processes: for instance, their about their rules, perceptions and **self-talk**. Sometimes you may challenge client perceptions and provide feedback. Furthermore, at appropriate junctures, you may summarize the ground recently covered. Towards the end of the understanding stage, counsellors and helpers may take one of two directions. First, you may summarize all the main points elicited so far and check with clients about the accuracy of their summary and whether they wish to modify, add or subtract anything. Second, you may try to identify at least one mind skills weakness and at least one communication/action skill weakness and translate them into goals for the work of stage three (Montgomery, 2006).

The client in the process
Often, clients are glad that they are working on tangible situations. In the past they may have felt stuck in relation to their situations. Clients can still feel the counselling or helping relationship is comfortable even though counsellors question them. Nevertheless, sometimes clients may feel vulnerable about some aspects of their situations and not reveal everything. Being able to get many of their thoughts, feelings and physical reactions systematically out into the open helps clients to get in touch with and reflect upon them. Clients can also find it useful to examine specific verbal, vocal and bodily dimensions of their communication rather than just talk in vague terms about them.

Clients can appreciate brief counsellor or helper summaries along the way that give them pause for thought and reflection. In addition, clients can find composite summaries, pulling together what they have been saying about their problem situations, particularly enlightening and thought provoking. As the understanding stage progresses, clients may start thinking that perhaps they can do something constructive about their situations after all. This may especially be the case where clients' problems have been broken down into mind skills goals and communication/action skills goals for them to address.

Stage 3: the Changing stage

The counsellor/helper in the process
Two somewhat overlapping approaches that counsellors, helpers and clients can take to the changing stage are the problem solving approach and the developing specific mind skills and communication/action skills approach. In the problem solving approach, counsellors and helpers assist clients to clarify goals for problem situations, generate and explore options to attain them, and then to develop and implement action plans.

In the developing specific mind skills and communication/action skills approach, clients can be assisted to attain specific goals. Frequently, counsellors and helpers act as client-centred coaches who assist clients to develop more effective verbal, vocal and bodily communication skills for their problem situations. You need to be careful to keep clients 'owning' their problems and to draw out clients' ideas and resources in dealing with them.

Sometimes coaching includes **role playing**. Some counsellors and helpers incorporate the use of the whiteboard into their coaching: for instance, jointly formulating with a client a clear verbal request for someone to change their behaviour and then pinpointing desirable vocal and bodily communication to back up this request.

In addition, counsellors and helpers can encourage clients to think more effectively. For instance, once clients have identified useful ways of communicating in their problem situations, counsellors can coach them in helpful self-talk for rehearsing and enacting this behaviour in real life. Furthermore, counsellors can assist clients to challenge unrealistic rules and perceptions and replace them with more realistic ones.

Counsellors and helpers can assist clients to rehearse and practise their new skills of thinking and communicating between sessions and then report back at the start of subsequent sessions. You encourage clients to assume responsibility for changing their behaviour both now and in future. Before ending, counsellors, helpers and clients review ways that clients can maintain their skills afterwards.

The client in the process
Often, clients appreciate their need to think more clearly about what they want to achieve in situations. They also may be very aware of the need to avoid repeating behaviours that have worsened situations in the past. Many clients have never taken a systematic approach to analyzing and changing how they communicate and act. They can find it useful to have their communication broken down into its verbal, vocal and bodily elements so that they can improve it bit by bit. Clients who are visually oriented like working with counsellors and helpers who outline desirable communications on the whiteboard. During the changing stage, many clients start getting more of a sense that they can take control of their communication. In addition, clients appreciate attention being paid to how they think, realizing that a stronger inner game can lead to a better outer game. In the past, many clients have allowed themselves to be too easily discouraged and distracted from their goals. Most clients can recognize the importance of being responsible for their mind skills and communication/action skills and also for maintaining their gains once counselling or helping ends.

Example 4.1 Case illustrations

Example 1   Helping a shy pupil to become more social

Sarah, 35, a counsellor at a secondary school, meets with Craig, 16, who is worried about not getting on well with girls. Sarah allows Craig to talk about his life and his home and school relationships and he gradually starts opening up to her. Craig tells Sarah that he comes from a reasonably happy home background, but that both his parents work hard and do not socialize much. He has always been rather shy. Now he thinks that girls will not be interested in him and he tends to avoid them. Sarah helps Craig to realize that he can talk to girls without feeling the pressure to ask them out. Craig practises this with Sarah and in real life. As he starts making friends with girls, Craig gets the confidence to ask one for a date. By now Sarah has helped him to realize that even if he were to get turned down by one girl, there are still plenty of other girls he can ask.

Example 2   Helping a client look after her health better

Helen, 58, a real estate agent, is recovering from a heart attack and is referred by her doctor to see the counsellor, Guy, attached to the private practice. Initially, Helen is very skeptical about counselling and thinks that she does not need help. Guy facilitates Helen to talk about how she has been a heavy smoker since her youth, the stresses she is under at work and how she has been poor at setting limits on them, her generally good relationship with her husband Jon, her lack of any real outdoor activities, and what sort of future she wants for herself both now and when she retires from the business where she works. Helen realizes that she has been lucky this time in that no permanent damage has been done, but there is no guarantee that a future heart attack might not be either fatal or leave her physically incapacitated. With Guy's assistance, Helen decides to cut down from about 60 to 10 cigarettes a day and resume playing tennis, which she used to enjoy. Helen decides that she has been too perfectionist and needs to work to a more realistic schedule, especially since she has been taking on extra duties rather than been given them by management. Helen sees changing her behaviour as giving her more time with Jon, which she regards very positively. Helen agrees to see Guy regularly since she realizes that it is extremely important that she changes how she thinks and acts.

Example 3   Helping a client to become more assertive

Kim, 24, and Neil, 25, have lived together for four months, but there is a growing problem in their relationship. Kim comes to see a helper, Kate, who discovers that, while the couple get on quite well, Kim feels that she is doing most of the cleaning and looking after their apartment and she is starting to resent this. On probing further, Kate discovers that Kim and Neil have yet to have a real talk about how to share the apartment chores. Kim discusses her fears of bringing up the topic, in particular, the fact that she might lose Neil.

Example 4.1 Case illustrations – cont'd

Kate helps Kim to break her problem down into mind skills and communication skills. Kim has a goal of overcoming her rule of needing to be approved all the time by Neil and testing the accuracy of her perception that he will not change if she brings the subject up and then persists. Kate works with Kim on the communication skills of how she might bring up the subject with Neil, in particular, assertively letting him know she wants the relationship to continue, but she also wants to discuss a more equal sharing of apartment duties.

Activity 4.1 Using the skilled client model

1 In what counselling or helping context(s) are you or do you see yourself using counselling skills?
2 To what extent do you think it realistic to work within a Relating–Understanding–Changing skilled client model in that context(s)?
3 How do you think you can make the relating stage work well when using counselling skills either on your course or in the context(s) mentioned above?
4 How do you think you can make the understanding stage work well when using counselling skills either on your course or in the context(s) mentioned above?
5 How do you think you can make the changing stage work well when using counselling skills either on your course or in the context(s) mentioned above?

5

Counselling and helping relationships

CHAPTER OUTCOMES

By studying and doing the activities in this chapter you should:
- be able to describe some key issues in defining counselling and helping relationships;
- understand that counselling and helping relationships are both public and private;
- understand communication processes and patterns in counselling and helping relationships;
- be able to describe some core conditions of counselling and helping relationships; and
- understand the need for flexibility in offering counselling and helping relationships.

Counselling and **helping relationships** are the human connections between you as counsellors and helpers and your clients, both face to face and in each other's minds. Connection is the essential characteristic of any relationship. When in a counselling and helping relationship you exist in some connection or association with another, be it in counselling, health care, human resource management, teaching, or voluntary agency work. In addition, your person-to-person contacts, however brief, offer you the prospect of a relationship that may continue in the minds of each of you, both between your meetings and even long after you stop meeting.

In the context of this book, counselling and helping relationships are those in which you use **counselling skills** mainly face to face to assist clients in any or all of the following ways: to feel supported and understood, to clarify and expand their under-standing, and to develop and implement strategies for changing how clients think, act, and feel so that they can attain life-affirming **goals**. These relationships tend not to imply matching between equals to meet both parties' needs: instead usually one of you is actively using counselling skills to assist the other person to attain her or his goals or, at the very least, to receive psychological comfort.

Despite common characteristics, there is no single way of describing effective coun-selling and helping relationships. Already the distinction has been made between being a **counsellor** and using counselling skills as part of other roles. Many of you reading this book are likely to use counselling skills as part of helping relationships connected with other roles. If so, your helping relationships are likely to take place in the context of other primary agendas – for example, health, business or education. Such helping relationships may well take place in out-of-office settings: for instance, talking with patients in hospital beds or with secondary school students between classes.

In addition, though all counselling approaches **stress** the importance of the relationship, they differ in how much they emphasize and use it. For example, in person-centred counselling, the quality of the counsellor–client relationship is considered both necessary and sufficient for change. In the cognitive-behavioural approaches, the relationship is regarded as necessary, but usually insufficient to bring about desired changes. In addition to offering good relationships, cognitive-behavioural counsellors require skills that focus on assessing and changing clients' specific thoughts and behaviours. In the psychoanalytic approach, the nature and use of the counsellor–client relationship differs again in that it can become a source of content to be talked about. Analysts may examine and interpret any significantly distorted **client perceptions** towards them.

If using the **Relating–Understanding–Changing (RUC) counselling and helping process model** described in Chapter 4, you adjust the counselling relationship for each stage of the process. In the relating stage, the counsellor offers a relationship that creates an emotional climate in which it is easy for clients to talk and feel understood on their own terms. In the understanding stage, while still offering a supportive relationship, the counsellor asks more **questions** and directs the conversation to a greater extent than in the relating stage. In the changing stage, the counsellor may also be a coach who uses the relationship to assist clients to gain confidence and skills and then to practice changing.

For those of you using counselling skills as part of other roles, your use of the counselling relationship at each stage of the Relating–Understanding–Changing model is likely to be heavily influenced by the contexts in which you work. Some of you may only have the opportunity for brief, but nevertheless important, helping contacts. You may be faced with difficult decisions about whether you just offer supportive relationships or attempt to use the relationship to foster change as well. In addition, you might experience conflicts within roles: for instance, personnel officers may face conflicts between doing performance appraisals for their organizations and putting their clients' interests first.

Dimensions of counselling and helping relationships

Mental processes and emotions

Counselling and helping relationships take place within participants' hearts and heads as well as face to face. Most obviously, **counselling relationships** are public and consist of observable verbal, **vocal** and **bodily communication** of varying degrees of intention. However, these relationships are also private and consist of counsellor or counselling skills student and client internal mental processing. For example, you each relate to your perceptions about one another and the relationship. Furthermore, you each create and edit thoughts both shared and left unstated. These thoughts may be 'there and then', 'there and now' and 'there and in future' thoughts about outside events as well as 'here and then', here and now', and 'here and in future' thoughts about events in counselling and helping.

Furthermore, the fact that counselling relationships are internal as well as external means that session material can be processed between sessions and when the external relationship ends. A consequence is that, if successful, knowledge and skills acquired in public now become the preserve and responsibility of private **self-helping** relationships.

Counselling relationships also consist of emotions, only some of which may be exhibited. For instance, both of you may hold and exhibit different degrees of trust and liking for one another. Furthermore, you may experience the relationship differ- ently: for example, as warm, lukewarm, tepid or cold.

Thinking influences feeling as well as the reverse. Both you and your client's **feelings** may be based on undistorted perceptions of one another as well as on distortions created by such factors as **anxiety** and reminders of past relationships. In the psychoan- alytic tradition, in particular, transfers of past feelings, perceptions and behaviours into present counselling and helping relationships are called **transference**, if by clients, and **counter-transference**, if by counsellors. An example of transference is that of clients, whose parents have been demanding, transferring anxiety about revealing personal **information** to them to sharing it with their counsellor now. As time goes by clients may perceive in less distorted ways and reveal more personal information.

Communication processes and patterns

The public or observable relationship consists of all the communications relevant to any particular counsellor– or helper–client relationship. During your contacts, both counselling skills student and client send and receive numerous verbal, vocal and body messages. In addition, counselling skills students may provide clients with written material, use a whiteboard, and sometimes make cassettes and/or videotapes. After coun- selling, there may be further face-to-face contact or contact by phone, letter or e-mail.

One way to look at the communication processes involved in counselling relation- ships is in terms of how counselling skills students and clients reward each another. For example, your communications like active **listening**, warmth, and invitations for clients to become involved in the process can each be rewarding to clients. Clients also provide rewards, for instance smiles and head nods.

As in any relationship, counselling skills students and clients can build up mutually reinforcing **communication patterns**, which can enhance or impede the process. A useful pattern of communication is one that is collaborative in attaining legitimate goals. For example, good empathic responses from students elicit honest self-exploring responses from clients which in turn elicit good empathic responses from students and so on. In addition, counselling skills students who quietly encourage clients to assume responsibility for their lives may get clients communicating in ways that do so.

On the other hand, counselling skills students who encourage **dependency** may have clients who are continually looking for answers outside of themselves. A simple example of a negative communication pattern is that of talkative counsellors who wonder why they have quiet clients. The demand–withdrawal pattern is another example of an unhelpful pattern of communication. Here, counsellors continually seek personal data from clients who constantly withdraw in the face of such attempts because they are not ready to reveal the required information. Sometimes, however, under-confident counsellors are too reticent in seeking information. Another negative communication pattern is that between charismatic or domineering counsellors and dependent clients.

Clients also try to influence how counselling skills students communicate. Often their attempts are useful, for instance by clarifying counsellor misunderstandings. On other occasions, clients may use flattery or play nice, unintelligent or dependent, as ways of trying to elicit caring communications. If successful, clients may elicit insufficiently **challenging** communication that helps them to stay stuck rather than to change.

Language of counselling and helping relationships

Each approach to counselling and helping has concepts described in its own specialist language, for instance in psychoanalytic, person-centred or cognitive-behavioural languages. The counselling relationship is a series of conversations requiring the necessary language and vocabulary. In any counselling relationship there are at least three kinds of conversations going on: namely, the public or overt client–counsellor conversation and each participant's private or internal conversation. All counsellors who operate out of explicit theoretical frameworks are likely to talk to themselves about clients privately in the language of that framework. Then, in varying degrees, your private language will be used in your face-to-face relationships with clients. However, counsellors may not always communicate with clients in the language they use in their private reflections. For example, much of the language in which **person-centred theory** is formulated, with concepts like organismic valuing process, subception and conditions of worth (Rogers, 1959), tends not to be shared with clients. Instead, person-centred counsellors try to reflect a client's personal content and its underlying meanings and nuances.

Cognitive-behavioural approaches, like **rational emotive behaviour therapy** and **cognitive therapy**, actively try to influence the language in which clients talk to themselves so that it becomes helpful rather than harmful. These approaches educate clients to converse with themselves creatively. Likewise in the skilled client model, counsellors and helpers think about your clients in the same language as the actual counselling conversation is conducted. Furthermore, collaboration with clients ensures that they understand how to talk to themselves once counselling ends so that they can maintain their skills. Useful elements of the counsellor's language are exported to and imported by clients so that they can become and remain more self-aware and increasingly self-reliant.

Relational depth

Though not focused on in this introductory book, Mearns and his colleagues have developed the notion of meeting the client at relational depth (for example, Mearns, 2003; Mearns and Cooper, 2005). Counsellors who are willing to work with clients at relational depth try to leave aside conventional ways of responding and project themselves fully into the clients' experiencing. Clients, too, may make suggestions as to how therapy may proceed. If and when clients feel convinced of their counsellors' ability to meet them at relational depth, they may feel the safety and companionship that allows them to share their very existence as they are experiencing it. Mearns writes of the client experiencing relational depth: 'In this territory he does not talk *about* his experiencing – he *is* his experiencing … In this existential process he cannot lie – lying belongs to a much more superficial level of relating' (Mearns, 2003: 5). In meeting clients at relational depth, the maxim of person–centred counselling that it is more about *being* than about *doing* holds true.

Activity 5.1 Defining counselling and helping relationships

Answer the following questions depending on whether you are interested in either counselling relationships or helping relationships.

1 How would you define the counselling/helping relationship?
2 Critically react to the notion that counselling/helping relationships involve internal as well as external relationships.
3 What is the role of mental processing in counselling/helping relationships
   a) on the part of counselling skills students
      · in strengthening the counselling/helping process?
      · in interfering with the counselling/helping process?
   b) on the part of clients
      · in strengthening the counselling/helping process?
      · in interfering with the counselling/helping process?
4 What is the role of emotions in counselling/helping relationships
   a) on the part of counselling skills students
      · in strengthening the counselling/helping process?
      · in interfering with the counselling/helping process?
   b) on the part of clients
      · in strengthening the counselling/helping process?
      · in interfering with the counselling/helping process?
5 Regarding communication processes and patterns in counselling/helping relationships
   a) how can counselling skills students communication influence client communication?
   b) how can client communication influence counselling skills student communication?
   c) how can counselling skills students and clients set up patterns of communication that
      · strengthen the counselling/helping process?
      · interfere with the counselling/helping process?

Core conditions for counselling and helping relationships

In 1957, Carl Rogers published a seminal article entitled 'The necessary and sufficient conditions of therapeutic personality change' (Rogers, 1957). Here Rogers identified six conditions for therapeutic change, three of which – empathic understanding, **unconditional positive regard** and **congruence** – are often referred to as the core conditions of counselling relationships. Rogers emphasized the client's perception of the counsellor's communication of the core conditions and not just the conditions themselves. He stressed that it was necessary for clients to perceive, at least to a minimal degree, empathic understanding and unconditional positive regard, though he omitted to mention congruence as well.

Rogers wrote his statement of the necessary and sufficient conditions in relation to **client-centred**, or what later became person-centred, counselling. Other counselling approaches, for instance cognitive-behavioural and psychoanalytic, attest to the importance of Rogers' conditions but adapt them and use additional skills as well. In the Relating–Understanding–Changing (RUC) process model the nature of the counselling and helping relationship differs according to stage. Counsellors are more likely to use the core conditions as Rogers intended in the relating stage and then modify use of them in the understanding and changing stages.

This book does not use the terms empathic understanding, unconditional positive regard and congruence, but has different terms to break down the counselling skills covered by these concepts. However, each of the core conditions gets briefly described for two main reasons. First, the concepts provide valuable insights into how to offer genuinely helpful relationships to clients that strengthen rather than interfere with developing the **working alliance**. Second, the terms **empathy**, unconditional positive regard and congruence are in such common use in the counselling and helping professions that you should know what they mean (Raskin, Rogers and Witty, 2008).

Empathy

Clients like to feel understood on their own terms by counsellors and helpers. Empathy is the capacity to identify mentally with and to comprehend another person's inner world. Counsellors may possess and be perceived to show empathic understanding in relation to single client statements, a series of client statements, the whole of a counselling session, or a series of counselling sessions. Rogers considered that counsellors should possess and show an empathic attitude. He stressed creating an empathic emotional climate rather than using empathy as a set of skills.

Rogers' use of the term empathy particularly focused on the construct of experiencing. He attempted to improve the quantity and quality of his clients' inner listening to the ongoing 'psycho-physiological' flow of experiencing within them. This flow is an inner referent to which individuals can repeatedly turn to discover the 'felt meaning' of their experience. As well as helping a client to get in touch with more obvious feelings, he attempted to help them sense 'meanings of which he/she is scarcely aware, but not trying to uncover feelings of which the person is totally unaware, since this would be too threatening' (Rogers, 1975: 4).

Empathy is an active process in which counsellors desire to know and reach out to receive clients' communications and meanings (Barrett-Lennard, 1998). Responding to individual client statements is a process of listening and observing, resonating, discriminating, communicating and checking understanding. Needless to say, the final dimension is that the client has, to some extent, perceived empathy. Even better is that empathy has enabled the client to get more in touch with the flow of her or his experiencing. Example 5.1, taken from a demonstration film with Rogers as the counsellor (Rogers, 1965), illustrates this process. The client, Gloria, is talking about how her father could never show he cared for her the way she would have liked.

Example 5.1 Dimensions of the empathy process

Client's statement: 'I don't know what it is. You know when I talk about it feels more flip. If I just sit still a minute, it feels like a great big hurt down there. Instead, I feel cheated.'

Counsellor's responding processes

Observing and listening: Observes and listens to the client's verbal, vocal and bodily communication.

Resonating: Feels some of the emotion that the client experiences.

Discriminating: Discriminates what is really important to the client and formulates this into a response.

Communicating: 'Its much easier to be a little flip because then you don't feel that big lump inside of hurt.'
Communicates a response that attempts to show understanding of the client's thoughts, feelings and personal meanings. Accompanies verbal with good vocal and bodily communication.

Checking: In this instance, the client quickly made her next statement that followed the train of her experiencing and thought. However, the counsellor could either have waited and allowed the client space to respond or could have enquired if the response was accurate.

Client perception of counsellor's responding
How the client reacted indicated she perceived that the counsellor showed excellent empathy and that she was able to continue getting more in touch with her experiencing.

Unconditional positive regard

Unconditional positive regard consists of two dimensions: level of **regard** and unconditionality of regard. Level of regard, or possibly more correctly level of positive regard, consists of positive counsellor or **helper** feelings towards the client like liking, caring and warmth. Unconditionality of regard consists of a non-judgmental acceptance of the client's experiencing and disclosures as their subjective reality. A key issue in unconditional positive regard is that as counsellors you are not trying to possess or control clients to meet your own needs. Instead, counsellors respect clients' separateness and accept their unique differences. Such acceptance gives clients permission to have and fully experience their thoughts and feelings.

Sometimes the notion of counsellors possessing unconditional positive regard is criticized because it implies acceptance of clients who exhibit unacceptable behaviours, for instance domestic violence or sexual abuse. Possible rejoinders to such criticism include the following points. Unconditional positive regard can mean accepting the validity of clients' subjective experiencing without agreeing with their behaviours. In addition, showing clients unconditional positive regard may be important in creating the conditions of psychological safety whereby they can acknowledge and question unacceptable behaviours for themselves. Furthermore, an important reason why clients may be behaving badly is that they have experienced insufficient unconditional positive regard in their pasts.

Another way of looking at unconditional positive regard is that counsellors respect and value the deeper core of clients and identify with their potential rather than with their current behaviours. Unconditional positive regard involves compassion for human frailty and an understanding of universal conditions that lead individuals to become less effective persons than desirable. Clients are more likely to blossom and change if loved for their human potential rather than rejected for their human failings. Though this observation may be setting very high standards, often the inability of counsellors and helpers to feel and show unconditional positive regard reflects their own insufficient personal development.

Congruence

Congruence or **genuineness** has both an internal and an external dimension. Internally, as counsellors and helpers you are able to accurately acknowledge your significant thoughts, feelings and experiences. You possess a high degree of **self-awareness**. This self-awareness may include acknowledging parts of yourself that are not ideal for helping: for example, 'I am afraid of this client'; or 'My attention is so focused on my own problems that I am scarcely able to listen to him' (Rogers, 1957: 97).

Externally, counsellors communicate to clients as real persons. What you say and how you say it rings true. You do not hide behind professional facades or wear polite social masks. Congruent communication is characterized by honesty and sincerity. For example, **compassionate** and caring counsellors live these qualities in helping encounters. Your verbal, vocal and bodily communication sends consistent caring messages. You are not portraying how you think you should be but communicating how you truly are in those moments.

Congruence does not mean 'letting it all hang out'. As counsellors you are able to use your **awareness** of your own thoughts and feelings to nurture and develop clients. Though congruence may include personal disclosures, these disclosures should be for the benefit of clients and in the interest of humanizing the helping process in such a way that it moves forward.

Flexibility in counselling and helping relationships

An important issue in offering counselling and helping relationships is that of how flexible to be. Should counsellors, helpers and students offer the same relationship to all clients or should you vary it? Noted American-based psychotherapist, Arnold Lazarus, observes that the first thing students learn in introductory **psychology** courses is that individual differences are paramount, yet many prominent counsellors show very little change in how they work with different clients across different sessions (Lazarus, 1993; 2008).

Let's look at clients as customers or consumers of counselling and helping services. If clients are to be best served, you require some flexibility in the relationships that you offer. For instance, a timid young teenager who has been dominated at home and is very afraid of any form of intimacy may require a much more gentle relationship than a confident teenager who comes for help in making a decision about which major subject to study at university. Another example is that of a recently bereaved person requiring more space to ventilate feelings than someone who is further along the process of coming to terms with loss. Still another example is that of clients who wish to discuss career decisions rationally and then have their **expectations** dashed by counsellors who insist on focusing on their feelings.

On the assumption of 'different strokes for different folks', counselling skills students can develop a comfortable style of relating that you vary when appropriate. Considerations for varying relationships include whether your role is that of either being a counsellor or using counselling skills as part of performing another role. Considerations for treating clients differently include their interpersonal styles, current emotional states, the nature of their problems and **problem situations**, what sort of relationship they expect, the stage of counselling they are in, and whether clients would be more comfortable with some variation in the relationship according to personal characteristics such as their culture and biological sex. While it is impossible to be all things to everyone, nevertheless the nature of the relationship can be thoughtfully varied to suit individual clients. All helping relationships, whether counselling relationships or relationships requiring the use of counselling skills as part of other roles, need to be created and lived afresh.

Activity 5.2 Core conditions for counselling and helping relationships

Answer the following questions depending on whether you are interested in either counselling relationships or helping relationships.

1 Critically discuss whether there are some central or core conditions operating in all effective counselling/helping relationships?
2 *Empathy*
   a) What does the term 'empathy' mean?
   b) Give an example of or briefly demonstrate offering empathy in a counselling/helping relationship.
3 *Unconditional positive regard*
   a) What does the term 'unconditional positive regard' mean?
   b) Give an example of offering unconditional positive regard in a counselling/helping relationship.
4 *Congruence*
   a) What does the term 'congruence' mean?
   b) Give an example of offering congruence in a counselling/helping relationship.

(Continued)

Activity 5.2 Core conditions for counselling and helping relationships – cont'd

5 *Client perceptions*

a) Why did Rogers stress the importance of clients perceiving the counsellor's or helper's communication of empathic understanding and unconditional positive regard?

b) Assuming counselling skills students offer good levels of empathic understanding and unconditional positive regard, what factors might influence how well clients perceive this?

PART TWO
THE RELATING STAGE

MAIN TASK: To start establishing a collaborative working relationship

Part Two covers the relating stage of the RUC model. Chapter 6 shows readers how to respond to clients from the internal as contrasted with the external frame of reference. Chapter 7 focuses on body messages for showing attention and interest. Chapter 8 trains readers in reflecting both feelings and also the reasons for them. Chapter 9 describes how to start the counselling and helping process and Chapter 10 deals with problems like managing resistant clients and making referrals.

6

Understanding the internal frame of reference

CHAPTER OUTCOMES

By studying and doing the activity in this chapter you should:
*   understand what the term 'active listening' means;
*   understand some reasons for the importance of active listening;
*   understand what it means to possess an attitude of respect and acceptance; and
*   become better at taking the client's perspective.

How many people do you know who listen to you properly? Most of us know very few. Quite apart from wanting air time to speak about their own thoughts, feelings and experiences, many people we know will put their own 'spin' on what we say rather than listen accurately and deeply to us. Egan (2007) observes that full **listening** means listening actively, listening accurately and listening for meaning. The single most important goal of any basic counselling and helping **skills** course is to improve the quality of students' listening. Experienced counsellors and helpers have to monitor the quality of their listening all the time

Using active listening

How, as a **counselling skills** student, can you create an emotional climate so that your **clients** feel safe and free to talk with you? Many of the component skills of creating collaborative working relationships come under the heading of **active listening**. A distinction exists between hearing and listening. *Hearing* involves the capacity to be aware of and to receive sounds. *Listening* involves not only receiving sounds but, as much as possible, accurately understanding their meaning. As such it entails hearing and memorizing words, being sensitive to vocal cues, observing body language, and taking into account the personal and social context of communications. However, counsellors and helpers can listen accurately without becoming rewarding listeners. *Active listening* entails not only accurately understanding speakers' communications, but also *showing* that you have understood. As such active listening involves skills in both receiving and sending communications.

Active listening is probably the central skill in developing and maintaining counselling and **helping relationships**. For clients who come to counselling, occasionally not being listened to may have created mild psychological pain; often not being listened to, moderate pain; and mostly not being listened to, severe pain.

Active listening by counselling skills students has a number of important consequences.

- *Establishing rapport* You are more likely to develop rapport with clients if they feel understood by you. For example, a study of helpful and non-helpful events in brief counselling identified eight kinds of events perceived as helpful by clients (Elliott, 1985). These helpful events were grouped into two super clusters corresponding to interpersonal and task aspects of counselling. Understanding was the predominant cluster in the interpersonal grouping.
- *Establishing trust* Trust is a major issue in any relationship. Dictionary definitions of trust focus on a firm belief in the honesty, integrity and reliability of another. Many clients come to counselling perceiving that significant others in their past or present lives have been untrustworthy. In addition, life teaches most people to be wary of being taken advantage of. In the face of at least a degree of clients' inevitable mistrust, as counselling skills students you need to establish your credentials of honesty, integrity and reliability.

  An important way of looking at trust in **counselling relationships** centres around clients' fears of rejection. The question becomes: 'Deep down can I trust this **counsellor** to accept me and not to hurt me intentionally?' Here the underlying issue is that of acceptance. A second way of looking at trust is in terms of respect. Here relevant **questions** are: 'Can I trust this counsellor to continue seeing me as a separate individual and not to distort their perception of me to meet her/his own needs?' and 'Can I trust this counsellor to encourage my growth as a separate person within the independence of our relationship?' A third way of looking at trust is in terms of duty of care and **competence**: 'Can I trust this counsellor to act in my best interests?'

  Trust in counselling and helping relationships is an interactive process. The degree to which each counsellor and client trust themselves, one another and the relationship influences the other person's trust. Counselling skills students can expedite the process of establishing trust and dissolving mistrust by listening carefully to clients and showing them that you understand them on their own terms.
- *Bridging differences* Every counselling skills student has a potential set of blinkers depending upon your circumstances. How can you know what it is like to be old, dying, female, male, **gay**, physically disabled, an immigrant, White, Black, Asian, Aboriginal or Maori, if the description does not fit you? However, if counselling someone with a different set of life's circumstances, using strong listening skills will greatly assist in understanding them. Showing good understanding of differences helps you to build bridges not walls.
- *Helping clients to disclose* Clients are often shy and anxious. They may be divulging highly sensitive **information**. Even if the information is not highly sensitive, clients may perceive disclosure as risky. Many clients are like boxers who have learned to keep their guards up for fear of getting hit if they reveal themselves. Previously they may have received much overt and subtle rejection for disclosing. Good listening helps clients to feel accepted, safe and understood which, in turn, helps them choose to tell their stories and to share their inner world.

- *Helping clients to experience feelings* Many, if not most, clients have been inadequately listened to in their pasts. Consequently, they may have relinquished, temporarily at least, some of their capacity for emotional responsiveness (Raskin, Rogers and Witty, 2008). Rewarding listening can help clients tune into and acknowledge the inner flow of their emotions. The message some clients may require is that it is 'okay' to experience and express feelings. They can become stronger and more centred if they can face and learn to deal with feelings than if they either block them out or only partially acknowledge them.

- *Gathering information* A facetious remark about a former psychologist colleague of mine was that he had to ask everyone whether they were male or female since he was incapable of gathering information without asking questions. If counsellors and helpers listen well, most clients collaborate in providing a good deal of relevant information about themselves. They do not require interrogation. Together, counsellor and client can build a working model of problems and **problematic skills** patterns. As part of this process clients provide and explore information about how they use their skills in their daily lives. Many novice counselling skills students question too much and listen too little. However, some ask too few or the wrong sorts of questions.

- *Creating an influence base* Counselling and helping using the skilled client model is a developmental education activity influencing clients to develop **self-helping** skills. Active listening is a way counselling skills students can build an influence base, so that clients are more likely to listen to you. Showing understanding to clients from different cultural groups can also contribute to your ascribed status and credibility. Social influence research points to active listening contributing to clients perceiving counsellors as competent, trustworthy and attractive (Strong, 1968). Studies of the counselling process indicate that successful counselling relationships start with high agreement, pass through a period of disagreement, and end with high agreement. The middle or disagreement stage results from counsellor efforts to generate change and client resistances to such efforts (Strong, Welsh, Cocoran and Hoyt, 1992). Counselling skills students who build social influence early on increase clients' willingness to accommodate your later efforts to generate change.

- *Helping clients to assume responsibility* Clients who are listened to sharply and supportively are more likely to assume responsibility for working on their problems and problematic skills than those who are not. One reason is that active listening may reduce defensiveness. Another reason is that active listening provides a base for offering well-timed challenges that encourage clients to assume – rather than to avoid – responsibility. Furthermore, active listening provides a climate in which clients can assume greater personal agency for constructing their actions and meanings (Strong, Yoder and Corcoran, 1995).

In short, active listening is the fundamental skill of any counselling and helping relationship. Nevertheless, throughout the Relating–Understanding–Changing process model, counselling skills students should adapt how you use active listening in the different stages of the model. Furthermore, if the model is unsuitable for the kind of helping contacts you have, you can adapt your skills of active listening accordingly. However, if as a counselling skills student you are unable to listen properly in the first place, you are poorly equipped to integrate active listening with other counselling skills, such as the ability to ask questions in an appropriate manner.

Possessing an attitude of respect and acceptance

Four kinds of listening take place in any person-to-person counselling or helping conversation. Listening takes place between counsellor and client and within each party. The quality of a counsellor's inner listening, or being appropriately sensitive to your own thoughts and feelings, may be vital to the quality of your outer listening. If either counsellor or client listen either poorly or excessively to yourselves, you listen less well to one another. Conversely, if either or both listen well to one another, this may help the quality of your inner listening.

An accepting attitude involves respecting clients as separate human beings with rights to their own thoughts and feelings. Such an attitude entails suspending judgment on clients' perceived goodness or badness. All humans are fallible and possess good and poor human being skills or capabilities that may result in either happiness or suffering for themselves and others. Respect comes from the Latin word *respicere* meaning 'to look at'. Respect means the ability to look at others as they are and to prize their unique individuality. Respect also means allowing other people to grow and develop on their own terms without exploitation and control. Though an accepting attitude involves respecting others as separate and unique human beings, this does not mean that counselling skills students need to agree with everything your clients say. However, you should be secure enough in yourself to respect what clients say as being their versions of reality.

Counselling skills students need to be psychologically present to clients. This entails absence of defensiveness and a willingness to allow clients' expressions and experiencing to affect you. As much as possible, you should be 'all there' – with your body, thoughts, senses and emotions. Psychological accessibility means having an accepting attitude not only towards clients, but to yourself. Put simply, a confident person's acceptance of self translates into acceptance of others, whereas the reverse is also true.

Understanding the client's internal frame of reference

Many clients come to counselling and helping feeling that they have no one who will really understand what is bothering them. They have either experienced being badly listened to or are afraid that this might happen. At the heart of good counselling is the idea of accurately listening to and understanding clients' verbal, voice and body **communication**. Counselling skills students require skills of taking the client's perspective or of understanding their **internal frame of reference**. There is an American Indian proverb that states: 'Don't judge any person until you have walked two moons in their moccasins'. If clients are to feel that they have been received loud and clear, counselling students need to develop the ability to 'walk in their moccasins', 'get inside their skins' and 'see the world through their eyes'. At the heart of active listening is a basic distinction between 'you' and 'me', between 'your view of you' and 'my view of you', and between 'your view of me' and 'my view of me'. 'Your view of you' and 'my view of me' are inside or internal perspectives, whereas 'your view of me' and 'my view of you' are outside or external perspectives.

The skill of listening to and understanding clients is based on choosing to acknowledge the separateness between 'me' and 'you' by getting inside clients' internal frame of reference rather than remaining in your own external frame of reference. If counselling skills students respond to what clients say in ways that show accurate understanding of their perspectives, you respond as if inside the client's internal frame of reference. However, if you choose not to show understanding of your clients' perspectives or lack the skills to understand them, you respond from the external frame of reference. Example 6.1 provides illustrations of individual responses from external and internal frames of reference.

Often counselling skills students can show that they are taking clients' internal frames of reference by starting their response with 'You'. However, as the statement 'You should have behaved ...' indicates, they can make responses starting with the word 'You' from the **external frame of reference** too.

Counselling skills students always have the choice of whether or not to respond as if inside a clients' internal frame of reference. Think of a three-link chain: client statement–counselling student response–client statement. Students who respond from clients' internal frames of reference allow them to choose either to continue on the same path or to change direction. However, if the response is from an external frame of reference, clients are influenced in such ways as to divert or block those trains of thoughts, feelings and experiences that they might otherwise have chosen.

Understanding the client's internal frame of reference and communicating this understanding in a way that the client feels understood is the main tool of person-centred counselling. This approach assumes that clients will more deeply and accurately get in touch with and be able to act on their unique experiencing this way. Other counselling approaches differ in how much and in what ways counsellors go beyond what clients say when they respond. For example, the cognitive-behavioural approaches aim to discover what thoughts and actions the client needs to change.

Example 6.1 Responses from internal and external frames of reference

External frame of reference responses.
'I wouldn't have done that.'
'You should have behaved ... [describes the behaviour].'
'I think you should ignore [her/him].'
'Stop letting yourself get depressed over small matters.'
'Don't be afraid to show your anger.'

Internal frame of reference responses.
'You feel happy that you've passed the test.'
'You feel sad that [she/he] has died.'
'You're uncertain about whether you should have been so forthright.'
'You're really in two minds as to whether you should invite [her/him] out.'
'You feel glad that you've got a good job at last.'

Some of the time cognitive-behavioural counsellors reflect what clients say, but on other occasions they ask questions and make interventions that come from their own frame of reference, albeit in response to what they perceive as the clients' problems and needs. The analytic school and approaches within it may take what clients say as a starting point for interpreting their thoughts, feelings and behaviour in accordance with the concepts of the approach being used. Sometimes they augment the clients' understanding with additional insights – often taking into account preconscious and unconscious processes.

The skilled client model described in this book begins with counsellors or helpers trying to stay in, or close to, the client's frame of reference. Then, as more information emerges, counsellors ask questions to clarify and understand problems better and then choose interventions depending on the nature of the problem(s). In short, you go out-side being strictly in the client's internal frame of reference. However, participation from your external frame of reference is intended to help clients to meet their **goals**.

Activity 6.1 Identifying the client's internal frame of reference

Below are some statement–response excerpts from formal and informal counselling and helping situations. Three counsellor/**helper** responses have been provided for each statement. Write 'IN' or 'EX' by each response according to whether it reflects the client's internal perspective or comes from the counsellor's/helper's external perspective. Some of the responses may seem artificial, but they have been chosen to highlight the point of the exercise. Answers are provided at the end of this chapter.

Example

Client to relationship counsellor

Client: Since I've started coming here I've increasingly realized that it is not all my partner's fault we've got problems.
Relationship counsellor:
EX (a) That will make it easier for us to work.
IN (b) You've increasingly become more aware that you too have a role in these problems.
EX (c) I think it is not a matter of blaming either of you.

1 Youth to youth worker

Youth: I hate it when my parents argue all the time.
Youth worker:
_____ (a) Can't you get away somewhere when it happens?
_____ (b) My parents used to argue a lot too.
_____ (c) You loathe it when your parents keep fighting.

(Continued)

Activity 6.1 Identifying the client's internal frame of reference – cont'd

2 Student to lecturer

Student: It seems as though there is so much work this term that I will have difficulty managing all of it.
Lecturer:
_____ (a) It helps if you can plan when to do it.
_____ (b) I think you can manage it.
_____ (c) You feel overwhelmed at the amount of work this term.

3 Patient to nurse

Patient: At last I'm starting to feel better and I'm very pleased.
Nurse:
_____ (a) You feel delighted because you are finally beginning to feel better.
_____ (b) Well, let's see how you feel tomorrow.
_____ (c) You should be able to leave the hospital soon.

Activity 6.2 Providing internal frame of reference responses

Provide an internal frame of reference response for each of the following statements.
1 **Client to social worker**
Client: I'm afraid of living in this area because I might get mugged.
2 **Worker to manager**
Worker: It's a difficult project, but we're gradually getting on top of it.
3 **Secondary school student to teacher**
Student: I find it hard to make friends here and feel on my own.

Answers

Activity 6.1

1 (a) EX (b) IN (c) EX
2 (a) EX (b) EX (c) IN
3 (a) IN (b) EX (c) EX

Activity 6.2

1 You feel frightened living here because of the risk of being attacked.
2 You're pleased that you're slowly but surely mastering this hard project.
3 You feel isolated because of your difficulty making friends here.

Other responses might be suitable too.

7

Showing attention and interest

CHAPTER OUTCOMES

By studying and doing the activities in this chapter you should:
- become more aware of good body message skills for listening closely to clients;
- know about cultural differences in sending bodily communication; and
- understand the importance of genuineness in counselling and helping.

When together people are always sending messages to one another. In Chapter 2, you were introduced to the idea of counsellors, helpers and clients sending **communication** and action messages by using verbal, **vocal** and **bodily communication**. The last chapter focused on understanding clients' **internal frame of reference** from the viewpoint of **counselling skills** students picking up verbal communication accurately. However, clients' verbal messages can be influenced by how well counsellors use vocal and bodily communication skills. When such communication is inappropriate, it can lead **clients** to edit what they say and even what comes into their **minds**.

   This chapter attempts to raise your **awareness** of **counsellor** and **helper** skills of sending good body messages to assist clients to communicate their internal frame of reference. During this process, counsellors' body messages as listeners are important both when **listening** to and responding to clients. To be a rewarding person with whom to talk you need physically to convey your emotional availability and interest. This often is referred to as **attending behaviour**.

   Body messages are probably the main category of counsellor or helper responses when clients are speaking. A simple example of what not to do may highlight the point. Imagine being a client who comes to a counsellor for assistance with a sensitive personal problem and, when the counsellor asks why you have come, she or he looks out of the window and puts her/his feet up on her/his desk. On a more serious note, when a counselling graduate student at Stanford University, I had an excellent client-centred counsellor who was the Director of what was then called the Counseling and Testing Center. Every now and then he would put his feet up on his desk in a relaxed manner. However, by then, I knew he was still attending closely to me and I did not find his behaviour at all off-putting.

   The following suggestions include some of the main body message skills that demonstrate interest and attention. In varying degrees, they provide non-verbal rewards for talking. This list of suggestions is offered with the proviso that counselling skills students who see clients in non-office settings will have to edit or adapt the suggestions to the different contexts. A further observation is that students can use some of the following suggestions to give the appearance of listening well, when this may not be the case. Deception in counselling and helping is not the sole preserve of clients.

Be clear about availability

Counselling skills students may sometimes rightly or wrongly be perceived as insufficiently available to help. You should avoid intentionally or unintentionally sending messages that create unnecessary distance. You may be overworked, but you should not also be poor at letting your availability or any limits on it be known. Where possible, you should send clear messages as to your availability in ordinary circumstances, including people who can stand in for you. In addition, it is especially important that you arrange adequate cover for emergencies. For instance, youth workers need to let their availability be clearly known to their clientele, both when they may be seen face to face and how to contact them, or if necessary someone else, when they are not immediately available or in an emergency.

Counselling skills students also physically need to provide messages to clients and others about availability and access. A simple way to show your approachability in informal helping settings is to go over and either be near or chat to people. In some settings another way is to arrange some well-advertised times where people can drop in and talk without an appointment. Those of you with secretaries can also make sure that they are sensitive to and good at dealing with new or old clients who need quick access.

Adopt a relaxed and open body posture

Counselling skills students require sensitivity to the impression that your bodies make on clients. A relaxed body posture, without slumping or slouching, contributes to the message that you are receptive. If as a counsellor you sit in a tense and uptight fashion, your clients may consciously or intuitively feel that you are too bound up in your personal agendas and **unfinished business** to be fully accessible.

One reason that counsellors and clients need to sit with an open body posture is so that you can easily see each another. Some counselling skills trainers recommend sitting square to clients – the helper's left shoulder opposite the client's right shoulder. Another option is to sit at a slight angle to clients. Here both of you can still receive all of one another's significant facial and bodily messages. The advantage of this is that it provides each of you with more discretion in varying the directness of your contact than if sitting opposite one another. Highly vulnerable clients may especially appreciate this seating arrangement.

How you use your arms and legs can enhance or detract from an open body posture. For example, crossed arms can be perceived as a barrier – sometimes, crossed legs can too. There is some research evidence that suggests that postural similarity, where two people take up mirror-image postures, is perceived as a sign of liking.

In many settings, counselling skills students – and sometimes clients too – may not be seated for some or all of their contact: for instance in hospitals or in school playgrounds. Nevertheless, you can try to ensure that your body posture is as open and relaxed as circumstances allow.

Lean slightly forward

Another aspect of body posture is that of whether counselling skills students lean forwards, backwards or sideways. If you lean too far forward you look odd and clients may experience an invasion of their personal space. However, in moments of intimate disclosure by clients, a marked forward lean may build rapport rather than be perceived as intrusive. If you lean too far back, clients may find this posture to be distancing. Especially at the start of counselling or **helping relationships**, a slight forward trunk lean can encourage clients, without threatening them. As the relationship progresses counselling skills students always require sensitivity to the different needs and reactions of individual clients.

Use appropriate gaze and eye contact

Gaze means looking at people in the area of their faces. Good gaze skills indicate a counselling student's interest and enable you to receive important facial messages. Clients' use of gaze can give them cues about when to stop listening and start responding. However, the main cues used in synchronizing conversation are verbal and voice messages rather than body messages.

Good eye contact skills involve counselling skills students looking in clients' directions in order to allow the possibility of your eyes meeting reasonably often. There is an equilibrium level for eye contact in any helping relationship depending on the degree of **anxiety** in each party, how developed the relationship is, and even the degree of attraction involved. Staring can threaten clients because they may feel dominated or seen through. Even a usual amount of eye contact can be too overpowering. I once had a client who started counselling by sitting with one hand shielding his eyes, looking 90 degrees from him, and only occasionally taking a quick peek in my direction. It took about eight sessions for this client gradually to move towards a normal amount of eye contact. Most clients want a usually appropriate amount of eye contact from those helping them and are likely to perceive counselling skills students looking down or away too often as tense or bored. However, always be prepared to make exceptions.

Convey appropriate facial expressions

Listening or responding accurately is not just a matter of hearing, it entails showing that you have heard the verbal content and picked up clients' vocal and bodily messages accurately. When discussing **feelings** in Chapter 2, seven important feelings were mentioned – happiness, interest, surprise, fear, sadness, anger, and disgust or contempt – each of which can be conveyed, or sometimes disguised, by facial expressions. People's faces are usually the main way that they send body messages about feelings. However, the same, or even contradictory, messages can be sent with other parts of the body as well – for instance, walking away in disgust.

Much facial **information** is conveyed through the mouth and eyebrows. A friendly and relaxed facial expression, accompanied by a smile in appropriate instances, usually demonstrates interest. However, as clients talk, counselling skills students' facial expressions need to show that you are tuned into what is being said. For instance, if clients are serious, weeping or angry, students need to adjust your facial expression to indicate that clients' feelings are understood. However, this must be done appropriately, both in response to the nature and intensity of the emotion and to how clients are likely to react.

Use good gestures

Gestures are body movements used to convey thoughts and feelings and can be used by counselling skills students for good or ill. Perhaps the head nod is the most common gesture in listening, with small ones to show continued attention, larger and repeated ones to indicate agreement. Head nods can be viewed as rewards to clients to continue talking. On the negative side, selective head nods can also be powerful ways of controlling clients. Then unconditional acceptance becomes conditional acceptance.

Gestures may also illustrate shapes, sizes or movements, particularly when these are difficult to describe in words. Counselling skills students can respond with arm and hand gestures to show attention and interest to clients. Often, however, it may be inappropriate to mirror clients' utterances mainly by gestures since better matching can be achieved by using good verbal responses. In addition, using expressive arm gestures too much or too little can be off-putting. Negative gestures that can display inattentiveness and discourage clients from communicating clearly include fidgeting with pens and pencils, clenched hands, finger drumming, fiddling with your hair, putting your hand over your mouth, ear tugging, and scratching yourself, among others.

Use touch sparingly

Touching some clients may be appropriate in counselling and helping, though great care needs to be taken that it is not an unwanted invasion of personal space. Furthermore, counselling skills students should always resist touching clients in sexual ways, including sexual intercourse. Touch can be a way of showing genuine caring and concern. For example, concerned counsellors may touch or hold clients' hands, arms, shoulders, and upper back. The intensity and duration of touch should be sufficient to establish contact, yet avoid discomfort and any hint of sexual interest. Part of being an active listener includes picking up messages about the limits and desirability of the use of touch. On occasion nearly touching a client can be an alternative to actually touching them, for instance putting an arm over the back of their chair as they reveal something very upsetting.

Be sensitive to personal space and height

Active listening entails respecting clients' personal space. Counselling skills students can be too close or too far away. Perhaps in interviews a comfortable physical distance for counsellors and clients is sitting with their heads about five feet apart. In Western cultures clients might perceive any shorter distance as too personal. If counsellors are physically too far away not only do clients have to talk louder, but they may also perceive you as emotionally distant. In helping contacts that take place in informal settings, helpers have to use judgment about what is a good distance, if different from about five feet, from clients in your particular circumstances.

The most comfortable height for counselling and helping conversations is with both of your heads at the same level. Counselling skills students who sit in higher and more elaborate chairs than your clients can contribute to them feeling less powerful in the relationship. Students who are taller than clients when standing may need to find ways of lessening the height difference, for instance by leaning towards clients or, if possible, finding appropriate seating.

Be careful about clothing and grooming

To a certain extent with all counsellors and helpers and to a large extent with some 'you are how you look.' First impressions can be heavily influenced not just by what helpers say and your facial expression but also by the messages sent by your clothing and where you see clients. Sometimes helpers' clothes are governed by the contexts in which you work, for instance doctors wear white coats and nurses wear uniforms in hospitals. On many other occasions counselling skills students can choose how to dress. Clothes and jewellery send messages that can influence how much and in which areas clients reveal themselves. These messages include social and occupational standing, sex-role identity, ethnicity, degree of conformity to peer group norms, rebelliousness and how outgoing or introverted they are. While maintaining individuality, counselling skills students need to dress appropriately for your clienteles: as mentioned in Chapter 2, delinquent teenagers may respond better to informally dressed people whereas stressed business executives may prefer people to be more formally dressed.

A counselling skills student's personal grooming also provides important information: for instance, you may be clean or dirty, neat or untidy. In addition, the length and styling of your hair sends messages to clients about you. Clients may have varying degrees of sensitivity as to how healthy they expect their counsellors to look. Though there can be medical reasons why people can be overweight or underweight, in general it is good for counsellors to be within the normal range. However, clients vary in their reaction to those who are outside this range and, if necessary, this can be brought up by either of you. Counselling skills students should always avoid interviewing when under the influence of drink or intoxicating drugs. In addition, you should be sensitive regarding periods when your health may be insufficiently good for you to genuinely help clients.

Cultural differences

Later in the book it is stressed that counsellors, helpers and clients may come from different cultures and that there are many different **goals** for multicultural counselling and helping. Most often the concept of culture refers to the patterns of thoughts, feelings and behaviours of different ethnic groupings. However, culture can be used more inclusively to refer to patterns related to different groupings: for instance, regional, social class, religious, and organizational. Here the main focus is on understanding and responding appropriately to differences in body language related to ethnic groupings.

A useful distinction exists between culture–deficit and the culture–sensitive approaches to using counselling skills. The culture–deficit approach assumes that the **rules**, **values** and behaviours of the dominant culture are normal and that variations observed in minorities are deficits. The culture–sensitive approach avoids the assumption that dominant group practices are proper and superior. Counsellors and helpers show respect for cultural differences and may emphasize positive features of cultural variation. You also show sensitivity to minority group members' different levels of, and wishes for, assimilation into the mainstream culture. Migrant clients are assisted to develop their own identities rather than either being crudely moulded or more subtly influenced into being 'true Brits' or 'dinky dye Aussies'.

The concept of rules is very important for understanding the appropriateness of body messages. However, rules governing behaviour in helping situations should not be straightjackets and, sometimes, counselling skills students may need to bend or break the rules to create genuinely collaborative helping relationships. Relationship rules differ across cultures. For instance, to some Australian Aboriginal people it is unacceptable to look others straight in the eye. Another example is that in India it is not uncommon for people either to nod *or* shake or to nod *and* shake their heads to mean 'yes' or 'no'. In short, counselling skills students require sensitivity to the body message rules of the social and cultural contexts in which you work as well as to your own and clients' individual needs.

The task of detailing cultural variations is too large and complex for this book. Instead, Example 7.1 tries to raise readers' awareness of the importance of culture differences in body language by highlighting aspects of Aboriginal bodily communication.

Example 7.1 Aspects of Aboriginal people's bodily communication

Eye contact To some Aboriginal people, it is unacceptable to look others straight in the eye.

Gaze Frequently Aborigines listen without looking and feel no strong obligation to look at the person talking to them.

Proximity Some Aboriginal lifestyles do not allow men and women to mix freely.

Attendance Attending interviews at specific times is far removed from the usual Aboriginal lifestyle.

Genuineness: creating consistent communications

Since counselling skills students and clients can create communications in so many different ways, **genuineness** becomes important. Both within students' body messages and also between students' body messages and your voice and verbal messages, consistency increases the chances of clients perceiving you as rewarding listeners. For instance, a counselling student may smile, yet at the same time either fidget or foot tap. The smile may indicate interest, the fidgeting and foot tapping impatience, and the overall message conveys insincerity. In addition, students may make good verbal responses that can be completely negated by poor bodily communication.

When sending messages it is possible to deceive others, yourselves or both. Human communication is often very complex and involves shades of grey. Counselling skills students with good skills in sending messages 'loud and clear' have bodily communication that matches your verbal and vocal communication. However, if you fail to send consistent verbal, vocal, and bodily messages you make it harder for clients to decode your overall communication accurately. Furthermore, you increase the chances of clients perceiving you as insincere. In general, verbal communication is easier to control than non-verbal communication. Thus, counselling skills students and clients can often pick up important messages about the real meaning of a communication by attending to how things are being said.

Activity 7.1 Assessing body messages for showing attention and interest

To the extent that they are relevant to the counselling/helping setting(s) in which you either use or will use counselling skills, assess yourself on each of the following body messages for showing attention and interest:
- being available
- adopting a relaxed and open body posture
- leaning slightly forward
- using appropriate gaze
- using appropriate eye contact
- conveying appropriate facial expressions
- using good gestures
- using touch sparingly
- being sensitive to personal space and height
- being careful about clothing and grooming
- cultural considerations in how you communicate with your body
- other important areas not listed above.

Set yourself specific goals, including setting a realistic time frame, for improving showing attention and interest when using counselling skills.

Activity 7.2 Improving showing attention and interest

Pick a specific body message for showing attention and interest that you think you might improve, for instance you may have a tendency to sit with too rigid a posture. Then hold a conversation with a partner where you work on improving your chosen body message. Either during or at the end of your conversation ask for feedback on how you are doing.

If appropriate, afterwards you and your partner reverse roles.

8

Reflecting feelings

CHAPTER OUTCOMES

By studying and doing the activities in this chapter you should:
- improve your verbal communication at reflecting feelings,
- improve your vocal communication at reflecting feelings,
- improve your bodily communication at reflecting feelings,
- become better at reflecting feelings and the reasons for them, and
- become better at understanding context and difference when responding.

Skilled counsellors and helpers are very sharp at picking up clients' **feelings**. **Reflecting feelings** entails your responding to clients' 'music' and not just to their words. To do this, **counsellor** responses incorporate appropriate voice and body messages. Reflecting feelings involves your feeling with a client's flow of emotions and experiencing and communicating this back. Often, **counselling skills** students have trouble in reflecting feelings. You may just talk about feelings rather than offer an expressive emotional companionship. Inadequately distinguishing between thoughts and feelings can be another problem for both clients and students. For example, 'I feel that equality between the sexes is essential' describes a thought rather than a feeling. On the other hand, 'I feel angry when I see sex discrimination' labels a feeling. This distinction between thoughts and feelings is important both in reflecting feelings and also when helping clients to influence how they feel by altering how they think. Constant reflections of feelings can run the risk of encouraging clients to wallow in feelings rather than to move on to how best to deal with them.

Reflecting feelings involves counselling skills students in having both receiver and sender skills. Receiver skills include understanding clients' verbal, vocal and body messages, tuning into the flow of your emotional reactions, taking into account the context of clients' messages, and sensing the surface and underlying meanings of clients' messages. Sender skills include responding in ways that pick up clients' feelings words and phrases, using expressive rather than wooden language to reword feelings appropriately, using vocal and body messages in ways that help reflect the emotions conveyed, and checking the accuracy of your understanding.

Pick up feelings words and phrases

A good but not infallible way to understand what clients feel is to listen to their feelings words and phrases. Feelings phrases are colloquial expressions used to describe feelings words. For example 'I've got the blues' is a feelings phrase describing the word 'depressed'. Picking up feelings words and phrases is similar to **paraphrasing**, but with a heightened focus on feelings rather than informational content. Sometimes counselling skills students ask, 'Well, what did you feel?' after clients have just told them. If so, you need to discipline your **listening** more. On occasion, feelings words are not the central message. For instance, Emma may say 'It's just great' that, after the break-up of a relationship, she is living on her own again, at the same time as her voice chokes, her face looks sad and the corners of her mouth are turned down.

Box 8.1 provides a list of feelings words. Incidentally, it is cumbersome, when reflecting feelings, always to put 'You feel' before feelings words: sometimes 'You're' is sufficient: for example, 'You're sad' instead of 'You feel sad.'

The following are some dimensions of reflecting feelings words and phrases.

- *Intensity* Mirror the intensity of clients' feelings words in reflections. For example, Kevin has just had a negative experience about which he might feel either 'devastated'

Box 8.1 List of feelings words

accepted	dependent	involved	supported
adventurous	depressed	irresponsible	suspicious
affectionate	discontented	jealous	tense
aggressive	embarrassed	joyful	tired
ambitious	energetic	lonely	trusting
angry	envious	loved	unambitious
anxious	excited	loving	unappreciated
apathetic	fit	optimistic	unassertive
appreciated	free	outgoing	unattractive
assertive	friendly	pessimistic	under-confident
attractive	frightened	powerful	uneasy
bored	grieving	powerless	unfit
carefree	guilt-free	rejected	unfree
cautious	guilty	relaxed	unfriendly
cheerful	happy	resentful	unloved
competitive	humiliated	responsible	unsupported
confident	hurt	sad	unwanted
confused	indecisive	secure	uptight
contented	independent	shy	vulnerable
cooperative	inferior	stressed	wanted
daring	insecure	strong	weak
decisive	interested	superior	worried

(strong intensity), 'upset' (moderate intensity) or 'slightly upset' (weak intensity). Corresponding mirroring words might be either 'sent reeling' (strong intensity), or 'distressed' (moderate intensity), or 'a little distressed' (weak intensity). It is possible to err on the side of either adding or subtracting intensity.

- *Multiple and mixed feelings* Sometimes clients use many words to describe their feelings. The words may form a cluster around the same theme, in which case the counselling skills student may choose only to reword the crux of the feeling. Alternatively, clients may have varying degrees of mixed feelings ranging from simple opposites, for instance, happy/sad to more complex combinations, for instance, hurt/angry. Good reflections pick up all key elements of feelings messages. For instance:

Client: I'm delighted, but also worried that she seems to finds me so attractive.
Counselling student: You feel thrilled, but also concerned that she is so keen on you.

Client: I both like working for him, but do not find him easy.
Counselling student: You're happy to be under him, but find him difficult too.

- *Assist labelling of feelings* Sometimes counselling skills students assist clients in finding the right feelings words. Here, reflecting feelings goes beyond reflecting feelings to helping choose feelings words that resonate for them.

Client: I don't quite know how to express my reaction to losing my job ... possibly angry ... upset, no that's not quite it ... bewildered ...
Counselling student: Hurt, anxious, confused, devastated ... are any of those words appropriate?
Client: Devastated, that's what I really feel.

Pick up voice and body messages

Much **information** about clients' feelings does not come from what they say, but from *how* they say it. Sometimes clients' verbal, voice and body messages are consistent. In such instances, it is relatively easy to label feelings and their intensity accurately. However, frequently clients' messages are heavily encoded. Clients may struggle to express what they *truly* feel in face of their conditioning about what they *should* feel. Furthermore, it takes time for clients to trust counsellors and helpers. Consequently, many emotional messages 'come out sideways' rather than loud and clear. Effective counsellors are skilled at listening with the 'third ear' to clients' voice and body messages and to what is left unsaid or camouflaged. In addition, they realize certain clients take time to develop skills of clearly identifying and articulating feelings. They are sensitive to the pace at which clients can work and understand that clients may require patience rather than pressure.

Counselling skills students unclear about clients' real or underlying feelings can check with them. For instance, you may make comments like 'I think I hear you saying [state feelings tentatively]... Am I right?' or 'I would like to understand what you're feeling, but I'm still not altogether clear. Can you help me?' Another option is to say: 'I'm getting a mixed message from you. On the one hand you are saying you do not mind. On the other hand you seem tearful?' After a pause, you might add: 'I'm wondering if you are putting on a brave face?'

A further consideration in picking up feelings is to understand whether and to what extent clients possess insight into their feelings. For instance, a counselling skills student may infer that a parent is absolutely furious with a child. However, the parent may not be able to handle such an observation since it clashes with his or her self-image of being a loving parent. Consequently, the student may need to pick up three feelings: first, the parent's stated feeling of unconditional love for the child; second, the underlying anger with the child; and third, the feeling of **threat** if the parent's self-picture were to be challenged by reflecting how intensely angry he or she was.

Sender skills of reflecting feelings

When reflecting feelings, counselling skills students may wonder how best to respond to the numerous verbal, voice and body messages that you receive. There are no simple answers. What you should try to do is (1) decode the overall message accurately, and (2) formulate an emotionally expressive response that communicates back the crux of the client's feelings. Here are a few guidelines for sending reflecting feelings messages.

- *Send back the crux of the client's message* Where possible, counselling skills students should show that you have understood the client's main message or messages. Whatever else you do, try to communicate back the core feeling.

  Client: We just argue and argue and don't seem to get anywhere. I don't know what to do. It's so frustrating. I wish I knew the answer. I don't seem to be able to handle our relationship.
  Counselling student: You feel extremely frustrated with constant unproductive arguments and not knowing how to improve matters.

- *State the client's main feeling at the front of the response* Even though clients may not start with their main feeling, they may feel better understood by counselling skills students who reflect their main feeling at the front of a response than if they reflect information first.

  Client: I've failed two of my exams and have to repeat them. I'm so disappointed.
  Counselling student: You're bitterly upset at having to retake the exams.

In the above example, the student as counsellor has tuned into feelings immediately. However, imagine the counselling student had replied: 'You failed your exams and are bitterly upset.' Here the student starts by responding from the head to the client's head. By the time the student reflects the feeling of disappointment, it may be too late for the client to experience being fully emotionally understood.

- *Be sensitive to clients' underlying feelings and agendas* Sometimes there are no hidden agendas in what clients communicate. On other occasions, counselling skills students may assist them to articulate underlying feelings. However, sometimes you may intentionally not respond to underlying feelings and agendas. For example, clients may require more space to acknowledge the feelings on their own. Alternatively, they may not be ready for a deeper reflection. Also, when making deeper reflections, there is a greater risk in being wrong than when making surface reflections.

- *Keep the response appropriately simple* Use simple and clear language. Avoid unnecessary words and qualifications. However, be prepared to state different parts of multiple and mixed messages.
- *Use voice and body messages to add expressiveness to verbal message(s)* Counselling skills students are not just talking about feelings, but reflecting feelings. For instance, if a hypothetical suicide-prone client says 'I feel terrible', you can adjust your voice and facial expression to mirror, to some extent, a sense of desperation. Consistency between verbal, voice and body messages is important. Clients receiving mixed messages may doubt the sincerity of those giving them.
- *Check understanding* Counselling skills students respond to client statements with different degrees of tentativeness depending on how clear the **communication** is and how confident you are about receiving messages accurately. However, all reflections should contain an element of checking whether you accurately understand clients' internal viewpoints. Sometimes you can check by slight voice inflections. On other occasions you can check more explicitly.

Activity 8.1 Reflecting feelings skills

For each of the following statements
(a) identify the words and phrases that the client has used to identify how she or he feels; and
(b) reflect the client's feelings, starting your responses with either 'You feel' or 'You're'.

Example

Nick to counsellor: I find doing my job so boring and dull that I am ready to quit.
    (a) Nick's feelings words and phrases: boring, dull.
    (b) Reflection of feelings: 'You feel your work is so uninteresting and tedious that you're thinking of leaving'.

Activity

1 *Bill to counsellor:* I get very down when I think of all the opportunities that I am missing.
    (a) Bill's feelings words and phrases
    (a) Your reflection of feelings
2 *Kim to helper:* I was sexually abused by my dad when I was nine. I've never forgiven him for betraying my trust and I'm still angry.
    (a) Kim's feelings words and phrases
    (b) Your reflection of feelings

(Continued)

Activity 8.1 Reflecting feelings skills – cont'd

3 *Chris to probation worker:* I get so angry when he does that that its all I can do
   to stop myself from hitting him.
   (a) Chris's feelings words and phrases
   (b) Your reflection of feelings

Reflect feelings and reasons

A useful variation in active listening is to reflect both feelings and the reasons for them
(Egan, 2007). Reflecting back reasons does not mean making an **interpretation** or
offering an explanation from the external viewpoint. Instead, where clients have already
provided reasons for a feeling, counsellors or helpers reflect these feelings back in a 'You
feel … because … ' statement that mirrors the internal viewpoint. Here is an example:

> **Katie:** I've struggled so hard to find a decent and affordable flat and now I'm happy
> I've finally succeeded.
> **Counsellor:** You're delighted because at last you've got a reasonable flat that's within
> your budget.
> **Katie:** Yes. I can now feel settled and able to get on with other things.

Here the counsellor's 'You feel … because … ' response shows more understanding of
Katie's predicament than if the response had stopped after 'You're delighted.' Katie was
able to emphasize that the meaning of finding the flat was not only getting a place to
stay, but the ability to get on with her life. Put another way, the 'because' part of the
counsellor's response identified the thinking contributing to Katie's feeling. Thus, 'You
feel … because … ' reflections are useful not only for helping clients tell their stories,
but also for assessing how clients' thinking contributes to their feelings.

Activity 8.2 Reflecting feelings and reasons

For each of the following client statements formulate a reflection of feelings that
strictly uses the 'You feel … because … ' format.

Example

Rachel to counsellor: I'm really happy that Roger and I don't fight so much. I feel
much better about our relationship.
Counsellor: You feel very pleased because you and Roger don't argue so much
and now you're much more optimistic about staying together.

Activity

1 *Becky to counsellor:* My parents keep on arguing and I get so worried about it.
   (a) You feel
   (b) because

Activity 8.2 Reflecting feelings and reasons – cont'd

2 *Naomi to social worker:* When he acts like he owns me I get so mad and upset.
(a) You feel
(b) because

3 *Andy to teacher:* At last I've got a good grade in a maths test and I'm relieved and happy.
(a) You feel
(b) because

Small verbal rewards

Small verbal rewards are brief expressions of interest designed to encourage clients to keep talking. Small verbal rewards are continuation messages. The message they convey is: 'I am with you. Please go on.' Counselling skills students can use small verbal rewards for good or ill. On the one hand you can reward clients for sharing and exploring their internal perspectives. For instance, when a client uses imagery to describe a feeling, you could say 'Tell me more about your image'. On the other hand, your use of small verbal rewards may subtly or crudely attempt to shape what clients say. For instance, you may reward clients for saying either positive or negative things about themselves – possibly rewarding them more for negative statements in early sessions and for positive statements later. Furthermore, you can selectively reward clients for talking about agendas of interest to you. Example 8.1 provides some illustrations of small verbal rewards, though perhaps the most frequently used, 'Uh-hum', is more vocal than verbal.

Open-ended questions

Counselling skills students may use **questions** in ways that either help clients to elaborate their internal perspectives or lead them out of their perspectives, possibly

Example 8.1 Small verbal rewards

'Uh-hum'	'Sure'
'Please continue'	'Indeed'
'Tell me more'	'And … '
'Go on'	'So … '
'I see'	'Really'
'Oh?'	'Right'
'Then … '	'Yes'
'I hear you'	

into yours. **Open-ended questions** allow clients to share their internal perspectives without curtailing their options. A good use of open-ended questions is in initial sessions when wanting to help clients to say why they have come. In subsequent sessions too, you are likely to find open-ended questions useful. Open-ended questions include 'Tell me about it?', 'Please elaborate?', and, slightly less open-ended, 'How do you feel about that?'

Open-ended questions may be contrasted with closed questions that curtail speakers' options: indeed they often give only two options, 'Yes' or 'No'.

> **Open-ended question:** 'How do you feel about your relationship?'
> **Closed question:** 'Is your relationship good or bad?'

Open-ended questions may also be contrasted with leading questions that put answers into clients' mouths:

> **Open-ended question:** 'What do you think about her?
> **Leading question:** 'She's a great person, isn't she?'

It is not suggested here that counselling skills students never use closed questions. It depends on the **goals** of your listening. Closed questions can be useful for collecting information. However, if wishing to help others share their worlds, restraint is required. You may also need to use open-ended questions sparingly. Leading questions are best avoided at all times since they show lack of respect for clients as separate persons with their own thoughts and feelings.

Possess understanding of context and difference skills

Counselling skills students require skills of understanding the contexts of clients and their problems. Issues of context and of clients' differences from you pervade counselling and helping. Clients with problems do not exist in vacuums. Rather they exist in networks of contextual variables whose relevance differs in each instance. A later chapter discusses the numerous personal characteristics that counsellors, helpers and clients bring into their contacts with each other. Clients vary in the number of contextual considerations relevant to identifying and clarifying their problems. Counsellors and helpers also vary in the range of clients they see. Most require a range of understanding context and difference skills, some of which are presented below.

Develop a knowledge base

When counselling skills students work with specific groups, for instance migrants from a certain country or **gay** and lesbian clients, you should be familiar with the assumptions, **values** and shared experiences of these groups. For instance, you should understand what are the major problems for any minority group with whom you are involved. In addition, you should understand the ways in which stereotyping and feelings of powerlessness may leave major scars. If not in possession of such knowledge, you can find it out. Even students possessing a good understanding of specific cultures and minority groups always need to update their knowledge. For example, those of you working with homosexual groups require the most up-to-date information about legislation concerning homosexual behaviour and about, for instance, the transmission and treatment of AIDS. In addition, you could become familiar with the 16 guidelines in the American Psychological Association's *Guidelines for psychotherapy with lesbian, gay and bisexual clients* (Division 44/Committee on Lesbian, Gay, and Bisexual Concerns Task Force, 2000).

Counselling skills students need to remain conscious of the assumptions underlying the sources from which information is gained. For instance, information and investigations about minority cultural groups may primarily reflect the perspective of members from the majority culture. The same may hold true for some, if not much, of the literature in other areas. You can also gain knowledge by speaking to leaders and members from the minority cultures or groups that you wish to target. Here, the risk is that the information may overly reflect the perspective of the minority culture. However, knowing what a predominant minority group perspective is, including its main variations, in itself is valuable in understanding clients who come from that group.

Demonstrate contextual empathy

Counselling skills students can show contextual **empathy** using voice, body, verbal and action messages. Take demonstrating cultural empathy as an example. British people tend to speak more softly than many Australians. Japanese do not use eye contact so much as people from Western cultures. Counselling skills students dealing with people from different cultures need the ability to send and receive both verbal and non-verbal messages accurately and appropriately. You should not assume that good intentions lead to good cross-cultural results.

In responding to verbal messages, counselling skills students need to be sensitive to topics that may have particular meaning to people from different cultures. For instance, a desire for harmonious family relationships often contains a much stronger cultural message when expressed by Asians than Anglo-Saxons. Sometimes high levels of empathy can only be offered by counsellors who speak clients' primary language. Counsellors whose linguistic skills do not match those of clients can either seek the service of translators with cultural knowledge or refer to bilingual counsellors, if appropriate people are available. Often, **cross-cultural sensitivity** is far more impor- tant than the cultural matching of clients and counsellors. On occasion, migrant clients may prefer counsellors from the majority culture because they perceive them as better able to assist their integration into it than people from their own culture.

An important skill in understanding clients' contexts and differences is that of assessing whether their 'problem' stems from either others' personal biases or from discriminatory bias in institutional structures. If so, counselling skills students can assist clients not to personalize problems inappropriately and then blame themselves. In addition, institutional intervention skills on behalf of clients can be used.

A related skill in understanding the impact of clients' contexts is the ability to assess when clients are using the context as a way of avoiding critically looking at their own behaviour. For instance, migrants who make little or no attempt to understand the language of their host country, contribute to their feelings of cultural alienation. In showing understanding, a delicate balance may need to be struck between acknowledging clients' internal viewpoints, yet not colluding in erroneous efforts to simplify themselves as victims of oppressive majority cultures. Even when majority cultures are oppressive, counselling skills students can empower clients with skills to manage their lives better in them. In addition, you can train clients in skills of counteracting institutional oppression.

Each client has a unique life history and way of interpreting the cultural and minority group influences that have affected her or him. Counselling skills students need to take care to avoid pigeon-holing clients into your version of cultural and minority group contexts rather than understanding them as individuals.

Give permission to discuss counsellor–client differences

Counsellors, helpers and clients come from different contexts. Counselling skills students may quickly become aware that you differ on significant characteristics from clients. One possibility is to acknowledge the difference – for instance racial or cultural – and ask what clients think and feel about this. A possible advantage of being direct is that it provides clients with opportunities to air and work through mistrust. A risk is that such questions may reflect more counsellors' than clients' concerns and, hence, de-focus clients. Possibly a more neutral way to unearth clients' concerns about obvious differences is to say: 'Are there any questions you would like to ask me?'

Give permission to discuss problems in terms of their broader contexts

Despite absence of counsellor skills student–client matching, you can show sensitivity to contextual issues in clients' problems. One way to do this is to acknowledge a possible deficiency in understanding the context of clients' problems and ask them to fill in the gaps (Poon, Nelson-Jones and Caputi, 1993). The following is a simplified illustration.

> **Asian student:** My father wants me to go into the family building business and I feel under a lot of pressure to continue on my building course to please him.
> **Counsellor:** It sounds as though you have mixed feelings. You have reservations about continuing your building course, yet don't want to go against your father's wishes. Cultural considerations are often important in understanding such problems and if you feel they are relevant to your case, please feel free to share them.

Ask questions to understand broader contexts

As part of their attempts to elicit relevant information, counselling skills students may use questions to understand the broader contexts of clients and their problems. Depending on what seems potentially relevant, questions can be asked that focus on one or more of the following contexts: cultural, racial, social class, family of origin, work/study, health/medical, gender, sexual preference, age, reference group, religion, and support network. This list is far from exhaustive.

Activity 8.3 Using basic facilitation skills

Divide into pairs or into triads (client, counsellor/helper and observer). One of you takes a turn to be the client. For at least five minutes, the counsellor/helper uses the following active listening skills to facilitate the client sharing her/his **internal frame of reference** about one or more **problem situations** in her/his helping or private life:

- good **attending behaviour**
- good vocal communication
- reflecting feelings
- small verbal rewards
- open-ended questions.

Since this is a training activity, along the way the client should 'feed' the counsellor/helper some feelings statements and pause every now and then to give her/him an opportunity to respond. Afterwards hold a debriefing session and reverse roles. Videotape feedback may add to the value of the activity. Clients can role play real clients if uncomfortable with sharing personal material.

Answers to activities

There is no single right reflection for each client statement in Activities 8.1 and 8.2.

Activity 8.1 Reflecting feelings skills

1. Bill's feelings words and phrases: 'very down', 'opportunities that I am missing'. Reflection of feelings: 'You feel very low when contemplating all the chances going by you.'
2. Kim's feelings words and phrases: 'never forgiven', 'betraying my trust', 'still angry'. Reflection of feelings: 'You're still mad and resentful at your father's extreme breach of faith in sexually abusing you.'
3. Chris's feelings words and phrases: 'so angry', 'stop myself from hitting him'. Reflection of feelings: 'You feel so mad when he behaves like that that you really have to force yourself not to strike him.'

Activity 8.2 Reflecting feelings and reasons

1. **You feel** extremely upset **because** your folks keep on fighting.
2. **You feel** so angry and furious **because** at times he treats you like his property.
3. **You feel** at ease and delighted **because** finally you've earned a good mark in a maths test.

9

Starting the counselling and helping process

CHAPTER OUTCOMES

By studying and doing the activities in this chapter you should:
- know the importance of preparing for counselling and helping sessions;
- have basic skills at meeting, greeting and seating clients;
- be able to make appropriate opening statements;
- possess basic summarizing skills;
- possess basic structuring skills; and
- assist clients to talk about why they have come for counselling and helping.

In this and subsequent chapters the Relating–Understanding–Changing (RUC) **counselling and helping process model** gets mainly presented as though you are on introductory **counselling skills** courses and training to become accredited counsellors. However, in all circumstances, both trainers and students should use the contents of this chapter according to the **goals** and stage of your introductory skills courses. Readers, such as teachers, pastoral care workers, and nurses, who may not conduct formal helping sessions can adapt the skills described here to the special nature of your helping contacts. The same advice holds for personnel officers, careers workers, speech therapists, and social workers and others who, without being accredited counsellors, may use counselling skills when conducting interviews as part of your roles.

The main task of stage 1 of the Relating–Understanding–Changing counselling and helping process model is to start establishing collaborative working relationships. By the end of stage 1 of the model, clients should have had the opportunity to elaborate on why they have come and to select a problem situation.

Preparation skills

Good preparation is important. It is easy for counselling skills students to get off to bad starts in sessions through poor preparation. Here, preparatory considerations for counselling and helping sessions in general are discussed, as well as comments made specifically to help you to avoid common pitfalls.

Pre-session contact

Counselling and helping takes place in settings of varying degrees of formality, for instance, counselling services, social work offices, personnel departments, careers services and so on. Horton (2006: 118) writes: 'Many practitioners believe that the therapeutic relationship actually begins before any face-to-face contact with clients'. Initial impressions are extremely important and usually start getting formed before counsellors, helpers and clients meet. Professional and voluntary services send messages about how user-friendly they are in how they advertise, in how the receptionist answers the phone, in what messages are given to clients on answer-phones, and in what sort of follow-up there is to answer-phone enquiries. If prospective clients perceive such messages negatively, they may either never use the service or else come along with potentially avoidable misgivings.

When clients come to counselling and helping settings, receptionists and waiting areas also send messages to clients about the service. I know from experience as a young vulnerable **client** when warm, friendly and efficient receptionists are worth their weight in gold. New clients can receive much-needed encouragement from sympathetic welcomes. Tact is vital. Receptionists should always remember that they are in a public area and not ask clients to reveal anything that might cause unnecessary embarrassment. Clients can also receive positive messages from waiting areas decorated in comfortable and quietly tasteful ways. On the other hand, clients receive negative messages from dreary, dirty and impersonal waiting areas.

Be prepared

At either the last moment or late some counselling skills students rush into sessions with clients. Instead, you should always try to arrive early to get the room ready and compose yourself properly. Preparatory considerations about the room include seeing that the seating is appropriate, coffee tables are clean and show no evidence of previous occupants, whiteboards are clear, and video-recording or audio-recording equipment is working and ready to start at the touch of a switch. If, for instance, a volunteer 'client' is already in the waiting area, politely let them stay outside while preparing the room. Allowing clients to see preparatory behaviour can negatively interfere with how competent they perceive their counsellors.

Arriving early also gives counselling skills students time to relax. This can be especially important for those worrying about holding and recording practise sessions. Furthermore, you can use the time to familiarize yourself with clients' names and check any **records** or referral letters about them. Then, when you go to ask clients to come in you are ready to focus solely on them.

Meeting, greeting and seating

The session starts at the moment of first contact with clients. Skilled counsellors and helpers possess good meeting, greeting and seating skills. Example 9.1 illustrates the difference between good and poor skills.

Example 9.1 Meeting, greeting and seating skills

Imagine two counsellors, both of whose offices are near the waiting area, wanting to meet and greet clients for the first time.

Poor skills
Counsellor A, who has just had an emotionally draining session with a client, decides to see the next client without any break. Still feeling distracted by **unfinished business** from the last client, she/he opens her/his office door, peers out, takes a few steps in the direction of the waiting area and calls the next client's surname correctly but without any warmth. When the client looks up, she/he offers no further introduction and in a neutral voice says: 'Come this way please.' Counsellor A then goes into the office first and, when the client enters, shuts the door and points a finger in the direction of a chair and says 'That's for you'.

Good skills
Counsellor B takes a moment to calm herself/himself down after an emotionally draining session with the previous client. Then she/he calmly comes out of the office, goes over to the waiting area, smiles and calls out either the client's first name and surname or the client's first name alone depending on the nature of the setting. The client gets up and the counsellor introduces herself/himself along the lines of 'Hello, I'm _____ [states name]. Please come this way' and then escorts the client to the office, smiles again as the client enters and then, with an open palm gesture, indicates where the client should sit and says 'Please sit down'.

Many counselling skills students require practise at becoming comfortable people for clients to meet from the moment of first contact. An issue that some students raise is whether or not to engage in small talk when first meeting clients. This is partly a matter of individual style. As long as the small talk is minimal and does not give the impression of a social relationship, it may humanize the meeting and greeting process. However, be sensitive to clients who are nervous about their conversational ability, those wanting to get straight into helping, and clients in crisis. You can convey many of the main messages of warmth, welcome and interest through good **bodily communication**.

Opening statements

Opening statements can have various functions, such as indicating the time dimensions of the session, checking 'where the client is at', and, if necessary, obtaining permission to record the session. Counselling skills students are not all knowing. Your opening remarks, openers or permissions to talk are brief statements indicating that you are prepared to listen. You try to build rapport by encouraging clients to share why they have come. Opening remarks are 'door openers' that give clients the message 'I'm interested and prepared to listen. Please share with me how you see things and feel.' A statement about how they work can be left until later.

Example 9.2 Opening statements

Acknowledging time boundaries
When the client is seated, you can first indicate the time boundaries of the session by saying something like 'We have about 45 minutes together' and then give permission to talk.

Permissions to talk
Please tell me why you've come?
Please tell me what brings you here?
Please tell me what's concerning you?
Please tell me what's the problem?
Please put me in the picture?
Where would you like to start?

Permission to talk acknowledging a referral
You've been referred by _____. Now how do you see your situation?

Permission to talk responding to client's bodily communication
You seem upset … Would you care to say what's bothering you?
You seem nervous …

Follow-up 'lubricating' comments
It's pretty hard to get started.
Take your time.
When you're ready.

Permission to record a session
Before giving a 'Permission to talk' remark, you may need to get permission to record the session along the lines of the following statement.

Would you mind if I videotaped this session for **supervision** purposes? Only my lecturer (if relevant add, 'and counselling skills training group') will see the video which will be scrubbed clean when it has been reviewed. If you wish we can turn the recorder off at any time.

Opening statements for use in informal helping settings
Is there something on your mind?
You seem tense today?
I'm available if you want to talk.

Counselling skills students are there to discover **information** about clients and to assist clients to discover information about themselves. You need to be careful about using common opening remarks like 'How can I help you?' or 'What can I do for you?' Such remarks can get initial sessions off to unfortunate starts by connoting that clients are dependent on you rather than on helping themselves.

When making opening remarks, good vocal and body **communication** is very important in indicating that counselling skills students are trustworthy persons with whom to talk. In trying to create a safe emotional climate, you should speak clearly and relatively slowly, be comfortably seated and look at the client, and avoid crossing your arms and legs. However, you can still sit with an open posture if you are crossing your ankles. Good vocal and body communication can also make it easier to obtain permission to record sessions. Counselling skills students who ask permission in nervous and hesitant ways are more likely to trigger doubts and resistances in clients than students who ask calmly and evenly.

Sometimes, counselling skills students may need to complete organizational requirements for gathering basic information before giving clients permission to talk. However, you require flexibility: for instance, clients in crisis require psychological comfort before bureaucratic form filling, which can come later. On occasion, limitations of **confidentiality** surrounding a session may need to be shared: for example, the need to report to a third party or any legal limitations. In addition, students who take notes may offer brief initial **explanations** for so doing or even ask clients' permission.

Many readers have informal contacts with clients outside of formal sessions, for instance correctional officers in facilities for delinquents, residential staff in half-way houses for former drug addicts, or nurses in hospitals. Here you may use permissions to talk when you sense that someone has a personal agenda that bothers them, but requires that extra bit of encouragement to share it.

Activity 9.1 Starting counselling and helping sessions

If appropriate, readers who work in informal settings can adapt this activity to suit your circumstances. In addition, those training to use counselling skills for roles other than being counsellors can adapt the exercise for maximum relevance.

Part A   Meeting, greeting and seating

Role play with a partner meeting a client in a waiting area, showing them to your office, and getting them seated – see Example 9.1 for suggestions. Then hold a feedback and discussion session and, if necessary, do more role plays until you feel confident about your performance.

Afterwards, reverse roles.

Part B   Making an opening statement

Role play with a partner making an opening statement – see Example 9.2 for suggestions. Then hold a feedback and discussion session and, if necessary, do more role plays until you feel confident about your performance.

Afterwards, reverse roles.

(Continued)

Activity 9.1 Starting counselling and helping sessions – cont'd

Part C   Combining meeting, greeting and seating and making an opening statement

Role play with a partner meeting a client in a waiting area, showing them to your office, getting them seated and making an opening statement. Then hold a feedback and discussion session and, if necessary, do more role plays until you feel confident about your performance.

Afterwards, reverse roles.

Summarizing skills

Summaries are brief statements about longer excerpts from counselling and helping sessions. Summaries pull together, clarify and reflect back different parts of a series of client statements either during a discussion unit, at the end of a discussion unit, or at the beginning or end of sessions.

 Here the focus is on summaries in the relating stage. Where possible these summaries serve to move the session forward. Such summaries may mirror back to clients segments of what they have said, check and clarify understanding, identify themes, problem areas and **problem situations**. Summaries may serve other purposes as well. If clients have had a lengthy period of talking, counselling skills students can summarize to establish your presence and make the helping conversation more two-way. Furthermore, if clients tell their stories very rapidly, students may deliver summaries at a measured speech rate to calm clients down.

When clients tell why they have come, counselling skills students may use summaries that reflect whole units of communication. Such summaries tie together the main feeling and content of what clients say. Reflection summaries serve a bridging function for clients, enabling them to continue with the same topic or move on to another. Other functions include making sure counsellors listen accurately, rewarding clients and clarifying your own and their understanding. A variation of the reflection summary is the **reflecting feelings** and reasons summary that links emotions with their perceived causes. Example 9.3 provides an illustration of a reflection summary.

 Who summarizes can be an issue. Generally, in the relating stage it is probably better for counselling skills students to do the **summarizing**. Clients are still finding their feet and appreciate it being made as easy as possible for them to share their internal frames of reference. In the understanding and changing stages, there may be occasions where clients can be invited to summarize: for instance, when checking their understanding of a strategy for changing how they think and/or communicate.

Structuring skills

Counselling and helping sessions are new experiences for many clients. Counselling skills students can try to make the process more comprehensible and less threatening.

Example 9.3 Reflection summary

Counsellor to student

You are really worried about your relationship with Chloe. You have known her for 6 months and have been living together for about 2 months. At first you got on really well, but now there are tense times that can last for days. She says that you do not care for her the way you used to and that you take her for granted. You think that you do about as much together as before, but that she has become more demanding. You are also finding that the time you spend together is becoming routine rather than exciting. You are wondering whether you can improve the relationship or whether you should leave it.

Structuring entails explaining the process to clients. Structuring is conveyed by vocal and body as well as by verbal communication. It can occur in each of the three stages of the Relating–Understanding-Changing counselling and helping process model. However, this section only covers structuring statements pertinent to the relating stage.

The relating stage may only last the first ten-to-fifteen minutes of initial counselling or helping sessions. Nevertheless, it is probably best to structure in two statements; an opening statement and a follow-up statement, rather than do it all at the beginning. Those offering the whole explanation at the beginning may fail to respond to clients who want emotional release or to share information with you.

In phased structuring, the opening statement provides the first occasion for structuring. Here, counselling skills students can establish time boundaries and the understanding that the client's main role for the time being is to talk and your main role is to help the client to do this. The second or follow-up structuring statement comes after clients have had an initial chance to say why they have come. Here, one briefly and simply explains the helping process to them. Example 9.4 provides two follow-up structuring statements providing a framework for the counselling and helping process model used in the book. The first statement is where the client clearly has only one main problem and the second statement is where the client has presented with more than one problem. If a specific situation has not already emerged, counselling skills students' follow-up statements should request clients to identify a situation within a main problem area on which to work together.

Structuring can strengthen the **working alliance** by establishing an agenda or goal for the counselling and helping process as well as obtaining agreement on how to proceed. Clients may require help in choosing a particular situation to work on that is important for them. Counselling skills students may also need to respond to **questions**. However, you should not allow yourself to be seduced into an intellectual discussion of the counselling process. If you make structuring statements in a comfortable and confident way, most clients will be happy to work within the framework that you suggest.

Example 9.4 Structuring statements

Opening statement
We have about 45 minutes together, please tell me why you've come?

Possible follow-up statements
a) Single problem
You've given me some idea why you have come. Now since time is limited, I wonder if together we can select a specific situation within your problem [specify] that we can work on. I will help you to understand the situation more fully and then we can examine strategies for dealing better with it. Is that okay with you?

b) More than one problem
After making an identification of problem areas summary, the counselling skills student says:
Which of these would you like to focus on? [The client states her or his choice]. Good. Now I wonder if we can identify a particular situation within this problem that it is important for you to manage better. Then we can explore this situation more fully and perhaps come up with some useful strategies for dealing with it. Is that all right with you?

Example 9.5 Illustration of the relating stage

Counsellor: We have about 45 minutes. Would you please tell me why you've come.
Client: Well it's not an easy thing for me to talk about …
Counsellor: Take your time …
Client: My friend suggested I come to the counselling service.
Counsellor: Your friend made the suggestion, but why did you choose to come?
Client: My problem is that I'm extremely shy.
Counsellor: Can you tell me more?
Client: My problem is that I have difficulty opening up to people.
Counsellor: So it's hard letting people get to know you … including me possibly.
Client: Yes … but I want to change. My mum is a shy person and I think I am rather like her. Dad's more hearty, but he is away on business much of the time.
Counsellor: You'd like to become more outgoing. More like Dad in that respect than Mum.

Example 9.5 Illustration of the relating stage – cont'd

Client: Yes. I'm getting worried now that my shyness is going to hold me back in life. Right now I get very lonely because I'm living away from home and find it difficult to make friends.

Counsellor: You feel isolated now and concerned about your future if you stay withdrawn.

Client: I'm twenty and want to have a girlfriend.

Counsellor: You think its high time for you to be dating.

Client: That's it. I see girls that I fancy, but just don't see how any of them could be interested in me.

Counsellor: So you have doubts about your attractiveness to women.

Client: Yes. It's not as though I'm bad looking, but I just lose confidence around women.

Counsellor: You feel your courage deserts you round women you fancy.

Client: I also have difficulty talking with my classmates.

Counsellor: Uh-hum … Can you say more.

Client: It's both when we are in the canteen and in class. I just seem to clam up. I do have things I'd like to say, but get frightened about what others will think.

Counsellor: You feel terrified about saying the wrong thing and so keep a low profile. Can I summarize the ground we have covered so far?

Client: Okay.

Counsellor: Right now you're lonely and worried that your shyness will cause you to miss out in life. You have difficulty socializing with your classmates, hold back on participating in class, and are bashful and under-confident with women. You want to change to become more outgoing. Is that about right?

Client: Yes … but can you help me?

Counsellor: You mentioned three problem areas: dating, socializing with classmates and participating in class. Are there any others?

Client: Those are the main ones.

Counsellor: Well let's select a specific situation that it is important for you to manage better in one of these areas. Then we can explore this situation more fully and perhaps come up with some useful strategies for dealing with it. Is that all right by you?

Client: But where to start …

Counsellor: Pick a situation that you can work on in the near future that may not be too difficult for you.

Client: Okay, I'd like to start with participating more in class.

Counsellor: Can you identify a specific situation?

Client: Yes. I hold back in my tutorial group.

Starting the counselling and helping process

In this and previous chapters many skills for beginning the initial session have been reviewed. Example 9.5 puts many of these skills together in an abbreviated illustration of the relating stage of the Relating–Understanding–Changing counselling and helping process model. The counsellor assists the client to tell his story and then select a problem situation for their further work. The setting is that of a college counselling centre.

Those counselling skills students training to use counselling skills as part of other roles or in informal helping are asked to alter the way the relating stage is presented so as to be maximally useful for your future work. Even students training to be counsellors should start by conducting mock ten-to-fifteen minute interviews just focusing on the relating stage.

Activity 9.2 Practising relating stage skills

Work with a partner. Each of you thinks of an area in your personal or work life that you are prepared to share in **role playing** the relating stage of an initial session. Alternatively, you can role play a client with a genuine concern. One of you acts as client. The counsellor/helper conducts an interview of up to 15 minutes using the following skills:

- preparation skills, for instance setting up the room and any recording equipment
- meeting, greeting and seating
- making an opening statement
- active **listening**
- summarizing
- structuring.

By the end of this relating stage section of the interview, the counsellor/helper should have assisted the client in identifying a specific situation for your future work together (see Example 9.5).

After the relating stage session, hold a feedback and discussion session, possibly illustrated by going through a videotape or audiotape of the session.

After a suitable interval, reverse roles.

10

Managing resistance and making referrals

CHAPTER OUTCOMES

By studying and doing the activities in this chapter you should:
- possess some strategies for dealing with different client characteristics;
- have some basic skills at handling reluctant and resistant clients;
- possess some knowledge and skills for referring clients; and
- understand how you can empower your mind in the relating stage.

Counsellors, helpers and **counselling** students need to address numerous issues in the relating stage. Some issues common to getting started with most **clients** were addressed in the previous chapters. This chapter explores issues of dealing with difference and with managing **reluctance** and **resistance** from individual clients. It also looks at how to make referrals and finishes by examining how **counselling skills** students can use either poor or good **mind skills** when beginning contact with clients.

Dealing with difference

Differences between counselling skills students and clients can become immediately obvious the moment you set eyes on one another: for example, race, gender, age and most physical disabilities. Other differences, such as culture, are less immediately obvious. Each case requires judging on its merits: for example, south Asians in Britain and south-east Asians in Australia are at varying degrees of assimilation to the host culture. One clue about whether clients come from different cultures can be found in their accents when speaking English. Still other counsellor–client differences are not apparent on the surface, for example sexual and affectionate orientation.

Should counselling skills students take the initiative and acknowledge such differences right at the start of their contact, or wait until their relationship progresses, or leave it to clients to bring up such issues? Furthermore, if you raise issues of difference, how do you go about it? One possibility is to directly acknowledge the difference at or near the start of helping and ask the client what they think about this. However, a risk of acknowledging difference right at the start is that this may not be 'where the client is at'. Such an acknowledgment may reflect more the counselling skills student's rather than the client's concerns and, hence, derail clients from revealing and exploring their internal frames of reference. Another option is to hold back and see what the client's concerns are before acknowledging differences. However, with some clients and in some settings immediate acknowledgment of difference may be best.

Another option is for counselling skills students, as clients start telling their stories, to invite them to provide assistance in understanding any aspects of their problems that may be influenced by differences between you. For example, a statement inviting attention to cultural issues might be: 'Cultural considerations can be important, so please help me to understand your culture when necessary.' Each client has a unique life history and way of interpreting the impact of their differences on how they function, so students need to be careful not to pigeon-hole clients into your **interpretation** of what the differences should mean. In addition, clients differ in the extent to which they are or have been victims of others' prejudices and of discriminatory structures and practices within institutions.

Activity 10.1 Dealing with difference

1 Consider your own experiences of difference. How have these experiences helped to shape you as a **counsellor/helper**?
2 Select one or more significant differences between you and the clients you are likely to counsel or help. For each area of difference you have selected, discuss each of the following skills for approaching it:
   · directly acknowledge the difference at the start of counselling/helping;
   · hold back and see what the clients' concerns are before acknowledging the difference;
   · invite the client to provide assistance in understanding the difference, if relevant;
   · other skills not mentioned above?

Managing resistance

Resistance may be broadly defined as anything that clients put in the way of the counselling and helping process. Resistance comprises clients' **feelings**, thoughts and **communications** that frustrate, impede, slow down and sometimes stop the process. Reluctance, which is unwillingness or disinclination on the part of potential or actual clients to enter into the process, is an aspect of being resistant. Some clients do not see the need for help. They reluctantly see counsellors to meet others' wishes: for instance, children sent by teachers or parents, or substance abusers and perpetrators of domestic violence sent by the courts. Many clients are ambivalent about discussing their problems. At the same time as wanting change, many may have anxieties about changing from their safe and known ways and also about the counselling and helping process: for instance, revealing personal **information**. Furthermore, clients may resist counsellors whose behaviour is too discrepant from their **expectations** and from what they think they need.

How to manage resistance

The following are some suggestions for understanding and dealing with resistance early on in counselling and helping. Many of these skills are also relevant for later sessions and contacts. Because there are so many variations and reasons for resistance within the broad range of contexts in which counselling students use introductory counselling skills, it is impossible to cover all contingencies.

Use active listening skills

Counselling skills students may wrongly attribute the sources of clients' resistance by being too quick to blame them for lack of cooperation and progress. Beginning and even more experienced helpers may both sustain and create clients' resistance through poor **listening** skills. Resistance can be a normal part of the early stages of helping. By using good active listening skills, students can do much to build the trust needed to lower resistance. Some clients' resistance manifests itself in aggression. Rather than feeling the need to justify yourself and risk becoming sucked into competitive contests, one approach to handling such aggression is to reflect it back, locating the feelings clearly in the client, but indicating loud and clear that you have picked up the anger. Where clients provide reasons for their hostility, students can reflect these too. Counselling skills students, by just showing clients that you understand their internal frames of reference, especially if this is done consistently, can diminish resistance.

Join with clients

Sometimes counselling skills students can lower clients' resistance by helping them to feel that they have a friend at court. For instance, you can initially listen and offer support to children expressing resentment about parents.

> **Toby** I think coming here is a waste of time. My mum and dad keep picking on me and they are the ones who need help.
> **Counselling skills student** You feel angry about coming here because your parents are the people with problems.
> **Toby** Yeah [and then proceeds to share his side of the story].

In the above instance the counselling skills student accepted Toby's focus on parental deficiencies and used his need to mention parental injustices to build the counselling relationship. Were the client to continue to complain about his parents, after an appropriate period of time the student might have built up enough trust and goodwill either for Toby to focus on his own behaviour of his own accord or for the student to assist him to make this switch.

Give permission to discuss reluctance and fears

If counselling skills students receive overt or subtle messages from clients that they have reservations about being seen, the agenda can be discussed in the open and given clients permission to elaborate. In the following example, a trainee parole officer responds to a juvenile delinquent's seeming reluctance to disclose anything significant.

> **Parole officer**   I detect you are unwilling to open up to me because I'm your parole officer. If I'm right, I'm wondering what specifically worries you about that?

Where appropriate, counselling skills students can also give clients permission to discuss differences in their characteristics, for instance culture and race, that may make it harder for some clients to participate.

Invite cooperation

Establishing good collaborative working relationships with clients both prevents and also overcomes much resistance. Counselling skills students can make statements early on in the counselling process that can aim to create the idea of a partnership, a shared endeavour in which work is undertaken together to assist clients to deal with their problems and thus to lead happier and more fulfilled lives.

Enlist client self-interest

Counselling skills students can assist clients to identify reasons or gains for them of participating in counselling and helping. For instance, children who perceive their parents as picking on them and as the ones with problems can be assisted to see that they themselves might be happier if they had better skills for **coping** with their parents. Furthermore, **questions** that challenge clients with the adequacy of their own behaviour may enlist self-interest. Such questions include 'Where is your current behaviour getting you?' and 'How is that behaviour helping you?' Questions that encourage clients to think about **goals** are also useful: for example, 'What are your goals in the situation?' and 'Wouldn't you like to be more in control of your life?'

Reward silent clients for talking

Some clients find it difficult to talk whether or not they are with counsellors and helpers. Others may find it particularly difficult to talk to you. Without coming on too strong, counselling skills students can respond more frequently and more obviously. For example, you may use more small rewards when clients talk. In addition, you can offer encouragement by reflecting and making the most of what clients say. Furthermore, you can reflect the difficulty certain clients have in talking, even though they may not have verbalized this themselves.

Counselling skills students require sensitivity to the pace at which different clients can develop the trust required for a good **working alliance**. Clients who feel pressured may become even more resistant and reinforce rather than lower their defenses. Flexibility, realism and tact are important attributes for dealing with reluctant and resistant clients.

Activity 10.2 Managing resistance

1 For a setting in which you either work, or might work, list the main ways clients might show resistance early on in counselling or helping.
2 Work with a partner who is resistant to participating in the beginning stages of counselling/helping. Help your partner to work by using one or more of the following kinds of managing resistance skills:
   · making a joining response
   · giving permission to discuss reluctance and fears
   · inviting cooperation
   · enlisting client self-interest
   · rewarding silent clients for talking
   · other skills not mentioned above.
   Afterwards, discuss and reverse roles.

Making referrals

Early on in their working relationships and also later, counselling students may face decisions about referring clients elsewhere. Even experienced practitioners have types of clients with whom they feel more competent and comfortable and others less so. Noted psychotherapist, Arnold Lazarus, states that an important principle is to 'Know your limitations and other clinicians' **strengths**' (Dryden, 1991: 30). Referrals should be made where other counsellors have skills that you do not possess or more appropriate personal styles for particular clients. Important **ethical issues** surround referral, especially where others have more expertise with specific problems, for instance with substance abuse or unwanted pregnancy.

Referral may not be an either/or matter. Sometimes it is possible to continue working with clients but also refer them to other professionals. Alternatively, counsellors may be the recipients of referrals from other professionals who continue working with the same client. Sometimes clients are referred to gain additional knowledge about their problems: for example, clients with concentration blocks or difficulty performing sexually might be sent for medical checks. Then, depending on the outcome of these checks, the counsellor or helper has relevant information about whether or not to continue seeing them either alone, or in conjunction with a physician, or not at all.

On many occasions it is possible to refer clients' problems rather than clients to others. For example, you can discuss with colleagues or supervisors how best to assist certain clients. Occasions when counselling skills students might refer clients' problems rather than clients include when you are the only helper available in an area, when clients state a clear preference for continuing to work with you, and when clients are unlikely to follow through on referrals.

How to refer

The following are some considerations and skills for making referrals. Counselling skills students can be too ready to refer clients and should avoid doing so unnecessarily.

Sometimes it is better for clients to continue working with you. Under-confident students should tune into their anxieties and fears about seeing certain clients. You can endeavour to build your confidence and skills to expand the range of clients with whom you can work. Wherever possible, you should ensure that you have adequate **supervision** and support.

As time goes by counselling skills students should try to develop a good feel for your strengths and limitations. You should be realistic about the kinds of clients with whom you work well and those with whom you are less skilled. You also need to be realistic about your workload and set an appropriate limit on it.

Good referrals are more likely to be made to people whom one knows and trusts rather than 'blind'. Counselling skills students and their supervisors should get to know the relevant resources available in their locations so that making referrals to counsellors about whose **competence** you are unsure is avoided. In addition, even if you do know the other counsellors, it may be wise to check if they have the time available for seeing new clients. Where possible, referrals are best made early on. If deferred longer than necessary, clients' and counselling skills students' time is wasted. Furthermore, it is preferable to refer clients before they emotionally bond with you.

When making referrals, calmly explain to clients why this may be a good idea. Where possible, support such **explanations** from information already provided by them. It is important that clients are absolutely clear about how to make contact with those to whom they are referred. You may either give clients people's business cards or write out the relevant addresses and phone numbers.

Be prepared to spend time discussing any queries and emotional reactions clients may have to referral suggestions. If the clients are in crisis, they may need accompaniment to another person's office. Also consider whether and what information should be provided for the next helper. Often such issues can be discussed with clients and, if necessary, their permission asked to share information.

Lastly, counselling skills students should consider building **support networks** for current and future work. Such networks provide professional support when you want to refer clients' problems rather than the clients themselves. Support networks are likely to overlap with referral networks, but some members' roles are different. For example, clients' problems can be discussed with supervisors and trainers, but the clients themselves are less likely to be referred to them.

Activity 10.3 Making referrals

In regard to either your current or future counselling/helping work:
1 When might you refer clients to others?
2 What categories of counsellors and helpers do you require in your referral network?
3 What categories of counsellors and helpers do you require in your support network – when you refer problems but not clients?
4 What are some considerations in making good referrals?
5 When might you be at risk of making unnecessary referrals?

Empowering your mind

At the start of practice sessions, some counselling skills students put extra pressure on yourselves by creating unhelpful – as contrasted with helpful – thoughts. Here, three common mind skills deficiencies of beginning students are reviewed.

Creating self-talk

When you feel a little unsure about yourself it is very easy to feel even more unsure if you start telling yourself negative statements. For example, when starting a session with a 'client', you may tell yourself 'I am going to make a mess of this', 'I don't know enough to perform competently' and 'My counselling skills are poor'. In addition, if you then start getting even more anxious, you may tell yourself that 'The situation is going to get out of control', 'The client will notice how anxious I am', and 'My **anxiety** is going to make my counselling skills even worse'.

    Already it has been suggested that counselling skills students arrive for sessions early to get prepared. During this period, you can create and tell yourself statements that calm you down: for instance, 'Calm down', 'Take a few slow deep breaths' and 'Take it easy'. Such calming statements have value in their own right and not only as correctives to negative **self-talk**.

    In addition, counselling skills students can coach yourselves in listening skills that help to take the pressure off. Many students find instructing yourselves to 'Speak slowly and clearly' useful since this self-talk creates both a relaxed atmosphere and more time to think. Counselling skills students can also self-coach to 'Give the client space to tell her/his story' rather than pressure clients because of your anxiety.

Creating rules

Counselling skills students can **stress** yourselves if you possess perfectionist **rules** along the lines of 'I must perform perfectly', 'I must be as good as all my classmates' and 'I must learn counselling skills immediately'. In addition, some students create rules demanding others' approval like 'My clients must approve of me', 'My peers must approve of me' and 'My trainer must approve of me'.

    In Chapter 3, it was mentioned that you can have either demanding rules, or **preferential rules**, or rules that are a mixture of being demanding and preferential. As counselling skills students, it can be important to detect and challenge any demanding rules that you have. Illustrative questions to ask include 'Is there such a thing as perfection?', 'Why should I as a learner of counselling skills expect that I exhibit a high level of competence right away?', and 'Why is it vital that my clients approve of me?' Then you can substitute a preferential for a demanding rule: for instance, 'The perfect is the enemy of the good' might be substituted for the rule 'I must perform perfectly'. Such a mental change can contribute to feeling and communicating in a more relaxed way.

Creating explanations

Another way that counselling skills students pressure yourselves is by assuming too much responsibility for the success of counselling and helping. The late Carl Rogers had great faith in the client's intrinsic tendencies towards personal growth if given the right counsellor–offered conditions. Even if students are not so optimistic about human nature as Rogers, it can still be acknowledged that clients have both a right and a responsibility to make the most of their lives. Your job is to help clients develop their potential and cope better with their problems and **problem situations** rather than to take over their lives.

Sometimes, I have had to help very well-intentioned students to see the limits of their responsibility to clients. Students can relax and help clients more when they acknowledge that counselling and helping is a cooperative endeavour in which the best that can be done is to offer competence rather than guaranteed results. Clients have to help themselves too. In addition, there are many environmental factors in clients' lives that may influence outcome.

Activity 10.4 Empowering your mind for the relating stage

Part A   Creating self-talk

1 Identify any negative self-talk that you may use when starting an initial counselling or helping session with a new client.
2 Create two each of
   · calming self-talk statements
   · coaching self-talk statements.
3 Rehearse and practise putting together your calming and coaching self-talk statements so that you feel more comfortable when getting started with a new client.

Part B   Creating rules

1 Identify any unrealistic or demanding rules you may be creating that puts extra pressure on you when starting an initial counselling or helping session with a new client.
2 For each of these rules
   · challenge and question it
   · create a preferential rule which you substitute for the demanding rule.
3 Rehearse and practise telling yourself your preferential rule(s) so that you feel more comfortable when getting started with a new client.

Part C   Creating explanations

1 Do you tend to assume too much of the responsibility for the success of counselling or helping when starting an initial session with a new client?
2 If so,
   · challenge and question your explanation(s) for the success of counselling/ helping
   · replace any unrealistic with more realistic explanations about why counselling/helping may or may not be successful.
3 Rehearse and practise telling yourself your more realistic explanation(s) so that you feel more comfortable when getting started with a new client.

PART THREE
THE UNDERSTANDING STAGE

MAIN TASK: To assess and agree on a shared definition of the client's problem(s)

Part Three covers the understanding stage of the RUC model. Chapters 11, 12 and 13 focus on assessing how clients feel and physically react, think, and communicate and act. Chapter 14 covers some additional skills, such as challenging clients, giving them feedback and self-disclosing to them. Chapter 15 looks at how to monitor clients' behaviour, make summaries as appropriate, and identify some mind skills and communication/action skills to improve.

11

Assessing feelings and physical reactions

CHAPTER OUTCOMES

By studying and doing the activities in this chapter you should:
- be introduced to the understanding stage of the Relating–Understanding–Changing model;
- know some of the main bodily changes accompanying feelings;
- know some things to look out for when assessing feelings; and
- possess some skills for eliciting and assessing feelings and physical reactions.

Welcome to stage 2 of the Relating–Understanding–Changing (RUC) **counselling and helping process model**. In stage 1, the relating stage, counsellors and helpers lay the foundation of a **working alliance** with **clients**. You build a relationship with clients by allowing them to tell their stories and share their internal worlds. During this process **counselling skills** students should act as comfortable companions who reduce the **threat** inherent in initial sessions and informal helping contacts so that clients feel more confident about 'leveling' or sharing their real agendas. You are in a receptive **listening** mode and hold back on probing clients to any great extent. Even if clients come with just one problem situation, students should make it easy for them to talk about this rather than emphasize getting them responding to **questions**. If clients come with multiple problems, you can ask them to choose in which area they want to focus and then encourage them to identify a specific problem situation in it for future work.

In stage 2, the understanding stage, counselling skills students maintain the emphasis on having good relationships with clients. However, in stage 2, you move the counselling and helping process forward by clarifying both the client's and your own understanding of the targeted **problem situation**. Staying in clients' internal frames of reference, you can help them to develop fuller pictures of problem situations than they would have developed alone.

Frequently, clients only look at part of the picture when thinking of problem situations. Emotions may cloud thought processes. In addition, sometimes significant others in clients' lives have vested interests in preventing them from formulating their own versions of reality. Clients may gain approval only if they anaesthetize or distort how they truly view situations. Consequently, on their own, clients may find it difficult to gain the kind of detached perspective they can often attain with skilled and supportive assistance. In stage 2, counselling skills students can calmly and fairly systematically try to assist clients to think more clearly about problem situations. This and the next chapters examine assist-ing clients to assess their **feelings** and **physical reactions**, thinking and communication.

Why assess feelings and physical reactions?

There are many reasons why counsellors and helpers assess feelings and physical reac-tions. Such **assessment** can enhance the relationship, in that clients perceive that you really 'get it' if their feelings are understood. In addition, by assessing feelings at the start, together you can establish baselines against which to evaluate changes. Furthermore, assessing feelings can provide useful leads to where clients' real problems and poor **skills** lie. Assessing feelings and physical reactions also performs protective functions: for example, identifying any suicide risk in clients and screening for medical and psychiatric considerations. Those of you who are not medically trained should acknowledge your limitations and, as appropriate, seek medical or psychiatric advice. Occasions to take medical and psychiatric considerations into account include where clients are on **medication** (Sexton and Legg, 1999), have a physical illness such as cancer that affects how they feel, show psycho-physiological symptoms like peptic ulcers and migraine headaches, exhibit the effects of substance abuse, and suffer from mental disorders (American Psychiatric Association, 2000).

Though the categories overlap, a useful way to think of assessing feelings is on whether the focus is on the person, their problem or problems or on a specific situa-tion. Put another way, when assessing feelings and physical reactions, three important questions are: 'What is the overall level of functioning of this person?', 'What feelings and physical reactions are associated with a particular problem(s)?', and 'What feelings and physical reactions are experienced in a specific situation?'

Depending upon their theoretical orientation, counsellors and helpers emphasize persons or problems and situations, or some combination of these. Person-centred counsellors focus on the person, cognitive and behavioural counsellors focus on prob-lems and situations. The skilled client model, which is something of a hybrid between the humanistic-existential and cognitive-behavioural orientations, advocates taking each case on its merits. Some badly wounded clients definitely require a healing relationship with a focus on affirming them as persons. However, counselling skills students and clients can still concentrate on particular problems and situations in their lives.

Dimensions of physical reactions

Physical reactions, or bodily sensations, both represent and accompany feelings and, in a sense, are indistinguishable. Assessing physical reactions is discussed prior to assessing feelings, since this ordering emphasizes that feelings are located in the body.

Word labels or linguistic symbols describing feelings are attached to different clusters of physical reactions. For example, physical reactions associated with the word shyness include dry mouth, blushing, nausea, feeling faint, perspiring, knotted stom-ach, pounding heart, shaking, **mind** going blank and shallow, rapid breathing. Most, if not all, of these feelings characterize **anxiety**. Often in the counselling and therapy literature, shyness gets called social anxiety. Sometimes clients react to their physical reactions. For example, in anxiety and panic attacks, clients may first feel tense and anxious and then become even more tense and anxious because of this initial feeling. Counselling skills students and clients need to develop skills of describing with appropriate words clients' physical reactions. Box 11.1 summarizes some of the main bodily changes before, during and after feelings.

Box 11.1 Some bodily changes associated with feelings

Galvanic skin response
Detectable electrical changes take place in the skin.

Blood pressure, distribution and composition
Blood pressure can rise. The distribution of blood may alter: for instance, in blushing (going red) or blanching (going white) the blood vessels near the skin's surface dilate or constrict, respectively. In addition, there can be changes in blood composition; for instance, blood sugar, acid-base balance, and adrenalin content.

Heart rate and pulse rate
A pounding heart and a rapid pulse characterize intense emotion.

Breathing
Shallow, rapid breathing can characterize anxiety.

Muscular tension
Muscular tension is associated with intensity of feeling. Clients can feel tension in different parts of their bodies. Sometimes trembling accompanies muscular tension.

Slower and quicker body movements
Body movements can slow down, for instance when depressed, or speed up, for instance when excited or anxious.

Dry mouth
Emotional excitation can produce a decrease in saliva.

Dilation of eye pupils
In moments of heightened feeling, for instance anger or sexual attraction, the eye pupils tend to dilate.

Stomach problems
Emotional excitement may contribute to nausea or diarrhoea. Persistent emotional excitement may lead to ulcers. Appetite may become poor.

Goose pimples
A response in which the hairs of the skin stand on end.

Thought blocking
Tension may contribute to clients' minds going totally or partially blank.

Speech difficulties
Heightened excitation can lead to stammering, speaking rapidly and slurring words. In extreme instances, the ability to speak may be temporarily lost.

Sleep difficulties
Sleep difficulties include time taken to get to sleep, disturbed sleep and early morning waking.

Sex difficulties
Complete or partial loss of desire is a common sex difficulty associated with tension.

An important aspect of clients' physical health and emotional well-being is their level of energy. Changes in energy level may precede, be concurrent or follow from changes in how clients feel and think. For example, energetic clients may feel more confident. However, once clients lose their confidence, they may feel less energetic. Counselling skills students and clients can assess how much mental and physical energy clients have and how vital or apathetic they are. If clients' energy levels are very low, you can ask them to check with their doctors for medical explanations.

Dimensions of feelings

In Chapter 2, it was mentioned that dictionary definitions of feelings tend to use words like 'physical sensation', 'emotions' and '**awareness**'. Mood is another term sometimes used to describe feelings. A mood is a state of mind or feeling associated with physical reactions. When assessing and helping clients to assess their feelings, counselling skills students need to look out for many things. Only some of the main ones are mentioned here.

Counselling skills students need to be aware of clients' ability to experience feelings (Mearns and Thorne, 2007; Rogers, 1961). Some clients lack emotional responsiveness across a wide range of feelings. Other clients may have difficulty experiencing specific feelings: for example, sexual feelings or anger. One of the outcomes of any extended counselling should be that clients become better at experiencing and expressing feelings.

Counselling skills students also need to be aware of clients' level of self-esteem or of confidence. Clients with very low self-esteem are potential suicide risks. Clients with reasonable self-esteem possess a useful asset for working on problems and skills they need to improve. Students can assess how anxious clients are and in what areas of their life anxiety occurs. Is their anxiety a pervasive trait or is it a state attached to specific situations? You can also assess how clients show anxiety, both in obvious ways and also in terms of their less obvious defensive processes or security operations.

Counselling skills students should assess the strength and persistence of feelings. Strong feelings can be indicated by unrestrained crying, explosive outbursts and rollicking gales of laughter (Mahrer et al., 1999). Often the intensity of a feeling is described by words like 'mild', 'moderate' or 'severe'. For example, clients may be mildly depressed, moderately depressed or severely depressed. However, there can be different **perceptions** of what is mild, moderate or severe between students and clients. Persistence or duration of feelings may be described by words like 'chronic' and 'acute'. Chronic implies persistent whereas acute implies sharp and short. In addition, disorders like **schizophrenia** may be in partial remission or full remission (American Psychiatric Association, 2000).

Feelings can be complex and often come in twos and threes. For example, anger may be accompanied by hurt and **guilt** or depression by anxiety and sadness. Feelings may also be layered: for example, anger may be the surface manifestation of underlying hurt. Though not always with the same intensity, feelings frequently are accompanied by their opposites. Ambivalent feeling states include happy–sad, love–hate, pleased–displeased, and approach–avoidance. Sometimes clients experience ambivalent feelings simultaneously and sometimes sequentially.

Counselling skills students should attempt to assess the appropriateness of feelings. Did the client experience an appropriate level of an appropriate feeling and was this appropriately expressed? Assessing the appropriateness of feelings must take into account clients' unique styles of expressing feelings and numerous situational, contextual and cultural considerations. One way of assessing the appropriateness of feelings is to assess their consequences for clients and others. To what extent and in what ways were there positive or negative emotional and behavioural consequences?

It is vital to be sensitive to cultural differences in showing feelings. Cultures differ greatly in the ways in which the expression of feelings is demonstrated. In addition, somatic symptoms – or physical reactions – associated with distress differ across cultures. In some cultures depression is experienced largely in somatic terms rather than with sadness or guilt. For example, in Chinese and Asian cultures, depressed people may complain of weakness, tiredness or 'imbalance'.

Clients invariably have feelings about counselling and counselling skills students. Clients' perceptions of those helping them as being similar or dissimilar because of cultural, racial, gender and social class characteristics may influence the degree to which they feel free to disclose feelings and physical reactions. In addition, clients may have a range of feelings about helpers such as like or dislike, trust or mistrust, and experiencing them as competent or incompetent. Sometimes clients express feelings that counselling skills students can find difficult to handle: for example liking, sexual attraction, anger or sadness.

Skills for eliciting and assessing feelings and physical reactions

Forming good collaborative working relationships with clients can help them to get in touch with, experience, express and explore their feelings. Assessing feelings and physical reactions can be a sensitive process in that clients' feelings, especially the more threatening and delicate ones, require particularly favourable conditions if they are to emerge and be shared. Clients' feelings may fluctuate and, hopefully, change for the better as counselling proceeds. Rather than being able to identify clients' feelings clearly, counselling skills students are forming hypotheses much of the time and either waiting for or eliciting further evidence to confirm or negate these hunches. Below are some skills useful for eliciting and assessing feelings.

Active listening

In supportive and trusting relationships, clients assist counselling skills students to understand how they feel. Active listening provides a safe emotional climate for clients to experience and share feelings. Students sensitive to clients' feelings and feeling nuances legitimize the importance of experiencing and discussing feelings. It requires good skills to pick up and reflect back the messages conveyed by feelings.

Receiver skills include paying attention to feelings words, observing voice and body messages, and being keenly attuned to any mismatch between voice, body and verbal messages. Sometimes feelings can be inferred from what is left unsaid or partially said.

Sender skills that students can use to help clients share feelings include showing attention with your voice and body messages, **reflecting feelings** and offering companionship to clients as they explore new and sometimes unexpected feelings.

Counselling skills students need to use tact and sensitivity when clients encounter feelings that are difficult either to experience or share and it is important at all times to remain aware of the pace at which clients wish to reveal feelings. Sometimes a box of tissues helps to facilitate the process! You can make the following kind of remarks to encourage clients to share feelings without pressurizing them.

'I realize that this may be a painful area for you to discuss.'
'You seem upset. Just take your time in sharing what you feel.'

Clients' voice and body messages probably provide the most valid source of **information** about how they feel. From the moment of first contact, it is important to observe body messages closely and listen attentively for vocal messages. Clients differ in how clearly they send messages. However, counselling skills students should both consciously and intuitively listen 'with the third ear' and observe 'with the third eye' for deviations, omissions and discrepancies in communications. You can look out for feeling fragments or occasional glimpses that are clues to more substantial and as yet unshared feelings.

Asking questions about feelings and physical reactions

Questions can assist clients in being specific about feelings and physical reactions. Frequently, since counselling skills students cannot assume a common meaning, it is necessary to clarify labels clients attach to feelings. For instance, follow-up questions to a client who says 'I am very depressed' might be: 'When you say you are very depressed, what exactly do you mean?' or 'When you say you are very depressed what are your specific feelings and physical reactions?' or 'You feel very depressed. Tell me more about that feeling?' Then the student can collaborate with the client to identify the relevant feelings and physical reactions. Sometimes you may directly check out specific feelings or physical reactions, for instance 'Do you feel suicidal sometimes?' or 'How is your appetite?'

Counselling skills students can assist clients to distinguish between feelings and thoughts. If clients respond to questions that focus on feelings with how they think, you may gently bring them back to focusing on feelings.

Client I feel very depressed.
Counsellor When you say you feel very depressed what exactly do you mean?
Client I am having problems in my job and in my marriage.
Counsellor You're having problems at work and at home. These are thoughts or reasons why you may be very depressed. However, could you tell me more about the actual depressed feelings you experience?

Frequently counselling skills students need to assist clients in expanding and elaborating their feelings and physical reactions. Example 11.1 provides some illustrative questions that focus on feelings.

Example 11.1 Questions that focus on feelings and physical reactions

When did you start feeling this way?
Tell me more about the feeling?
Describe how your body experiences the feeling?
In which part of your body do you experience the feeling?
Do you have any **visual images** that capture the feeling?
How has your mood been and how is it today?
Are there any other feelings that accompany or underlie that feeling?
How do you feel here and now?
On a scale of 0-to-10 (or 0-to-100) how strong is the feeling?
How persistent is the feeling?

Emotion-eliciting strategies

Sometimes counsellors and helpers deliberately attempt to induce feelings so that they and their clients can observe and assess them. Adequately supervised counselling skills students may use the same skills.

- *Visualizing* Clients can be asked to shut their eyes, visualize a scene and re-experience the emotions attached to it. For example, socially phobic clients can be asked to conjure up the images immediately before and during anxiety-provoking social situations.
- ***Role playing*** Counselling skills students may conduct mini role plays of scenes with clients, for example a parent arguing with a teenaged daughter or son who has come home much later than agreed. Then you can assist clients to identify and clarify the emotions elicited in these role plays.
- ***Self-disclosure*** To promote client insight into their feelings and to make it easier to talk about them, counselling skills students may share personal information about experiences similar to those of clients. Such disclosure always needs to have the clients' best interests in mind. Usually, it is preferable to talk about past experiences, where some emotional distance has been obtained, than about current experiences. In certain kinds of counselling and helping, such as in some alcohol and drug treatment programmes, peer self-disclosure is built into the process.
- *Live observation* Counselling skills students can take clients into difficult situations, observe their reactions and listen to what they say about how they feel. For example, a student might go with an agoraphobic client into a supermarket, offer support, and observe her or his reactions.
- *Task assignment* Counselling skills students and clients may agree on between-session tasks for clients: for instance, a recently divorced man asking someone for a date. Clients can record their feelings and physical reactions before, during and after these tasks.

Encouraging clients to monitor feelings

Counselling skills students can encourage clients to monitor their feelings and physical reactions on a regular basis. Such **monitoring** can raise **self-awareness** as well as help clients to learn a valuable skill: listening closely to their feelings.

One approach to doing this is to use daily rating forms. Clients can be asked to rate themselves daily on feelings such as mood (very happy to very depressed), anxiety level (not anxious at all to very anxious), feelings of stress (very relaxed to very stressed) and so on. Ratings may be on scales ranging from 0 to 3, 5, 7, 9, 10 or 100. In the example below clients are asked to give themselves a daily mood score using the following scale.

Very depressed   1   2   3   4   5   6   7 Very happy

Counselling skills students can train clients in the skills of identifying and rating the key or important feelings and physical reactions they experience in specific situations. In **cognitive therapy**, going from situation to feelings is a useful entry point for then examining the thoughts that contribute to the feelings (Beck and Weishaar, 2008; Greenberger and Padesky, 1995). Clients can also be asked to rate their feelings and physical reactions on either a 0-to-10 or 0-to-100 scale.

Example 11.2 shows a worksheet filled out by a client identifying and rating their key feelings and physical reactions during or immediately after being in a situation. This worksheet can be expanded in two ways. The same questions can be repeated for situation 1, situation 2 and so on. Alternatively, the worksheet can concentrate on a single situation and then examine the thoughts that were going through clients' minds just before they started to feel and physically react this way.

Another way to monitor feelings is to use brief questionnaires that clients can fill out daily. Greenberger and Padesky (1995) provide examples of a 19-item *Mind Over*

Example 11.2 Worksheet for identifying and rating key feelings and physical reactions regarding a situation

Situation
(Who? What? When? Where?)
Wednesday, 8.30pm
I come home late from work and my partner says 'Where on earth have you been?'

Key feeling(s) and physical reaction(s)
(What did I feel? How did I physically react? Rating for each key feeling and physical reaction (0-to-100%))
Angry   70%
Hurt   80%
Tense   65%

Mood Depression Inventory and a 24–item *Mind Over Mood Anxiety Inventory* that can be used for monitoring these feelings.

Waiting and seeing

A big risk in assessing feelings is to jump to premature conclusions on insufficient evidence. For example, counselling skills students may be too ready inaccurately to label women as hyper-emotional and men as hypo-emotional or lacking in emotion. Even with skilled counsellors and helpers, clients' feelings can take time to unfold. For example, clients either brought up to deny feelings or for whom expressing feelings was dangerous in their family of origin may change slowly. It is important to allow clients to share feelings and physical reactions at a pace comfortable for them. Almost invariably initial session assessments of feelings require updating. Sometimes counselling skills students will find that such assessments require substantial modification as you get to know clients better and as clients learn more about themselves.

Activity 11.1 Assessing feelings and physical reactions when counselling and helping

Part A   Pairs activity

Work with a partner with one of you acting as counsellor/helper and the other as client. Conduct a counselling session in which the counsellor/helper focuses mainly on helping the client experience, disclose, explore and assess her/his feelings and physical reactions about a specific problematic situation. Use skills such as active listening, reflection of feelings, questions focusing on feelings and physical reactions, and emotion-eliciting strategies, as appropriate. The session should be a minimum of five minutes and longer, as necessary. Towards the end of the session, the counsellor/helper shares and discusses her/his hypotheses about feelings and physical reactions with the client.

Afterwards, discuss and reverse roles.

Part B   Group activity

One person acts as client who presents a specific problematic situation to the group. The remainder of the group, say up to six people, sit in a semi-circle round the client and counsel/help the client in such a way as to elicit and assess her/his feelings and physical reactions relevant to the situation. One approach is for the group members to take brief turns as counsellor or helper. Every now and then stop and discuss both what's happened and where to go next. Before ending, the group shares and discusses their hypotheses about feelings and physical reactions with the client.

The group can repeat this exercise with other 'clients'.

Activity 11.2 Assisting a client to identify and rate feelings and physical reactions regarding a situation

Part A   Monitoring the past

Make up a worksheet similar to the one below. Counsel a partner who acts as a client and presents you with a situation in which she or he has experienced unwanted feelings. With the aim of assisting your client to learn how to do this for themselves, assist her or him to fill out the worksheet in which she or he describes the situation, identifies her or his key feelings and physical reactions, and rates each of them on a 0-to-100 scale.

Afterwards, discuss and reverse roles.

Worksheet for identifying and rating key feelings and physical reactions for a situation

Situation

(Who? What? When? Where?)

_____

_____

_____

Key feeling(s) and physical reaction(s)

(What did I feel? How did I physically react? Rating for each key feeling and physical reaction (0-to-100%))

_____

_____

_____

Part B   Monitoring the present

Make up a worksheet similar to the one in Part A of this activity. However, this time allow for at least four situations (situation 1, situation 2 and so on). Counsel the same client as for Part A of this activity. Discuss with your client using this worksheet for self-monitoring purposes. Ask your client to agree that, during the next week, she or he will fill out the worksheet shortly after current situations in which she or he experiences strong feelings/physical reactions and rate the intensity of each key feeling/physical reaction on a 0-to-100 scale. Answer any questions your client may have about how to proceed.

Afterwards, discuss and reverse roles.

12

Assessing thinking

CHAPTER OUTCOMES

By studying and doing the activities in this chapter you should:
*   understand the importance of assessing and assisting clients to assess their thinking;
*   know some questions to ask when assessing clients' thinking; and
*   know about a repertoire of other interventions for eliciting and assessing thinking.

How clients think deeply influences their **feelings, physical reactions, communication** and actions (see Persons, Roberts and Zalecki, 2003; Westbrook and Kirk, 2005). Therefore counsellors and helpers need to ask: 'What thoughts and **mind skills** engender or fail to engender feelings, physical reactions, communication and actions conducive to this **client**'s well-being rather than causing her/him distress?' **Counselling skills** students need to learn to develop hypotheses about those poor mind skills that contribute to maintaining problems. Assessing thinking is a vital step in formulating shared definitions of problems acceptable to both clients and those helping them. Few counselling skills students think about how people think in **skills** terms. That is why Chapter 3 focused on introducing mind skills from the viewpoint of students. The time is now ripe for looking at skills for eliciting and assessing clients' thoughts and mind skills.

Skills for eliciting and assessing thinking

When eliciting and assessing thinking, counselling skills students and clients need to develop and maintain good collaborative relationships. Both should participate actively in the detective work of discovering clients' self-defeating thoughts, including their **visual images** and poor mind skills. Since clients are unlikely to be skilled at thinking about their thinking, they will often not realize the significance of what they are reporting about their thoughts in identifying how they are sabotaging their happiness.

Counselling skills students need to develop skills in knowing and spotting the clues for the various poor mind skills. Then, if necessary, further investigation can develop more accurate hypotheses about clients' self-defeating thoughts and poor mind skills.

Assessing thinking is a continuing process. At best, all you may be able to do in a first session is to form some initial ideas about where clients may need to focus in future. Thoughts interweave with feelings and, as counselling proceeds, clients often become clearer about what they feel and think. Furthermore, in successful counselling, clients become better at developing the **self-helping** skills of **monitoring** and changing how they think. The following are some skills for eliciting and assessing thinking.

Building a knowledge base

It is essential that counselling skills students wishing to work with clients' mind skills develop your knowledge of how people think. You cannot help clients if you do not know what to look for. In addition, you may limit your effectiveness if you only focus on one or two mind skills. However, focusing on just a few mind skills can be a good way to start.

How can counselling skills students develop their knowledge base? First, you can read the works of cognitive therapists, the two main ones being Ellis (Ellis, 2001; 2003; 2008) and Beck (Beck, 1988; Beck and Weishaar, 2008). Second, secondary sources, such as self-help books, like Greenberger and Padesky's (1995) excellent client manual for **cognitive therapy** *Mind Over Mood*, and textbooks, like my *Theory and Practice of Counselling and Therapy* (Nelson-Jones, 2006) can be read. Third, students can work on your own thinking skills either independently, in personal therapy or in training groups. Fourth, work with clients, preferably at first under **supervision**.

Important cognitive theorists like Beck and Ellis rarely use the word 'skills' when writing about how clients think. However, some of their followers are much more explicit about teaching skills. For example, Greenberger and Padesky write: '*Mind Over Mood* teaches you skills that are necessary to make fundamental changes in your moods, behaviours, and relationships' (1995: 2). The Relating–Understanding–Changing (RUC) **counselling and helping process model** incorporates a similar teaching of skills emphasis. However, counsellors, helpers and students require caution and tact in how to introduce the concept of skills to clients.

Asking questions about thoughts

Counselling skills students can help clients to reveal their thoughts by asking appropriate **questions**. One approach to asking questions about thinking is called 'Think aloud'. Think aloud involves encouraging clients to speak aloud their thought processes in relation to specific situations. For instance, you can ask clients to reveal in slow motion their thoughts and feelings in relation to specific anxiety-evoking experiences.

When asking questions, it is important that you use **active listening** skills. Clients feel interrogated when counselling skills students ask a series of questions in quick succession. Though you should not follow this guideline slavishly, you can greatly soften your questioning if you pause to see if clients wish to continue responding and then reflect each response. Interspersing active listening has the added advantage of ensuring the accuracy of your understanding.

Sometimes, counselling skills students can access thinking from feelings, for instance 'What thoughts preceded or accompanied those feelings?' On other occasions you may choose to access thinking from a client's or from another person's behaviour, for example 'When you did that what were you thinking?' or 'When s/he said that what went through your mind?' Students can also ask follow-up questions, such as 'Were there any other thoughts or images?'

Another way to look at thoughts is in terms of their strength. One way to do this is to label thoughts as cool, warm or hot. In particular, counselling skills students should assist clients to look out for hot thoughts that may trigger unwanted feelings and self-defeating communications. Often clients' thoughts about what other people are thinking can be the hot thoughts that drive their poor communication, for example following the thought 'She or he is out to get me' with an angry outburst against her/him. Example 12.1 provides some illustrative questions focusing on clients' thinking.

Thought-eliciting strategies

Counselling skills students can use the same strategies to elicit thoughts and images as you use to elicit feelings and physical reactions.

- *Visualizing* You can ask clients to conjure up images that elicit feelings and then ask them to identify the accompanying thoughts. Clients can visualize past, present or future scenes and get in touch with harmful and helpful thoughts.
- **Role playing** You can conduct role plays with clients, for instance telephoning someone for a date, and then you can explore their thoughts and feelings.

Example 12.1 Some questions focusing on thinking

What thoughts did you have before/during/after the situation?
What images do you get in the situation?
Go in slow motion through your thoughts in the situation?
How frequently do you get those thoughts?
When she or he acted like that what did you think?
Which of those thoughts is the hot thought?
What do you think she or he was thinking?
What resources or **strengths** do you have in the situation?
Where is the evidence for this thought?
Are there other ways of looking at the situation?
What is the worst thing that could happen?
In addition, asking specific questions about **rules, perceptions, self-talk,** visual images, **explanations** and **expectations**

- *Live observation* You can accompany clients into situations that cause them diffi-culty, for instance returning something to a store or driving a car after an accident, and ask them to recount their thoughts.
- *Task assignment* You can encourage clients to perform feared tasks in between sessions and afterwards to record their thoughts and feelings. Clients can view such tasks as personal **experiments** to collect evidence about themselves.

Activity 12.1 Assessing thinking when counselling and helping

Part A   Pairs activity

Conduct a counselling session with a partner in which the counsellor/helper first briefly focuses on helping the client share her/his feelings and physical reactions about a specific problematic situation. Then mainly focus on helping the client share and assess her/his thoughts and images before and during the situation. The counsellor/helper uses skills such as active listening, asking questions about feelings, thoughts and images, and thought-eliciting strategies, as appropriate. The session should be a minimum of five minutes and longer, as necessary. Towards the end of the counselling session, the counsellor/helper shares and discusses her/his mind skills hypotheses with the client.

Afterwards, reverse roles.

Part B   Group activity

One person acts as a client who presents a specific problematic situation to the group. The remainder of the group, say up to six people, sit in a semi-circle round the client and counsel the client in such a way as to assess her/his thoughts and images before and during the situation. One approach is for the group members to take brief turns as counsellor/helper. Every now and then stop and discuss both what's happened and where to go next. Before ending the group shares and discusses their mind skills hypotheses with the client.

The group can repeat this activity with other 'clients'.

Encouraging clients to monitor their thoughts and perceptions

Counselling skills students can encourage clients to monitor their thoughts, perceptions and images. Sometimes such monitoring is in conjunction with monitoring feelings and physical reactions as well. One approach to monitoring thoughts is to ask clients to count every time they get a specific self–defeating perception, for instance 'I'm no good'. Sometimes clients use wrist counters for this purpose. Counting can help clients to become aware of the repetitive nature of their thinking. Clients may then record over a period of time the daily frequency of targeted thoughts and perceptions.

Another approach to monitoring thoughts is to expand the worksheet for identifying key feelings and physical reactions in a situation to include perceptions and images. Example 12.2 provides an example of such a worksheet. Here the client is asked to put a star by the hot perception most associated with the feelings and physical reactions. Students can train clients in how to complete the worksheet, possibly by **working**

Example 12.2 Worksheet for identifying and rating key feelings, physical reactions, perceptions and images in a situation

Situation
(Who? What? When? Where?)
Wednesday, 8.30pm
I come home late from work and my partner says 'Where on earth have you been?'

Key feeling(s) and physical reaction(s)
(What did I feel? How did I physically react? Rating for each key feeling and physical reaction (0-to-100%))
Angry   70%
Hurt   80%
Tense   65%

Perceptions and images
(What perceptions and images did I have just before I started to feel and physically react this way? Place a star by any hot perceptions.)
She/he is angry with me.
*She/he never gives me the benefit of the doubt.
I was looking forward to getting home.
Home is not the safe haven it should be.
An image of our previous fight about this issue.

through an example with them on a whiteboard in the interview room. Clients can be asked to fill out separate worksheets for difficult situations they faced **between sessions**.

Activity 12.2 Assisting a client to identify perceptions and images in a situation

Make up a worksheet similar to that in Example 12.2. Counsel a partner who acts as a client and presents you with a situation in which she/he has experienced distressing feelings. With the aim of assisting your client to learn how to do this for themselves, assist her/him to fill out the worksheet in which she/he describes the situation, identifies her/his key feelings and physical reactions and rates each on a 0-to-100 scale, lists her/his perceptions and images immediately before starting to have these feelings/physical reactions, and puts a star by any hot perceptions and images.

Afterwards, discuss and reverse roles.

A further approach to monitoring thinking is that of the **STC framework** that can be used by counselling skills students and clients alike as a tool for analyzing how thoughts mediate between situations and how clients feel, physically react, communicate and act about them. In this framework:

S = Situation (situations clients face)
T = Thoughts (thoughts and visual images)
C = Consequences (feelings, physical reactions, communications and actions)

The idea is that clients do not go automatically from the situation (S) to the consequences of the situation (C). Instead the consequences (C) of the situation (S) are mediated by what and how clients think (T). Thus, clients' feelings, physical reactions, communications and actions are mediated for good or ill by their thoughts and mental processes.

Example 12.3 provides an STC worksheet that clients can use both during counselling sessions and between sessions to monitor and analyze their thoughts in situations. Again, counselling skills students can show clients how to complete the worksheet during the session, possibly using a whiteboard as an aid. The demonstration worksheet has been filled out for Vanessa, a 25-year-old counselling student, who is very anxious about an upcoming driver's licence test and thinks in negative ways. The mind skills represented by each of Vanessa's thoughts have been placed in parentheses.

Example 12.3 STC (Situation–Thoughts–Consequences) worksheet

Situation
State my problem situation clearly and succinctly.
Next Tuesday, in five days, I'm going to be taking my driver's licence test.

Thoughts
Record my thoughts about the situation.

'I must pass the test.'	(creating rules)
'I'm no good at taking tests.'	(creating perceptions)
'I am afraid that I will fail.'	(creating expectations)

Consequences
What are the consequences of my thoughts about the situation?
My feelings and physical reactions
Feelings: very anxious
Physical reactions: **tension** in my stomach, not sleeping properly

My communications and actions
In the past I have avoided getting a driver's licence.
I have started withdrawing from my friends.

Activity 12.3 Assisting a client to identify thoughts and consequences in a situation

Make up a worksheet similar to that in Example 12.3. Counsel a partner who acts as a client and presents you with a situation in which she/he has experienced distressing feelings. With the aim of assisting your client to learn how to do this for themselves, assist her/him to fill out the STC worksheet in which she/he describes the situation, lists her/his main thoughts and images in relation to it, and identifies the feelings/physical reactions consequences and the communication/action consequences of these thoughts and images.

Afterwards, discuss and reverse roles.

Forming hypotheses about mind skills to improve

For some counsellors and helpers all roads lead to Rome and they focus on one important mind skill. For example, rational emotive behaviour therapists focus on altering irrational beliefs or rules and cognitive therapists focus on improving clients' ability to test the reality of their perceptions.

Clients rarely, if ever, tell their counsellors and helpers: 'Look, I've got this poor mind skill I need to improve! [and then proceed to name it]'. Counselling skills students who think that many clients may need to improve more than one mind skill make inferences and form hypotheses about these possible poor skills. Inferences about thinking may stem from clients' words, feelings and actions. In the understanding stage counselling skills students can be on the lookout for clues that clients may be creating negative or unhelpful thoughts. In this section, some key indicators that clients may possess unhelpful thoughts are reviewed for three mind skills areas: creating rules, creating perceptions and creating self-talk. Often negative thinking needs to be inferred since clients are unlikely to relate directly 'I have this particular problem with how I think...' and then specify it.

Another point to remember is that negative thinking is rarely an either/or matter. Clients mix helpful with unhelpful thinking and it may only be the 20 or 30 per cent of a client's thinking that is unhelpful. For example, 80 per cent of a client's thinking may be about attaining realistically high levels of **competence**, whereas the remaining 20 per cent is about attaining unrealistically high levels of perfection. It is changing this 20 per cent that counselling skills students need to learn to address.

Counselling skills students can identify and collect evidence that helps you to form hypotheses about clients' poor mind skills. As part of the process of assessing thinking, you may collect further **information** that either **supports** or negates your hypotheses. Conversely, you may choose not to collect further information about some hypotheses.

Creating rules
The following are some indicators or signals for demanding rather than **preferential** **rules**. Counselling skills students can pay attention to signs of inappropriate language. For example, demanding rules tend to be characterized by 'musts', 'oughts', 'shoulds' and 'have to's': for example, 'I must have approval' or 'Others should do what I want'.

Persistent inappropriate feelings can signal that clients possess a demanding rule. The dividing line between appropriate and inappropriate feelings is not always clear. Life can be difficult, so appropriate feelings cannot simply be equated with 'positive' feelings like happiness, joy and accomplishment. Some 'negative' feelings like sadness, grief, fear and anger can be entirely appropriate for the contexts in which they occur. Students have to ask yourselves questions like: 'Is this feeling appropriate for the situation?' and 'Is keeping feeling this way helping or harming the client?' Physical reactions may also signal demanding rules; for instance persistent muscular tension could signal clients putting pressure on themselves for perfection or universal approval.

Inappropriate feelings, physical reactions and communications/actions are interrelated. If clients feel excessively angry because of a demanding rule, their physical level of arousal can impair their judgment to the point where they act violently and worsen rather than help their position. Relevant questions for counselling skills students to ask yourselves, and possibly clients too, include: 'Are clients' communications or actions helping or harming themselves or others?', 'Are they overreacting?', and 'Is their behaviour self-defeating?'

Creating perceptions

In Chapter 3, I mentioned the importance of being able to distinguish fact from inference and guarding against the tendency to jump to unwarranted conclusions. Counselling skills students can closely observe how much evidence clients provide to support assertions about how they and others behave. When clients make statements like: 'I have no friends', 'I'm no good at maths', 'She/he never does anything for me', and 'My boss hates me', students can ask clients to generate evidence to support or negate their statements.

Students can also look out for characteristic tricks of the mind that might indicate clients are creating insufficiently accurate perceptions (Beck, 1988; Beck and Weishaar, 2008). Especially when feeling under **stress**, clients are likely to perceive inaccurately. Using the STC framework, six mind tricks follow that clients may use at T that lead to negative feelings, physical reactions and communication consequences at C.

- *Making unsupported inferences* Drawing conclusions without adequate supporting evidence.
- *Using **tunnel vision*** Narrowly focusing on only a portion of the available information in a situation rather than taking into account all significant information. For example, clients focus mainly on the positive aspects of a new job and select out potentially negative information.
- *Thinking in black-and-white terms* Perceiving in all or nothing terms: for example, a client gives the impression 'Either my relationship with my employer is a total success or a total failure.'
- *Magnifying and minimizing relevant information* Seeing things as far more important or less important than they really are. For instance, magnifying minor upsets into disasters or minimizing negative events – for instance, either exaggerating or down-playing the implications of being diagnosed with cancer.
- *Overgeneralising* Making general comments that clients probably would not be able to support if they bothered to check the evidence. For example, 'My partner never appreciates me' and 'I always try to understand my partner's viewpoint.'

- *Being overly negative* Attaching unduly negative and critical labels to oneself and to others. Overemphasizing the negative at the expense of the positive or neutral. Going beyond useful ratings of specific characteristics to devaluing one's own or another's whole worth as a person.

Creating self-talk

When asking clients what is going through their minds before, during and after specific **problem situations**, counselling skills students can look out for self-talk that increases the likelihood of harmful feelings and self-defeating actions. For example, **anxiety**-arousing self-talk may include the following elements: emphasizing mastery rather than **coping**, catastrophizing or imagining the worst, adversely reacting to physical symptoms or getting anxious about getting anxious, and being overly self-conscious about what others think. Anger-arousing self-talk may include jumping to negative conclusions about others' intentions, focusing on other people's shortcomings, and feeling sorry for oneself. In addition to presence of harmful self-talk, look out for absence of helpful self-talk, for instance absence of calming and of cooling self-instructions.

Counselling skills students can also look out for absence of or insufficient coaching self-talk. Clients may not realize the importance of coaching themselves in how to communicate and act appropriately in problem situations. They may insufficiently clarify their **goals**, fail to think in terms of a step-by-step approach to situations, and insufficiently focus on coaching themselves in sending good **vocal** and **bodily communication**.

Clients can also lower their self-esteem by talking to themselves as if they were their own worst enemies. For instance, they may tell themselves how stupid, incompetent, uninteresting and ugly they are. In addition, they may fail to remind themselves of their strengths and of supportive people in their lives.

Case example

Below is a case study in which the counsellor makes hypotheses about which mind skills a client might improve. Though only three mind skills were discussed above, for didactic purposes, here the counsellor makes hypotheses that cover the six central mind skills reviewed in Chapter 3. In real life, counsellor and client might focus on improving the one, two or three mind skills they consider the most important to change.

> ### Case study: Forming hypotheses about mind skills Jim needs to improve
>
> Jim, 28, is deputy manager of a large supermarket. Jim got on well with his previous boss, Pamela. However, three months ago Pamela was transferred to another branch and Paul, 44, was appointed to replace him. Jim has not developed such a good relationship with Paul and is considering leaving his position after a run-in with him.
>
> The counsellor's **assessment** is that Jim is disturbing himself through his faulty thinking to the point where he might make the mistake of resigning

(Continued)

Case study: Forming hypotheses about mind skills Jim needs to improve – cont'd

prematurely from a good job and then still not know how to cope with similar pressures in succeeding jobs. It might be much better for Jim to learn to become mentally more skilfull early in his career.

Creating rules Jim can detect, challenge and alter his subconscious demanding rule that his boss must approve of everything he does all the time.

Creating perceptions Jim can get a more balanced perception of Paul: for instance, he can remember that Paul has praised him in the past, drives everyone including himself very hard, and that Paul's angry feelings may be transient.

Creating self-talk Jim can talk to himself with calming statements and with statements that help him to stay focused on goals that are important both in this particular mini-crisis and in his overall career.

Creating visual images Jim can use visual images both to calm himself down and to rehearse in his imagination how he might communicate more effectively in his future dealings with Paul.

Creating explanations Jim can regain confidence by explaining to himself that much of Paul's angry reactions could be related to both the realistic and self-inflicted pressures he feels under to make a success of the supermarket.

Creating expectations Jim can also learn to correct his tendency, when feeling emotionally vulnerable, to create unrealistic expectations about how badly

Activity 12.4 Identifying unhelpful thinking

Part A   Creating rules

For a specific problem situation in either your own or a client's life, how you might be able to identify the presence of one or more unhelpful rules:
- by attending to inappropriate language
- by noticing persistent inappropriate feelings
- by noticing unwanted physical reactions
- by becoming aware of self-defeating communication/actions.

Part B   Creating perceptions

For a specific problem situation in either your own or a client's life, how you might be able to identify the presence of one or more inaccurate perceptions:
- by observing how much evidence you/the client provide(s) to support assertions about your/their behaviour
- by observing the following characteristic tricks of the mind
    making unsupported inferences
    using tunnel vision

Activity 12.4 Identifying unhelpful thinking – cont'd

thinking in black-and-white terms
magnifying and minimizing relevant information
overgeneralizing
being overly negative.

Part C   Creating self-talk

For a specific problem situation in either your own or a client's life, deliberately
formulate unhelpful self-talk statements that might
- cause you/the client to feel anxious
- cause you/the client to feel angry
- coach you/the client in self-defeating communication or actions.

13

Assessing communication and actions

CHAPTER OUTCOMES

By studying and doing the activity in this chapter you should:
- understand the importance of assessing communication and actions;
- develop some skills for assessing and getting clients to assess how they communicate and act; and
- assist clients to form hypotheses about improving communication and action skills.

Counsellors and **helpers** need to pay close attention to **communication** and actions because, if **clients** are to manage most problems better, they must change how they behave. **Communication** and **action skills** interact with thinking and feeling. Improved thinking needs to be followed by effective communication and action. Furthermore, if clients are to feel better, they frequently need to change how they communicate and act to achieve their **goals**: for example, developing friendship skills so as to become less lonely.

Generally, **counselling skills** students find it easier to think in terms of communication and action skills than thinking skills. However, a common mistake is to focus only on verbal skills. Communication and action skills involve five main message categories: verbal, voice, body, touch and taking action. The first four message categories usually assume face-to-face contact. The fifth category, taking action messages, does not require direct contact: for instance, sending flowers to someone one loves.

Skills for eliciting and assessing communication and actions

When counsellors and helpers assess communication and actions they seek both to identify which skills are important and also to evaluate how skilfully clients perform in them. Below are some skills for assessing clients' communication and actions and for helping clients monitor and assess themselves.

Building a knowledge base

Counselling skills students require knowledge of the relevant communication and action skills for the client populations that you service. As with **mind skills**, if you do not know what constitutes skilled behaviour in an area you cannot assess it with any accuracy. For example, those of you working with people with relationship problems require knowledge of communication skills such as disclosing appropriately, **listening** well, sharing intimacy, enjoying sex, managing anger and communicating assertively. Students working with people seeking jobs require knowledge of how to make résumés and take part in interviews. Counselling skills students working with school and university students' work problems require knowledge of **study skills**, such as reading efficiently, taking good notes and sitting exams effectively.

Gathering information inside and outside of counselling and helping sessions

Counselling skills students can gather information about observable communication and actions either inside or outside of counselling sessions. There are a number of ways in which such information can be collected in interviews. First, there is client self-report. Clients can tell you how they behave outside the interview. A limitation of client self-report is that you do not observe client behaviour directly and so have to rely on their versions of events, which may be incomplete and/or inaccurate. Clients may edit what they say to protect their self-pictures.

Second, counselling skills students can observe clients in the counselling room or helping setting. Depending on the areas of clients' problems, you may learn much from observing their verbal, voice and action messages. For example, clients may exhibit communication difficulties, such as shyness, in your presence. Third, you can listen to your own experiencing of how you feel when clients communicate in certain ways

and use this as additional information for **assessment**: for instance, you may directly experience the impact of a client's annoying mannerism.

Students may wish to supplement interview information with that gathered in clients' natural or home environments. Sometimes you can go with clients into situations in which they experience difficulty and observe how they behave: for instance, when requesting a drink in a bar or relating to children at home.

Though possibly not in initial training, later on and with permission counselling skills students may also collect information about how clients communicate and act from third parties: for instance, spouses, parents, siblings, or peers. You need to be mindful of, and consider exploring, differences between third parties' and your clients' own observations. Students may need to train third parties in what to look for and in how to observe systematically.

Asking questions about communications and actions

Questions about clients' communication and actions aim to elicit specific details of how they behave. Often, clients' reports are vague and they require assistance in becoming more specific. However, many counselling skills students are poor at helping

Example 13.1 Some questions focusing on communication/actions

How did you behave?
What did you say?
How were you communicating with your voice?
How were you communicating with your body language?
How did she/he react when you did that [specify]?
What is the pattern of communication that develops between you when you row?
In what situations do you behave like that?
What happened before you did that?
What were the consequences of doing that?
When does it happen?
Where does it happen?
How many times a day/week/month do you ... ?
Over what period were you ... ?

clients to discover what actually happened in situations and so the vagueness can persist. Example 13.1 provides some questions focusing on communication and actions.

A further question focusing on communications and actions is 'Show me?' Counselling skills students can invite clients to illustrate the verbal, vocal and body messages they used in an interaction either on their own or in a role play with you playing the other party. For instance, parents who experience difficulty in disciplining their children can show the counselling skills student how they attempt this. Role play allows the possibility of exploring patterns of communication that extend beyond an initial 'show me' response focused on just one unit of interaction. Students can also video-record role plays and play them back to clients to illustrate points and develop clients' skills of observing themselves.

Encouraging clients to monitor their communication and actions

Counselling skills students can encourage clients to become more aware of how they communicate and act in problem areas. Sometimes you will agree with clients on **between-session** homework tasks, for instance telephoning to ask for a date, and ask clients to record how they behave.

Clients can take away and fill in worksheets for **monitoring** how they communicate and act. The simplest version of such a worksheet asks clients to describe the situation first and then report how they communicate/act in the situation. When filling in worksheets, clients need to pay attention to vocal and bodily as well as verbal communication. More elaborate worksheets include having a situation, **feelings**, thoughts and communication/actions format or adopting the STC (Situation–Thoughts–Consequences) format. When using the STC format, clients record how they communicate and act in the consequences section.

Filling out activity sheets or schedules in which clients record what they do throughout the day is another way that clients can monitor their actions. When using activity schedules with depressed patients, Beck and his colleagues ask them to provide ratings on 0-to-10 scales for feelings of mastery and of pleasure experienced during each activity (Beck and Weishaar, 2008).

Forming hypotheses about communication and action skills to improve

As counselling skills students listen to clients and collect information, communication and action skills hypotheses are formed. You may feel confident about some hypotheses at the end of an initial session, but make other hypotheses more tentatively. Still further hypotheses emerge as counselling and helping progresses. Clients may also share ideas about unhelpful communication and actions. Such observations always merit attention, not least because clients are assuming some responsibility for their problems and **problematic skills**.

Counselling skills students may formulate many hypotheses concerning broad areas in which clients may need to develop skills. You may make some of these hypotheses in the initial session, but often you will defer detailed assessment of specific skills deficiencies until subsequent sessions when there is more time to do the job thoroughly. Furthermore, by then, students and clients may have prioritized which skills areas require detailed attention. In the following case study, the **counsellor** identifies just one communication/action skill to improve and illustrates it with some verbal, **vocal** and **bodily communications** that the client might change.

Case study: Forming hypotheses about communication/action skills Jim needs to improve.

This is a continuation of the case study presented in the last chapter identifying how Jim might improve his mind skills.

Regarding communication/action skills hypotheses, the counsellor considers that Jim needs to improve his assertion skills when relating to Paul. The counsellor has noted the following as actual or potential assertion skills deficiencies.

Verbal communication Insufficiently using 'I' **statements** that briefly and clearly explain his viewpoint on specific issues. Failing to express appreciation for positive actions by Paul in the past.

Vocal communication Speaking too quickly and not speaking sufficiently clearly and firmly.

Bodily communication Slouching slightly by not having his shoulders sufficiently back. Making insufficient eye contact.

Activity 13.1 Gathering information and forming communication skills hypotheses

Part A Pairs activity

Counsel a partner who discusses a problem entailing how she/he behaves towards another person. Your focus in this session is to work with your client in identifying and assessing her/his communication and skills in a specific problem situation. Counsel in an open-ended manner for the first two or three minutes and then intersperse focusing on communication questions with reflective responses. As you proceed, incorporate role play into your information gathering. Aim to obtain a clear picture of her/his verbal, vocal and bodily communication in the situation and of any unhelpful patterns of communication. During this process, form communication skills hypotheses about how she/he may contribute to making the situation problematic. The session should be a minimum of five minutes and longer, as necessary. Towards the end of the counselling/helping session, share and discuss your communication skills hypotheses with the client.

Afterwards, reverse roles.

Part B Group activity

One person acts as a client who presents a specific problematic situation to the group. The remainder of the group, say up to six people, sit in a semi-circle round the client and counsel the client in such a way as to assess her/his communications/actions before and during the situation. One approach is for the group members to take brief turns as counsellor/helper. Every now and then stop and discuss both what's happened and where to go next. Before ending the group shares and discusses their communication/action skills hypotheses with the client.

The group can repeat this activity with other 'clients'.

14

Challenges, feedback and self-disclosure

CHAPTER OUTCOMES

By studying and doing the activities in this chapter you should:
- possess some skills for challenging clients' perspectives;
- have some basic feedback skills;
- have some knowledge and skills for talking about yourself; and
- be able to assist clients to monitor themselves between sessions.

The previous chapters focused on **skills** for assessing and clarifying **feelings**, **physical reactions**, thinking, **communication** and actions. These skills are the 'bread and butter' skills of the understanding stage of the Relating–Understanding–Changing helping process model. This chapter reviews some additional skills counselling skills students can use to expand **clients'** and your own understanding.

Challenging skills

Challenging is perhaps a more gentle word than confronting, which conjures up images of clients sitting in hot sets having their self-protective habits remorselessly stripped away by aggressive counsellors and helpers. Counselling skills students can challenge clients from the **external frame of reference** with the aim of helping them to develop new and better perspectives about themselves, others and their **problem situations**. Skilled challenges invite clients to examine discrepancies in their feelings, thoughts and communications about which, for various reasons, they remain insufficiently aware. The challenges advocated here have two distinctive characteristics: first, they tend to be fairly close to clients' existing perspectives; and second, they are given in a relatively non-threatening manner. As Example 14.1 illustrates, challenges can come in many shapes and sizes.

How to challenge

Verbal messages for challenges include: 'On the one hand … on the other … ', 'On the one hand … but … '; 'You say… but … ' and 'I'm getting two messages … ' or 'I'm getting a mixed message … ' Counselling skills students' vocal and body communication

Example 14.1 Illustrations of challenging inconsistencies

- *Inconsistency between verbal, **vocal** and **bodily communication***
  'On the one hand you're saying you're all right but I catch a note of pain in your voice and your eyes look a little weepy.'

- *Inconsistency between words and actions*
  'You say that your kids are the most important thing in the world to you, but you seem to rarely go to see them.'

- *Inconsistency between negative self-picture and positive evidence*
  'You say you are no good with people, yet you seem to have some very good friends.'

- *Inconsistency between **goals** and actions*
  'You say you want to get a job and gain financial independence, however you're also telling me you've done little about looking for one.'

- *Inconsistency between earlier and present statements*
  'A moment ago you said you were uneasy about your social work course, but now you're saying it is quite good.'

- *Inconsistency between statements and evidence*
  'You said your boyfriend never does anything for you, but now you've just told me that he took you out to dinner on your birthday.'

- *Inconsistency between thoughts, feelings and actual communication*
  'You get extremely tense about going to parties, but you're also saying that you manage to perform so that it is hard for people to notice how uptight you get.'

- *Inconsistency between own and others' evaluations*
  'I'm getting two messages. You feel that you are hopeless at cooking, but the feedback from your girlfriend seems to be that she is pleased with your efforts.'

should remain relaxed and friendly. Beginning students should restrict yourselves to making mildly threatening challenges to clients since there are dangers if inexperienced students make strong challenges.

When challenging it is important to keep clients' ears open to a different viewpoint. Offer challenges as an equal and avoid talking down to clients. Remember, challenges are invitations for exploration. A major risk in offering challenges to clients is that they get perceived as put-downs.

Counselling students should use a minimum amount of 'muscle'. Strong challenges can create resistances. Although sometimes necessary, even with skilled counsellors and helpers such challenges are generally best avoided – especially in initial sessions where rapport and trust is not yet well established. Strategies that clients can use to resist challenges include discrediting challengers, persuading you to change your views, devaluing the issue, seeking support elsewhere for views being challenged, and agreeing with the challenge inside helping but then doing nothing about it outside.

The ultimate responsibility for assessing the value of challenges should be left with clients. They can decide whether challenges actually help them to move forward in their explorations. Often, challenges are only mildly discrepant to clients' existing **perceptions**. If well timed and tactfully worded, such challenges are unlikely to elicit a high degree of defensiveness.

Counselling skills students should be careful not to overdo challenging. Nobody likes being persistently challenged. If you challenge skilfully, you can help clients enlarge their understanding and act more effectively. However, if you challenge too often and too clumsily, you can block clients and harm creating a good **working alliance**.

Activity 14.1 Challenging skills

1 What does the concept of challenging clients mean to you? What are the advantages and disadvantages in initial counselling and helping sessions of challenges to clients:
   - by counselling skills students
   - by experienced counsellors/helpers.

2 Using Example 14.1 as a guide, formulate a challenging response in each of the following areas:
   - inconsistency between verbal, vocal and bodily communication
   - inconsistency between words and actions
   - inconsistency between negative self-picture and positive evidence
   - inconsistency between goals and actions
   - inconsistency between earlier and present statements
   - inconsistency between statements and evidence
   - inconsistency between thoughts, feelings and actual communication
   - inconsistency between own and others' evaluations.

Feedback skills

Feedback skills and challenging skills overlap. However, challenging skills are used in response to clients' inconsistencies, whereas there is no assumption of inconsistency in this section on feedback skills. Here, a distinction is made between observational feedback, 'I observe you as … ', and experiential feedback, 'I experience you as … '.

Observational feedback

Counselling skills students observing clients' communication may see it differently and possibly more accurately than clients themselves. When working together to try to understand clients' problem situations, there may be occasions where feedback might be provided to clients based on your observations. Take clients who have just shown how they communicate in a specific situation. After participating in mini role plays, clients may show some insight into their communication. However, as an observer, the counselling skills student wishes to bring something else to their attention.

Many of the same skills used when training counselling skills are relevant to giving feedback to clients: for example, using 'I' messages; being specific and, where possible, stating feedback in the positive; using confirmatory as well as corrective feedback; considering demonstrating feedback; and providing opportunities for clients to respond to feedback.

After a mini role play it can be a good idea to ask clients to evaluate themselves before providing any feedback. Reasons for this include keeping clients as active participants, reducing the need for external feedback since clients may have noticed the points anyway, building clients' skills of self-observation, and sensing that clients are more likely to be receptive to feedback if they have first had the opportunity to assess themselves. For instance, after inviting clients to comment on their performance and

listening to their responses, you can summarize and enquire 'Would you mind if I added one or two observations … ?' and then, if given permission, you can succinctly provide feedback.

Experiential feedback

Feedback can also involve counselling skills students in using your experiencing of clients as the springboard for making observations about both the client and the counselling process. To an extent counselling and helping sessions are microcosms of outside life. Clients can bring to the sessions the same patterns of communication that create

difficulties for them outside of them. However, you have to be very careful not to let your own personal **unfinished business** interfere with how you experience clients.

Counselling skills students may not need to engage in role plays to experience how clients may come across to others in their problem situations. For example, I once had a very bright and able businesswoman client, Louise, who was repeatedly getting turned down at interviews. I used questioning and **active listening** to explore what might be going on in these situations. However, the most powerful **information** came from my feelings of being overpowered by Louise's bombastic and lecturing interpersonal style. My first decision was 'Should I share this experientially based information or sit on it?' Having decided I might try to share the information, the second decision was 'How do I provide this experiential feedback to Louise who has shown limited insight so far?'

I tentatively suggested to Louise that I experienced her as coming across rather strong as she talked with me and that this might be relevant to panel members' reactions at her interviews. Furthermore, I fed back to her that she had a fairly booming voice. I could have done this more tactfully if I had remembered a comment that she had made about the possibility that she was 'too educational' at interviews. I could then have introduced this feedback about her booming voice as a hypothesis to clarify an aspect of her comment about being 'too educational'. Had I done this, this feedback would have been closer to her perspective and less from my own.

Instances where counselling skills students' experiencing of clients' interpersonal style may throw light on their problems outside include not coming on time for interviews, speaking in distant ways, being aggressive, and disparaging themselves. Giving positive experiential feedback to clients with low self-esteem can sometimes be helpful: for example 'I experience you as having some strength to deal with the situation' or

'I experience you as having much to offer a friend'. Such comments need to be gen-uine feedback rather than superficial reassurance.

Counselling skills students can also provide experiential feedback concerning the counselling or helping process. For example, if a client is repetitively going over the same ground, the student might say: 'I experience you as having taken that topic as far as you can go at the moment and it might be profitable to move on. What do you think?' Another example is that of a student who shares her or his experiencing of a client who uses humour as a distancing device whenever topics become too personal: for instance, 'I get the sense that this topic is getting too close for comfort and so you're starting to act the clown to avoid dealing with it directly.' Needless to say, tact and good **timing** is very important if clients are to use such experiential feedback to move forwards rather than backwards.

Activity 14.2 Feedback skills

Part A   Observational feedback

- Work in threes, Partner A as 'client', Partner B as '**counsellor**' and Partner C as observer. Partner A selects a problem situation involving another person where she/he thinks she/he might communicate better.
- Partners A and B conduct a mini role play in which Partner B, the counsellor, plays the other person and Partner A, the client, shows how she/he currently communicates in the situation.
- Afterwards, Partner B invites Partner A to comment on her/his own communi-cation. Then Partner B gives observational feedback to Partner A.
- Next hold a discussion in which Partner C, the observer, first asks Partner B to evaluate her/his giving feedback skills and then gives observational feedback to Partner B on her/his use of feedback skills.
- Then change roles until everyone has had the opportunity to be client, counsel-lor and observer.

Part B   Experiential feedback

a) What does the concept of experiential feedback mean to you? What are the advantages and disadvantages in initial counselling and helping sessions of experiential feedback to clients:
- by counselling skills students
- by experienced counsellors/helpers?

b) Formulate one or more experiential feedback statements.

Disclosing yourself skills

Should counselling skills students talk at all about yourselves in counselling and helping sessions? How can you show **genuineness** and humanity if you stay as a blank screen to clients? **Self-disclosure** relates to the ways in which people let themselves be known to one another. Usually the term refers to intentional verbal disclosure.

A useful distinction exists between disclosures showing involvement and those sharing personal experiences.

Counselling skills students' self-disclosure, even in brief contact with clients, can be for good or ill. Possible positive consequences to such disclosure include providing new insights and perspectives, demonstrating a useful skill, equalizing and humanizing the helping relationship, normalizing clients' difficulties, giving encouragement, and reassurance.

However, there can be grave dangers if counselling skills students inappropriately self-disclose. Boundaries may get blurred as you burden clients with your problems and shift the focus of the helping conversation to yourself. You may come across as weak and unstable when clients who feel vulnerable want a **helper** who has 'got her/his act together'. In addition, students may either intentionally or unintentionally use self-disclosure to manipulate clients to meet your own needs for approval, intimacy and sex.

Showing involvement

Disclosures that show counselling skills students' involvement can humanize counselling and helping so that clients feel they relate to real people. There is a 'here-and-now' quality in showing involvement by sharing reactions to clients. Three areas for disclosing involvement are responding to specific client disclosures, responding to clients as people, and responding to clients' vulnerability. Example 14.2 provides illustrative statements for each area.

Students who show involvement can help clients feel that you genuinely care. Positive self-involving statements that express positive rather than negative feelings about clients can draw favourable reactions (Watkins, 1990). However, students need to be careful about being too gushing and nice. Clients want detached involvement rather than involvement with psychological hooks attached. Furthermore, some clients may need tough alongside tender love.

Sharing personal experiences

Sharing personal experiences may help clients feel that a counselling skills student understands what they are going through. For instance, unemployed people might feel differently about those who share that they too have been unemployed. In some types of counselling and helping, disclosure of shared experiences is an important part of the process: for instance Alcoholics Anonymous and some drug addiction programmes.

Counselling skills students have many choices in sharing personal experiences. Included among these are whether to mention them or not, whether to restrict yourself to past experiences or discuss current experiences, how honest to be, whether to go beyond disclosing facts to disclosing feelings – for instance not only having been unemployed but then having to struggle against feelings of depression and uselessness, how you coped with your experience, and how you feel about it now. In the kind of brief counselling and helping assumed initially by the Relating–Understanding–Changing process model you will not have the opportunity to develop the 'relational depth' that some helpers achieve with some clients later in a series of helping sessions (Mearns and Cooper, 2005; Mearns and Thorne, 2007).

Example 14.2 Some counsellor and helper disclosures

Showing involvement

Illustrative responses include:

- *Responding to specific disclosures*
  'I'm delighted', 'That's great', 'That's terrible', 'I'm really sorry to hear that'

- *Responding to clients as people*
  'I admire your courage', 'I appreciate your honesty'

- *Responding to clients' vulnerability*
  'I'm available if you get really low', 'I'm very concerned about what you're going through'

Sharing personal experiences

Dina, at one stage in my life I was unemployed too and found it a very scary and difficult time. Though clearly our experiences differ, I think I do have some idea of what you're going through.

Below are some guidelines for appropriate sharing of personal experiences. An illustration is included in Example 14.2.

- *Talk about yourself* Do not disclose the experience of third parties whom you know.
- *Talk about past experiences* You may not have sufficient emotional distance from current experiences, for instance going through a messy divorce.
- *Be to the point* Personal disclosures should follow similar client disclosures. Avoid slowing down or defocusing the counselling or helping session through lack of relevance or talking too much.
- *Be sensitive to clients' reactions* Have sufficient **awareness** to realize when disclosures might be helpful to the client and when they might be unwelcome or a burden.
- *Share personal experiences sparingly* Be careful not to switch the focus of counselling and helping from clients to yourself.

Activity 14.3 Disclosing skills

Part A Showing involvement

1 With respect to your present or future counselling and helping work, write down the sorts of situations in which it might be appropriate for you to show involvement to clients in initial sessions.
2 Using Example 14.2 as a guide, formulate one or more disclosures showing involvement in each of the following areas:
  a responding to specific client disclosures
  b responding to clients as people
  c responding to clients' vulnerability.

(Continued)

Activity 14.3 Disclosing skills – cont'd

Part B   Sharing personal information

1 With regard to your present or future counselling and helping work, write down the sorts of situations in which it might be appropriate for you to share personal information with clients in initial sessions.

2 Using Example 14.2 as a guide, for each situation formulate one or more sharing personal information statements.

15

Monitoring, summarizing and identifying skills

CHAPTER OUTCOMES

By studying and doing the activities in this chapter you should:
- be able to assist clients to monitor themselves between sessions;
- intersperse active listening with questions;
- know about providing basic summaries of problem situations; and
- know about identifying some mind skills and communication/action skills for improvement.

This chapter concludes the discussion of stage 2 of the Relating–Understanding–Changing (RUC) **counselling and helping process model**. After reviewing some **monitoring skills** and questioning skills, I examine how to summarize **problem situations** and also how to identify **clients'** underlying skills weaknesses that may be causing them to sustain problems.

Monitoring skills

Counsellors, **helpers** and counselling skills students may need to encourage clients to gather more **information** to clarify and expand mutual understanding of their problem situations. In initial sessions, clients are likely to provide useful information, but it may still help to gather even more. Here, I discuss some simple monitoring methods and how to assist clients to use them.

Monitoring methods

The following are some methods whereby clients can monitor their **feelings**, **physical reactions**, **mind** and **communication**/actions in problem situations. Where appropriate, counselling skills students can tailor-make recording sheets to the particular needs of clients.

- *Diaries and journals* Some clients keep diaries and journals anyway. Clients can pay special attention to writing up specific instances of their problem situations. Although diaries and journals may be useful to some clients, others are likely to find this approach too easy to ignore and too unsystematic.

- *Frequency charts* Frequency charts focus on how many times clients think a thought or enact a specific behaviour in a given time period, say each day between the first and second counselling sessions and overall during this period. For example, in regard to thoughts, clients may tally how many times they engage in negative **self-talk** about a problem situation. In regard to communications and actions, unemployed executives frightened about making cold calls to prospective employers can record each time they manage to make such calls.

- *Situation, thoughts and consequences (STC) logs* Filling in three-column situation, thoughts and consequences (STC) logs can highlight clients' thought processes and help them to see the connections between what they thought and how they felt and communicated/acted (see Example 15.1, Part 1).

- *Verbal, **vocal** and **bodily communication** logs* Frequently, clients possess a low **awareness** of their verbal, vocal and bodily communication. During the understanding stage, counselling skills students and clients may become aware of some areas that may be important to understanding problem situations. For instance, a student works with a teenager, Antonia, whose problem situation is that of difficulty setting limits on her one year older brother Justin, who repeatedly wants to borrow money from her. Example 15.1, Part 2, contains a possible format for a log to collect information about how Antonia communicates. Antonia could be cued in advance to observe specific aspects of her vocal and bodily communication.

Example 15.1 Formats for monitoring logs

Part 1   Situation, thoughts and consequences log

Situation	Thoughts	Consequences
(What happened and when?)	(What I thought?)	(How I felt and communicated/acted)

Part 2   Verbal, vocal and bodily communication log

Situation 1 (provide basic details including when)

My words

My voice

My body language

Consequences for myself and others

Situation 2 (provide basic details including when)
(as for Situation 1)

How to assist clients' monitoring

Clients are not in the **habit** of systematically recording observations about how they feel, physically react, think and communicate/act. Counselling skills students may need to motivate them to do so. For instance, a student might explain to Antonia: 'Systematically writing down how you communicate with your words, voice and body each time Justin attempts to borrow money from you provides us with information to develop useful strategies for setting limits on him.'

Counselling skills students should always either supply the monitoring logs yourselves or, before the initial session ends, supervise clients in setting up the format for a log. You should not expect clients to make logs on their own. Clients may not do so in the first place and, if they do, they may get them wrong.

Clients are not naturally accurate self-observers. Consequently, you may need to train them in how to discriminate and record specific behaviours. Clients require clarity not only about what to record, but also about how to record it. In addition, clients require awareness of any tendencies they have to misperceive or selectively perceive their actions: for instance, being more inclined to notice weaknesses than **strengths**.

Remember to reward clients with interest and praise when they fill in logs. This guideline is based on the basic behavioural principle that actions that are rewarding are more likely to be repeated. Furthermore, always reward clients for their efforts by debriefing them.

Interspersing active listening with questions

Sometimes in counselling skills classes, I would seat student and client side by side to indicate the kind of working together relationship desirable in counselling and helping. In the understanding stage, students and clients are both moving towards the common goal of helping one another understand the problem situation more fully. They are detectives on the lookout for relevant information and clues concerning what makes situations into problems for clients.

Counselling skills students require clients' cooperation to conduct the understanding stage. If you can establish a good emotional climate clients are likely to reveal much more – both in answer to **questions** and of their own accord. Not only will clients feel freer, they will also be more comfortable about acknowledging to themselves their own thoughts, feelings and experiencing.

Clients feel interrogated when counselling skills students ask a series of questions in quick succession. You can greatly soften questioning if you pause to see if clients wish to continue responding and then reflect each response. Interspersing **active listening** has the added advantage of ensuring that you check the accuracy of your understanding. Example 15.2 illustrates the difference between interrogation and interspersing active listening with questions. Though these are only short excerpts, the first shows the counsellor controlling and dominating the client. In the second excerpt, the counsellor facilitates Lucy's description of her **internal frame of reference**. The emotional climate in the first excerpt is 'in the head'. In the second excerpt Lucy is encouraged to share her experiencing of her feelings and physical reactions.

Example 15.2 Interspersing active listening with questions

Problem situation
At the start of her final semester, Lucy, a 21-year-old final year student, comes to her counsellor worried about not getting a job at the end of her university course.

Interrogation

Lucy	I'm getting very anxious that I will not have a job when I finish here.
Counsellor	What makes you so anxious?
Lucy	The fact that I may not find employment.
Counsellor	What makes you think that you will be unemployed?
Lucy	I have not got a job so far.
Counsellor	Why are you so afraid of being unemployed?
Lucy	Because then I will have wasted my time here.
Counsellor	Well, why do you think getting a job is the only thing that counts?

Interspersing active listening with questions

Lucy	I'm getting very anxious that I will not have a job when I finish here.
Counsellor	You're increasingly worried about not getting a job ... Can you tell me more ...?
Lucy	Yes, I get tense just thinking about it.
Counsellor	You feel tense ... Where?
Lucy	In my head and in my chest. One of the reasons I came to study was so that I would get a really good job.
Counsellor	So you're worried about not meeting that goal?
Lucy	I'm not sleeping well and listless much of the time. I've never felt this anxious before.
Counsellor	It's really getting to you and affecting your sleep and energy level too. Can you describe not sleeping well and being listless more fully?

Note that the interrogating counsellor in Example 15.2 engages in jack-rabbitting or quickly hopping from one topic to another. Counselling skills students should always listen carefully to and respect what clients have just said. Frequently, your next question can follow on from and encourage clients to build upon the last response. Questioning that is logically linked to clients' responses creates a feeling of working together rather than of being directed by the student.

How counselling skills students question is very important in addition to what you say. For example, if your voice is loud and harsh clients may feel overwhelmed. If you use little eye contact and have a stiff body posture, clients may also feel less inclined to answer questions. When questioning, it is important to use good volume, articulation, pitch, emphasis and speech rate. Furthermore, counselling skills students' body messages should clearly show your interest in clients' answers.

Activity 15.1 Interspersing active listening with questions

Part A   Pairs activity

Work with a partner.
- Each partner picks a problem situation.
- Partner A acts as counsellor/helper and Partner B acts as client.
- Partner A spends a minimum of five minutes, longer if necessary, interspersing questions with active listening as together she or he clarifies Partner B's problem situation by asking questions about:
  - feelings and physical reactions
  - thinking
  - communication and actions
  - anything else that she or he considers relevant.
- At the end Partner A summarizes the main details covered so far using everyday language.
- Hold a sharing and feedback session.
- Afterwards, if feasible, reverse roles and repeat the activity.

Part B   Group activity

- Each student picks a problem situation that they feel safe in revealing to the group.
- A volunteer acts as client who presents her/his problem situation to the group who, as counsellors/helpers, sit in a semi-circle facing the client.
- After an opening statement by one counsellor/helper, go around the semi-circle and take turns in responding to the client, first by reflecting her/his previous response and then by asking a question to clarify her/his problem situation. When the client answers, the next counsellor/helper reflects the answer and then asks a question and so on.
- The trainer can stop the activity along the way and get the group discussing the ground covered so far and where to go next.
- When finished, hold a sharing and discussion session.
- Students can take turns as the client.

Summarizing information from questions

In the understanding stage, questions seek to 'flush out' details of clients' problem situations. For instance, in addition to her feelings, physical reactions and thoughts, relevant information for clients like Lucy with **anxiety** about getting a job include what steps that she has taken to find employment so far, what job seeking skills she has and how confident she is in using them, what her financial situation will be if she does not get a good job, how strong a student she is, and what other course and personal stresses she is under.

Counselling skills students can choose to summarize information along the way: for instance, a summary for each of feelings/physical reactions, thoughts and

Example 15.3 Summarizing a client's problem situation

The problem situation

The client Debbie, a single mum, comes for help about her uneasy relationship with Rob, her 15-year-old son. One area of the problem is that Debbie wants Rob to do more household chores. The specific situation that the client wishes to work on is how to ask Rob to mow the lawn once a week. Debbie has recently made an unsuccessful request for Rob to do this job.

Summary to clarify understanding

Well Debbie, I think it might be helpful if I tried to pull together the ground we have covered so far. Basically you love Rob, are proud of him and think he's a good kid. However, you get very anxious over asserting yourself with him by requesting that he does jobs like mowing the lawn. You tense up before you ask him and feel resentful when he does not cooperate. You also tense up because you are afraid that you might lose some of his affection to his dad who gives you no support in disciplining him. When you tense up you feel this in your neck and get red flushes in your neck and face. You want Rob to behave more like an adult and think that the time has come to stop mollycoddling him. You think Rob is afraid that if he gives a little ground in doing jobs for you he will be over-whelmed by more requests.

   When we looked at how you actually communicated with Rob, it seemed as though rather than make a direct request along the lines of 'Please mow the lawn once a week', you blurred it by saying 'Why don't you mow the lawn?' Your voice was not particularly firm and you probably made insufficient eye contact. Then, when Rob turned you down, you sulked and whiningly told him he did not appreciate how much you did for him. Is that about right?

communication/actions. In addition, you can provide a clarification of problem situation summary that pulls together significant information that you and your client have generated. Example 15.3 provides an illustration of **summarizing** a client's problem situation, namely that of client Debbie in relation to her son Rob.

An issue that will almost invariably arise is how to remember significant information generated by questions for summarizing at the end of the understanding stage. One option is to take brief notes discretely throughout the asking questions process. For instance, a counselling skills student could take an A4 pad and put four subheadings at intervals down the page – feelings, physical reactions, mind, communication/actions – and when relevant information emerges write it down.

Many counselling skills students dislike taking notes since they fear it blocks their relationships with clients. Some of you may want to start learning how to question without the added burden of learning how to take notes. Those on short introductory counselling skills courses have little time to learn about taking notes. Furthermore, if you see clients in informal contacts, taking notes is probably inappropriate.

However, taking notes in initial sessions can enable many counsellors and helpers to be more, not less, psychologically present to clients since it relieves the pressure to memorize information. For example, when the time comes to discuss strategies for change, then you have a written record to which you can refer back. Counselling skills students can develop skills of taking notes unobtrusively and of knowing when it is important to show clients undivided attention with your bodily communication. A suggestion for those doing mock interviews on medium length to longer introductory counselling skills courses is that, once you have had some experience of questioning without taking notes, to try jotting down important points rather than dismissing taking notes out of hand.

Identifying mind skills and communication/action skills for improvement

In Chapter 4, I mentioned that one approach to the understanding stage of the Relating–Understanding–Changing (RUC) counselling and helping process model requires counselling skills students to identify at least one **mind skills** weakness and at least one communication/**action skills** weakness for improvement. These weaknesses get translated into **goals** for stage three, the changing stage of the model. In the **clarifying/understanding** stage of the **RUC model**, students can go beyond describing the dimensions of clients' problem situations more fully to helping them identify specific communications and thoughts on which to work. Your suggestions about such communications and thoughts should flow easily out of what clients have told you during the relating and understanding stages. Students need to make sure that clients consider the communications and thoughts identified as **problematic skills** are relevant. Where appropriate, you should negotiate which ones are acceptable to work on.

The counsellor in Example 15.4 starts by offering a clarifying understanding summary for Debbie, the single mum, whose problem situation concerned how to ask her 15-year-old son Rob to mow the lawn once a week. The counsellor then moves on to negotiate with the client about **communication skills** and mind skills for improvement.

Example 15.4 Identifying communication skills and mind skills for improvement

The problem situation
The client Debbie, a single mum, comes for help about her uneasy relationship with Rob, her 15-year-old son. One area of the problem is that Debbie wants Rob to do more household chores. The specific situation that the client wishes to work on is how to ask Rob to mow the lawn once a week. Debbie has recently made an unsuccessful request for Rob to do this job.

Summary to clarify understanding
Well Debbie, I think it might be helpful if I tried to pull together the ground we have covered so far. Basically you love Rob, are proud of him and think he's a good kid.

(Continued)

Example 15.4 Identifying communication skills and mind skills for improvement – cont'd

However, you get very anxious over asserting yourself with him by requesting that he does jobs like mowing the lawn. You tense up before you ask him and feel resentful when he does not cooperate. You also tense up because you are afraid that you might lose some of his affection to his Dad who gives you no support in disciplining him. When you tense up you feel this in your neck and get red flushes in your neck and face. You want Rob to behave more like an adult and think that the time has come to stop mollycoddling him. You think Rob is afraid that if he gives a little ground in doing jobs for you he will be overwhelmed by more requests.

Identifying skills for improvement

When we looked at how you actually communicated with Rob, it seemed as though you could be making your request more assertively. With your words, you could be making a direct request. Instead of saying 'Why don't you mow the lawn', you could say something like 'Please mow the lawn once a week'. Your voice was not particularly firm and you probably made insufficient eye contact, so these aspects or skills require improving too. What do you think about this feedback?

[Client has the opportunity to contribute]

Looking at your mind skills or thinking skills, when Rob turned you down, you said you sulked and whiningly told him he did not appreciate how much you did for him. I think you may be creating **rules** that demand that Rob does what you want and demand that he shows affection. It is probably better that you think of your wishes as preferences, 'What I would prefer', rather than demands, 'What he must do'.

[Client has the opportunity to contribute]

Also, the way you talk to yourself insufficiently coached you in how to make your request assertively, so you probably need to alter this too.

[Client has the opportunity to contribute]

Activity 15.2 Identifying mind skills and communication/action skills weaknesses

Part A   Pairs activity

Work with a partner.
- Each partner picks a problem situation.
- Partner A acts as counsellor/helper and Partner B acts as client.

Activity 15.2 Identifying mind skills and communication/ action skills weaknesses – cont'd

- Partner A spends a minimum of five minutes, longer if necessary, interspersing questions with active listening as together she or he clarifies Partner B's problem situation by asking questions about:
  - feelings and physical reactions
  - thinking
  - communication and actions
  - anything else that she or he considers relevant.
- At the end Partner A summarizes and identifies at least one mind skill weakness and one communication/action skill weakness.
- Hold a sharing and feedback session.
- Afterwards, if feasible, reverse roles and repeat the activity.

Part B   Group activity

- One person acts as client who presents a specific problematic situation to the remainder of the group who act as counsellors/helpers.
- The group counsel the client by interspersing questions with active listening as together they clarify the client's problem situation by asking questions about:
  - feelings and physical reactions
  - thoughts
  - communications and actions
  - anything else they consider relevant.
- At the end of the questioning, one or more of the group summarizes and identifies at least one mind skills weakness and one communication/action skills weakness.
- Then hold a sharing and feedback session.

The group can repeat this activity with other 'clients'.

PART FOUR
THE CHANGING STAGE

MAIN TASK: To assist the client to change so that the problems and problem situations are addressed more effectively than in the past

Part Four covers the RUC model's changing stage. Chapter 16 deals with the 'how to solve problems' approach in which counsellors or helpers facilitate clients to change. Chapter 17 describes the coaching skills of speaking, demonstrating and rehearsing clients in changed ways of thinking and communicating. Chapters 18 and 19 present a series of interventions for improving how clients communicate and act and also for improving their mind skills, for instance creating rules, perceptions and self-talk. Chapter 20 on negotiating homework, Chapter 21 on conducting middle sessions, and Chapter 22 on terminating counselling and helping each provide you with practical information on how to perform these tasks.

16

Helping to solve problems

CHAPTER OUTCOMES

By studying and doing the activity in this chapter you should:
• possess some skills in helping clients to clarify goals in problem situations;
• know how to help clients in generating and exploring options; and
• be able to facilitate clients in planning how to communicate or act.

Welcome to the changing stage of the Relating–Understanding–Changing **(RUC) counselling and helping process model**. The preceding stage probably ended with a summary of the main ground covered so far and may have indicated some areas for change. In the changing stage, the focus moves from 'What's going on in the situation?' to 'What can I constructively do about it?'

Throughout the book I have assumed that introductory **counselling skills** courses differ in purpose and length. In relating and understanding stages in particular, students on short courses or at the beginning of longer courses should concentrate on developing good **active listening** skills, even if it means asking less **questions** and covering fewer **skills**.

There are two approaches to the changing stage: (1) a helping to solve problems approach and (2) a changing specific **mind skills** and **communication/action skills** approach. To some extent the two approaches overlap. However, in the helping to solve problems approach, I encourage counselling skills students to stay close to **clients' internal frames of reference** and mainly draw upon clients' suggestions for change. For this reason, the helping to solve problems approach lends itself to short introductory courses and for the beginning phases of longer courses. Later on in longer introductory courses, students can develop some basic skills in stating mind skills and communication/action skills as sub-goals and in assisting clients to **plan** strategies to attain their sub-goals. Here, to a greater extent than in the helping to solve problems approach, students are more active in assessing clients and in delivering strategies to them. The role of **counsellors** and **helpers** in the helping to solve problems approach to stage three is mainly that of facilitators. The role of counsellors and helpers in the changing mind skills and communication/action skills approach is both that of facilitators and user-friendly coaches.

Helping to solve problems

The helping to solve problems approach to stage three of the Relating–Understanding–Changing (RUC) counselling and helping process model is not restricted to beginning counselling skills students. Experienced counsellors and helpers can be very skilled at combining active listening skills with probes designed to clarify **goals**, explore options for attaining them and develop plans to implement a chosen option. Counselling skills students can develop similar skills. Furthermore, once you become more experienced, the helping to solve problems approach to the changing stage may remain some students' preferred way of working.

Clarifying goals

Locke and Latham (2002) summarized 35 years of empirical research on goal setting. They found that setting goals empowered clients in four ways: helping them focus attention and action, helping them mobilize energy and effort, providing incentives for them to search for strategies to accomplish their goals, and clear and specific goals helping them to increase persistence.

When some clients clarify their understanding of the key dimensions of their problems and **problem situations** of their own accord they then clarify goals and proceed to attain them. Counselling skills students can use good active listening skills to facilitate these clients to tap into their own resources and act appropriately in problem situations. The main thrust of Carl Rogers' person-centred approach is that counsellors should provide the facilitative conditions and emotional climate so that clients can get in touch with what they truly feel as a basis for taking effective action in their lives. Counselling skills students can be sensitive to the extent that clients just want you to be there as skilled listeners while they do their own work.

On other occasions, counselling skills students can follow up summaries that pull together the main dimensions of problem situations with questions that assist clients to clarify their goals in dealing with them. On first meeting, some clients are so overwhelmed that they lose sight of what they really want to achieve. As time goes by, many clients will have calmed down sufficiently so that they can think fairly rationally about their goals. However, these clients may still require assistance to articulate these goals.

Counselling skills students might start assisting clients to address issues of change with a **structuring** statement along the lines of 'Now we have clarified and summarized many of the main dimensions of your problem situation, perhaps we can now try and clarify your goals in it. Do you think this would be helpful?' Many clients will answer 'Yes' right away. Some might answer 'What do you mean?' If so, students can tactfully explain to clients that clarifying where they want to go makes it easier to decide how to get there.

Counselling skills students can distinguish between outcome goals, 'Where do I want to go?' and process goals, 'What are my sub-goals or steps in getting where I want to go?' Here the focus is on outcome goals. Often, when practising as a counselling psychologist, I found that clients started by being insufficiently creative when thinking about goals for specific situations. Rather than latch on to the first goal that comes to mind, students can assist clients to generate and consider a range of goals by asking 'What are your options in setting goals?' Such goals can be both positive, 'What do I want to achieve?' and negative 'What do I want to avoid?' and are often a mixture of the two. Example 16.1 lists some questions that can assist clients in clarifying their goals in problem situations.

Counselling skills students should avoid bombarding clients with questions about goals. In most instances, small is beautiful. A few well-chosen questions that get to the heart of what clients want to achieve and avoid are all that is necessary. Such goals should be specific enough to be verifiable and drive action, realistic in regard to resources, set in an attainable time frame and sustainable over an adequate time period (Egan, 2007). Sometimes students may need to facilitate clients in exploring deeper goals and the **values** that underpin them rather than surface goals. In all instances, you should respect clients' rights to set their own goals and also intersperse active listening with your questions to clarify goals. In addition, you should check that clients are committed to achieving the goals.

Generating and exploring options

Questions that clarify goals are about ends. Questions for generating and exploring options are about the means to achieve the clients' ends. Just as clients can latch on to the first goal that comes into mind, so they can latch on to the first method of achieving a goal that comes into their heads.

Example 16.2 is a case illustration that highlights the outcomes of using generating and exploring options questions to assist clients to attain goals. Often, once clients set goals, they feel stuck and do not know how to proceed. Skilled questioning to help clients to generate and explore options assists them to put on their thinking caps and

---

Example 16.1 Some questions for clarifying goals

What are your goals in the situation?
What would you consider a successful outcome?
What are your options in setting goals?
What do you want to achieve in the situation:
    for yourself
    for one or more others
    for your relationship, if appropriate?
What do you want to avoid in the situation:
    for yourself
    for one or more others
    for your relationship, if appropriate?
Are your goals realistic?
Are your goals specific enough?
What is the time frame for attaining your goals?

Example 16.2 Generating options to attain goals: case illustration

The problem situation

Dianne, 20, has been in a relationship with Adrian, 21, for the past three terms at university. Though they never lived together, frequently Adrian used to come round to her flat and spend time with her, sometimes sleeping with her. For some time, the relationship has been cooling as far as Dianne is concerned and she has decided to end it. However, when Adrian comes around, Dianne tells him she thinks it better that they split, but eventually ends up letting him come into the flat and so he is still in her life. Dianne has recently started in counselling with Rhonda and tells her that she really does want to end her relationship with Adrian and seek a new boyfriend.

Dianne's goals

Goals that Dianne wants to achieve now and within the next month:
1   To end my relationship with Adrian.
2   To have more friends in and out of university and ultimately get a new boyfriend.

Dianne's options

With the assistance of Rhonda, the following are some of the options that Dianne generates to attain her goals.

Goal 1 Options for ending my relationship with Adrian:
- writing down the reasons and making a firm commitment to myself to end the relationship
- stopping blaming myself for ending the relationship
- seeing Adrian as needing to assume responsibility for his life
- phoning Adrian and telling him clearly the relationship is over
- next time Adrian comes around, telling him the relationship is over
- not talking with Adrian at the door to my flat
- definitely not allowing Adrian into the flat
- getting a friend to support me at the flat next time Adrian is likely to come
- speaking in a much firmer voice to Adrian.

Goal 2 Options for having more friends in and out of university and ultimately getting a new boyfriend:
- stopping feeling guilty about socializing with other young men
- letting existing friends know that the relationship with Adrian is over and that I want to meet new people
- going out to parties and discos more
- talking more with other students at university
- possibly moving either to a university residence or to a different flat with other students.

use their **minds** creatively. Many clients are wiser than they know, but have insuffi-cient confidence and skills to get their wisdom out into the open.

Counselling skills students may need to assist clients to think about the conse-quences of options. Often it is best to generate options first and assess consequences afterwards. Prematurely assessing the consequences of options can interfere with the creative process of generating them.

Questions and comments for generating and exploring options include: 'Given your goal of _____ [specify goal] what ways might you attain it?', 'Just let the ideas flow without editing them too much', 'Are there any other ways that you might approach the situation?', and 'What might be the consequences of doing that?' Notice that all of these questions and comments put the onus of coming up with ideas on the client. Resist the temptation to take over and own clients' problem situations.

When working with clients, counselling skills students should start by keeping mat-ters simple. For instance, you might focus on exploring options to attain one goal and then only assist the client to generate a few options. If necessary, students should consider using either notepads or whiteboards. It is well nigh impossible for you and your clients to keep in your heads the kind of detail illustrated in the Dianne case example.

Assisting planning

Once clients have generated options, they need to choose those that they are prepared to implement. Plans can range from the simple to the detailed. Counselling skills students' skills for facilitating planning include assisting clients to choose options for attaining their goals, encouraging them to be specific about how they can implement the options, and, where appropriate, sequencing them into a step-by-step plan which has a time frame. When plans have been formulated, students can explore clients' commitments to implementing them, including how to deal with any anticipated difficulties and setbacks. Furthermore, you can encourage clients to write down plans to make them easier to remember. If clients are returning for subsequent sessions or helping contacts, students can assist them in **monitoring** progress and in adjusting plans, if necessary. Example 16.3 illustrates a plan that Dianne and her counsellor, Rhonda, formulated to meet her goal of ending her relationship with Adrian.

Alongside and as part of the plan for ending the relationship with Adrian, Dianne also decides to pursue her other goal of having more friends in and out of university with the intention of ultimately getting a new boyfriend. In particular, she thinks it will be helpful if she lets her friends know that her relationship with Adrian is over and that she wants to meet new people. Dianne also thinks that she needs to work on her tendency to blame herself for ending the relationship.

Sometimes counselling skills students and clients either have or think that there is little time to develop plans. For example, clients may have situations on their hands that require immediate action: for example, an upcoming exam or an imminent job interview. Just having someone calm to talk over the problem with may be of help to some clients. In addition, students can assist clients to try to think the situations through so they are less likely to engage in destructive thinking and self-defeating actions. For example, you might help someone going for a job interview to challenge

Example 16.3 Illustration of a plan

Dianne's goal
To end my relationship with Adrian.

Dianne's plan
Step 1 Before this evening, to write down the reasons why I have decided to end the relationship.
Step 2 From now on, to keep telling myself that I must assume responsibility for my life and Adrian must assume responsibility for his.
Step 3 If and when Adrian comes around, not letting him into the flat, quietly but firmly telling him that our relationship has ended, and not holding a conversation afterwards.
Step 4 If Adrian comes around to the flat again, repeat step 3.
Step 5 If Adrian comes around yet again, just calmly shut the door.

her or his thinking that this is the only job that it is important to get. In addition, you might attempt to teach the client some basic calming and coaching **self-talk** for handling interviews adequately.

Activity 16.1 Helping to solve problems

1 Work with a partner who presents either a problem situation of her/his own or one based on a client seen elsewhere.
2 Conduct the relating stage of a counselling/helping session in which you build a collaborative working relationship with the client.
3 Conduct the understanding stage in which together you clarify the problem situation and then you summarize and check out your understanding of the client's problem situation.
4 When you come to the changing stage of the counselling and helping process, adopt a helping to solve problems approach with the client including:
   · clarifying goals
   · generating and exploring options for attaining goals
   · developing a plan
   · exploring the client's commitment to and anticipating difficulties in implementing the plan.
5 After the session ends, hold a sharing and feedback discussion. It can be a good idea to videotape the session and play it back as part of the sharing and feedback.
6 If appropriate, reverse roles.

17

Coaching skills: speaking, demonstrating and rehearsing

CHAPTER OUTCOMES

By studying and doing the activities in this chapter you should:
*   understand the importance of client-centred coaching;
*   develop your speaking skills;
*   develop your demonstration skills; and
*   develop your rehearsing and practising skills.

In the last chapter it was mentioned that, to some extent, the helping to solve problems approach and the changing specific **mind skills** and **communication/action skills** approach overlap. In the helping to solve problems approach, **counselling skills** students can be assisting clients to think and act better without going as far as attempting to train them in skills. Though this chapter is written more from the viewpoint of helping clients to develop specific skills, much of it can be adapted to helping clients to change how they think and behave without using the concept of skills. This chapter is about adding training skills to counselling skills students' repertoire of counselling and helping skills. In particular, the chapter focuses on coaching, demonstrating and **rehearsing skills**.

Being a trainer

Despite many counselling approaches either explicitly or implicitly imparting skills to **clients**, to date there has been relatively little emphasis on how to impart skills systematically to clients. Skilled **counsellors** and **helpers** possess both good **facilitation** and good training skills and know how to combine them to best effect. Though facilitation skills provide the foundation for counselling and helping, counselling skills students can add training skills to help attend to the needs of a greater range of clients. Students often have a tendency to be either too facilitative or too didactic and many require assistance in getting the balance right.

In combining training with facilitation skills, counselling skills students can remember to assist clients to acquire and improve applied 'how to' skills, not academic knowledge. Clients' emotions are often heavily involved and they may need to calm down before they are willing to work systematically on improving **skills**. The understanding stage of the **Relating–Understanding–Changing (RUC) model** may end with descriptions of one or more mind skills and communication/action skills for improvement. Keeping the emotional climate human and personal, often students then need to train thoroughly at the same time as avoiding trying to do too much. You can respect clients by allowing them to have the final say in whether and how best to use the targeted skills in addressing their difficulties.

Coaching skills

When training clients in improving how they communicate, act and think, it is important that counselling skills students allow them to retain ownership of their problems and **problem situations**. Furthermore, students should always strive to maintain good collaborative working relationships. Sometimes the urge to teach and instruct can override respect for clients' potentials to lead their own lives and make the decisions that work best for them.

A useful distinction is that between counsellor-centred coaching and **client-centred coaching**. Counsellor-centred coaching essentially takes the jug and mug approach: counselling skills students are the jugs pouring knowledge and skills into clients' mugs. Students are in control and their comments take the form: 'First you do this, then you do that, then you do that ...' and so on. Clients are passive receptacles who are allowed to assume little responsibility for the pace and direction of their learning. In reality, very few students would work as crudely as this depiction.

Client-centred coaching respects clients as autonomous human beings. Counselling skills students as client-centred coaches develop plans to attain **goals** in conjunction with clients and draw out and build upon clients' existing knowledge and skills. Furthermore, clients participate in decisions about the pace and direction of learning, and are assisted to improve their knowledge and skills in such ways that they can help themselves after terminating counselling.

Take the example of providing feedback about clients' performances when rehearsing how to improve their verbal, vocal and body messages in a specific situation. Counsellor-centred coaches provide the feedback themselves as though they are the experts. Client-centred coaches try to develop the expertise of clients by asking them to evaluate their own performances before providing feedback themselves. Even when providing feedback, client-centred coaches are prepared to discuss it and leave clients with the final say regarding its validity for them.

Within the context of collaborative working relationships, counselling skills students impart applied skills, which are agreed upon with clients, by focusing on the three dimensions of 'tell', 'show', and 'do'.

Speaking skills

One approach to assisting clients to change is to facilitate them and allow them to come to their own conclusions as to how they might think and communicate better. This approach tends to characterize the helping to solve problems approach described in the previous chapter rather than the changing specific mind skills and communication/action skills approach focused on here. In this second approach, there are many occasions when counselling skills students require **speaking skills** when assisting clients to develop their skills, including when:

- offering reasons for developing skills
- initially describing component parts of skills
- providing commentaries for skills demonstrations
- coaching clients as they rehearse skills
- answering clients' **questions** about skills
- negotiating **homework** assignments.

Speaking skills for training are somewhat different than those for **active listening**. Some counselling skills students experience difficulty switching from the more passive role of active listening to the more active role of imparting **information**, where you are unable to feed off clients' most recent utterances. Without overwhelming clients, students can communicate information as clearly and as interestingly as possible. Furthermore, you can remain conscious that the best learning requires clients to develop their own capacity for **self-talk** about how to implement skills.

Prepare clear content

Clients cannot be expected to comprehend poorly presented skills, let alone know them well enough to instruct themselves once counselling and helping ends. Many counselling skills students experience difficulty in explaining skills clearly. Some are aware of this, others less so. In some cases, **anxiety** is a factor. Unfortunately, all too often students do not properly understand the skills being presented. Consequently, your **explanations** are either muddled or clearly inaccurate. On other occasions, you may understand the skills, but communicate them insufficiently clearly.

Counselling skills students require the skills of introducing and describing the key points of any human being skill or life skill that they impart. Systematic preparation is desirable, especially for beginners. Such preparation should not lead to rigid presentations. Rather, when clear in your own mind, often you can better address individual clients' needs and learning rates.

Counselling skills students' presentations can focus on the mechanics of how to perform a skill or sub-skill. They are not academic discourses. Students should use simple language: for instance *active listening* is probably better than *empathic listening*. In addition, you should be concise and specific aiming to describe skills as clearly as possible so that clients can easily describe the skills to themselves. Students should also avoid long sentences – the language of speech uses shorter sentences than written language. Furthermore, the longer the sentences become, the fewer are the clients who can comprehend them.

Develop delivery skills

Preparation of clear content is only part of the way to introducing and describing skills effectively. Counselling skills students still need to put the message across. Presenting information to individuals or couples does not require the theatrical performance skills of presenting information to larger numbers. Nevertheless, even in individual counselling, your voice and body are delivery tools for holding interest, emphasizing points and enlisting motivation.

Students should consider using visual as well as aural presentation. Audiovisual aids, for instance the whiteboard, may help present information more clearly than if just spoken. However, you need to think carefully about how to integrate audiovisual aids into your presentations so that they do not disrupt them.

Send effective voice messages

Let's take the VAPER acronym and suggest how counselling skills students may use volume, articulation, pitch, emphasis and speech rate when you deliver content rather than respond to clients.

- *Volume* When presenting skills, counselling skills students are under less obligation to adjust your volume to reflect that of clients than when responding as listeners. Without overwhelming clients, you need to speak reasonably loudly, possibly louder than when you respond. Some students may be better at being gentle listeners than outgoing talkers. Such students may need to project your voices when presenting skills in individual counselling and helping.
- *Articulation* Clear articulation may be even more important when presenting information than when responding. If counselling skills students enunciate poorly when sending listening responses, clients at least are able to put what you say in the context of their previous utterances. They do not have this opportunity when students present information for the first time. Instead they may be struggling to understand both delivery and content. Also, the longer speakers talk, the more poor enunciation distracts.
- *Pitch* Pitch errors that counselling skills students possess – for instance uncomfortable highness, lowness or narrowness of range – may be more pronounced when presenting information than when responding. One reason is that, when responding, students may modify pitch to match a client's pitch. Another reason is that, when presenting information, you may be less conscious of pitch because you are thinking of what to say. Furthermore, students have more scope for pitch errors since you are likely to speak for longer when presenting material than when responding.
- *Emphasis* When counselling skills students use reflections when responding as listeners, you emphasize the same words and phrases that clients emphasize. As presenters of information you emphasize words and phrases highlighting your own main points. Your use of emphasis should convey interest and commitment.
- *Rate* When describing skills, counselling skills students should speak fairly slowly. A slow, but comfortable, speech rate gives you time to think and gives clients time to comprehend. Effective use of pauses can both clarify and emphasize what students say and also allow clients to ask questions. Pause errors include too many, too few, too long, too short, and making extraneous sounds such as 'uhms' and 'ers'.

Send effective body messages

Sending effective body messages when describing a human being skill is partly a matter of avoiding interfering messages and partly a matter of sending good messages.

Many body messages for attending to clients when listening are still appropriate when delivering content: for instance relaxed body posture, physical openness, sensitivity to physical proximity and height, appropriate clothing and grooming, and appropriate facial expressions. Following are some additional suggestions for using effective body messages when presenting skills.

- *Gestures* Counselling skills students should use gestures economically to help explain what is being said. Fischer (1972) states there are three main types of gestures: *emphatic* gestures, such as pointing your finger, designed to make it clear that what you are saying is important; *descriptive* gestures, for instance stretching your arms out when saying that marital partners are poles apart, designed to help illustrate points; and *symbolic* gestures to which a commonly understood meaning has been ascribed, for instance shaking your head to say 'no'. Another broad category of gestures is that of *distracting* gestures: touching your head, scratching your nose, pulling lint off your cuff, waving your arms around, tugging your hair and so on. Students can learn to use gestures to work for, rather than against, training messages.
- *Gaze and eye contact* Talkers tend to use much less gaze and eye contact than listeners. Nevertheless, when presenting, counselling skills students require an adequate gaze level to read clients' reactions. You can present skills as though conversing with clients rather than talking at them. Use of gaze and eye contact is a most important way of relating directly to clients when making learning points. Gaze and eye contact errors include looking down too much and keeping turned away when writing on whiteboards rather than checking client reactions.

Put content and delivery together

Counselling skills students may practise long and hard to develop active listening skills so that clients want to talk to you. The same conscientiousness is required for developing sender skills of imparting information so that clients want to hear it. An analogy may be made with effective parenting: parents not only need to listen so that their kids will talk, they also need to talk so that their kids will listen. Students may need to rehearse and practise gaining fluency in describing different skills to clients. Furthermore, effective counsellors and helpers combine talking and listening skills in such a way that clients feel valued parts of the training process and not just receptacles of others' knowledge.

Counselling skills students can use speaking skills to help clients develop self-instruction skills. Ideally, when learning new skills, clients start by being receptive to the instructor's voice in their heads. However, they then need to replace the instructor's voice with their own voices.

Demonstrating

One of the main ways in which people learn is from observational learning or learning from models (Bandura, 1986). In real life, much **modelling** is unintentional. However, counselling skills students can consciously promote observational learning of desired skills and sub-skills. Here, the more everyday word 'demonstrating' is preferred to modelling. Students can use **demonstrations** to assist clients to develop different and better ways of communicating/acting and thinking. Furthermore, you can demonstrate how to accompany communicating or acting differently with appropriate self-talk.

Methods of demonstration
The following are some ways that counselling skills students can use demonstrations of improved ways of behaving.

- *Live* Probably most counselling and helping demonstrations are live. Counselling skills students may demonstrate live when initially presenting skills, when coaching clients afterwards and when working with current material that clients bring into later sessions. Live demonstrations have the advantage of here-and-now communication. Clients can receive verbal, voice and body messages as they occur. In addition, students can interact with clients and, if appropriate, show different or simpler ways to enact skills.

  Live demonstrations have limitations as well as advantages. Unless demonstrations are recorded, clients have no copies to listen to or watch on their own. Another limitation is that in live demonstrations it can be difficult to portray scenes involving more than one or two persons.

  A variation of live demonstration is to encourage clients to observe good and poor demonstrators of targeted skills in their everyday lives. For instance, clients with difficulty initiating contact with others can look out for how socially skilled people do this. Clients with poor parenting skills can be asked to observe parents they admire.
- *Written* Written demonstrations are more appropriate for helping clients to change how they think than to change how they communicate and act. However, written demonstrations that contain **visual images**, such as cartoon characters, can convey desirable communications and actions. It is possible for counselling skills students to demonstrate mind skills on whiteboards or notepads in sessions. Skills can also be demonstrated through the written page – be it either from handouts or from passages in books and training manuals. Written demonstrations can be used as examples for homework assignments. Furthermore, they can often be easily stored and retrieved.
- *Recorded* Recorded demonstrations can use audiocassettes and videotapes. Audiocassettes and videotapes can either be integral parts of initial skills demonstrations or used for homework assignments. Advantages of audiocassette and videotape demonstrations include that they can be reproduced, loaned to clients, and that they lend themselves to playback and to repeated viewing.

  Audiocassettes are particularly useful for demonstrating mind skills. With audiocassettes as contrasted to videotapes, clients can be taken through the sequences of choices entailed in targeted skills without visual distractions. Clients probably require repeated listening to demonstrations for the mind skills to become part of their everyday repertoires. Disadvantages of audiocassette demonstrations are that they are not always as spontaneous as live demonstrations and that they may be insufficiently geared to individual clients' needs.

  A major advantage of videotape over audiocassette demonstration is that clients observe body messages. During sessions you may use videotapes to demonstrate **communication skills**: for instance, excerpts of how either to make an assertive request for a behaviour change or to answer questions at job interviews. Clients may also self-administer demonstration videotapes as part of homework.

Many training audiocassettes and videotapes are already on the market. However, commercial videotapes may be neither available nor suitable. Counselling skills students who make demonstration videotapes have the choice of whether or not to bring in outside resources.

• *Visualized* Counselling skills students can ask clients to visualize or imagine the demonstration scenes that you describe. Clients can be asked to visualize either themselves or someone else performing the targeted communications or actions. Visualized demonstrations are only appropriate for clients who can imagine scenes adequately. A potential drawback is that, even when instructions are given well, there may be important differences between what helpers describe and what clients imagine. In general, clients visualize best when relaxed.

Demonstrator skills

Beyond speaking well, what follows are some demonstrator skills. Even live demonstrations require adequate preparation. Counselling skills students must know your material well to integrate good demonstrations into skills presentations. You need to pay attention to characteristics of the demonstration and not just of the demonstrator. One issue is whether to demonstrate incorrect as well as correct behaviours. You may **plan** briefly to demonstrate negative behaviours as a way of highlighting positive ones. However, you should make sure not to confuse clients and always place the emphasis on correct rather than incorrect skills.

Students should take care how to introduce demonstrations. Your initial demonstration of a skill is likely to be part of a 'tell', 'show', 'do' sequence. You may increase clients' attention by telling them what to look out for and also informing them that afterwards they will perform demonstrated behaviours.

During and at the end, counselling skills students may ask clients whether they understand the points demonstrated. In addition, you can ask clients to summarize the main points of demonstrations. Observers actively **summarizing** the main points of demonstrations are usually better able to learn and retain this information. Probably, the best way to check clients' learning is to observe and coach them as they perform demonstrated behaviours.

Activity 17.1 Using demonstrating skills

Work with a partner, with one of you taking the role of counsellor/helper and the other taking the role of client. Client and counsellor/helper hold a discussion to choose a specific communication that the client wants to improve. Do not attempt too much. The counsellor/helper then goes through the following steps in a demonstration:
• cuing the client on what to observe
• demonstrating each of the verbal, vocal and body message components of the communication for the client and then putting all three together (your partner is the client as you demonstrate)
• asking the client to summarize the main points of the demonstration.

(Continued)

Activity 17.1 Using demonstrating skills – cont'd

Afterwards hold a sharing and discussion session focused on the counsellor/helper's use of demonstration skills. If necessary repeat the demon-stration until the counsellor/helper feels she/he has obtained some degree of **competence** in using demonstration skills.

Then, reverse roles.

Rehearsing

Rehearsing is a possibly less threatening expression than **role playing**. Some clients become uncomfortable at the idea of role playing. Feeling shy and vulnerable already, they think they will further expose themselves in role plays. Counselling skills students may need to explain to clients that rehearsing can help them by allowing them to try out communicating differently in an environment where mistakes do not really matter. As such rehearsing can provide knowledge and confidence for communicating effectively in actual problem situations.

Skills for assisting rehearsing
The following are some skills for rehearsing clients.

- *Explain reasons for rehearsal* Some clients find the idea of rehearsal off-putting. For example, they may be self-conscious about their acting skills. Explain reasons for rehearsals to ease clients' anxieties and help motivate them. Here is a ration-ale for using role play rehearsal with a client, Oliver, who gets excessively angry when his teenage daughter, Ellie, comes home late.

  Oliver, I think it would be helpful if we rehearsed how you might use your new skills to cope better with Ellie next time she comes home late. I realize that it may seem artificial acting the scene here. However, role playing gives us the chance to rehearse different ways you might behave – your words, voice messages, and body messages – so that you are better prepared for the real event. It is safer to make mistakes here where it doesn't count for real. There is no substitute for learning by doing. What do you think about this approach?

- *Set the scene* Elicit information about the physical setting of proposed scenes, what other characters are involved, and how they behave. If the counselling skills student is to rehearse how to deal with someone, for instance Ellie, collect suffi-cient information about Ellie's verbal, voice and body messages to get into the role. Depending on what sort of office you are using, you may move furniture around to create a 'stage', for instance a family living room.
- *Assess current skills* Sometimes time is well spent if you conduct initial role plays in which clients demonstrate how they currently communicate in problem situa-tions. For instance, you can elicit much relevant information about non-verbal communication that may not be apparent if clients only talk about how they act. **Assessment** role plays can also reveal how clients think in situations.

- *Formulate changed communication* Counselling skills students can cooperate with clients to formulate new and better ways of communicating that both use targeted skills and yet feel 'comfortable'. You should facilitate clients' contributions to the discussion prior to making suggestions. As part of this process students can demonstrate the different verbal, vocal and body message components of appropriate communication skills. In addition, you can explore with clients how to cope with different responses by others.
- *Rehearse changed skills* Once clients are reasonably clear of their new roles and counselling skills students understand your 'parts', trial enactments or rehearsals take place. Avoid trying to do too much or anything too difficult too soon. Students may allow role plays to run their course. Alternatively, you may intervene at one or more points along the way to provide feedback and coaching. Role play rehearsals are dry runs of how to use communication skills in specific situations. Video feedback may be used as part of coaching both during and after role plays. You may need a number of rehearsals to build clients' skills. Some of these rehearsals may involve clients in responding to different situations. For example, clients asking for dates may get accepted, postponed or rejected in separate rehearsals.

  Role reversal and mirroring are **psychodrama** techniques that counselling skills students may use (Blatner, 2005). In role reversal, you get clients to play the other person in interactions. Role reversals force clients to get some way into another's **internal frame of reference**. With mirroring, you 'mirror back' clients' verbal, voice and body messages. Clients see themselves as others experience them.

  Clients may also rehearse changing their mind skills along with their communication skills. For example, clients may learn to use the calming and coaching dimensions of self-talk to accompany new communication skills. In addition, students can rehearse clients in other mind skills relevant to targeted communication skills.
- *Process rehearsals* Processing involves spending time dealing with clients' thoughts and **feelings** generated by rehearsals. Together, counselling skills students and clients can discuss learnings from them, and make plans to transfer rehearsed skills to daily life. You can ask clients processing questions like: 'How were you feeling in that rehearsal?', 'How well do you think you used your skills in that rehearsal?', 'What have you learned in that role play that is useful for real life?', and 'What difficulties do you anticipate in implementing your changed behaviour and how can you overcome them?' After processing the previous rehearsal, students and clients may move on to the next one either regarding the same or with another problem situation.

Activity 17.2 Using rehearsing skills

Work with a partner, with one of you taking the role of counsellor/helper and the other taking the role of client. Either for a specific communication that was demonstrated in Activity 17.1 or for another specific communication that the client wants to improve, go through the following sequence:

- cuing the client on what to observe
- demonstrating each of the verbal, vocal and body message components of the communication and then putting all three together (your partner is the client as you demonstrate)

(Continued)

Activity 17.2 Using rehearsing skills – cont'd

- asking the client to summarize the main points of the demonstration
- introducing the idea of rehearsing the communication to the client
- rehearsing and coaching the client to the point where, within the limits of this activity, she/he feels competent to perform the communication in real life competently. Audiocassette or videotape playback may be used as part of the rehearsing process.

Afterwards hold a sharing and discussion session focused on the counsellor/helper's use of rehearsing skills. If necessary, allow the counsellor/helper to rehearse some more until she/he feels she/he has obtained some degree of competence in using rehearsing skills.

Then, reverse roles.

Example 17.1 Illustration of coaching

Will, 19, initially comes to see a counsellor, Charlotte, at university, because he finds himself getting very depressed and this is adversely affecting his studying and ability to get good grades. One of Will's issues is that he has a very poor social life, partly because he feels extremely shy about asking women out. Right now, in his English literature class, there is a student called Jessica, 19, with whom at times Will sits and they talk a little. Will likes Jessica very much and thinks that the feeling may be mutual. However, to date, Will has been far too scared to make a move towards Jessica that might allow their relationship to develop. Will asks Charlotte if she can help him. Together, Will and Charlotte discuss how Will might find out whether Jessica would like a closer relationship with him. Will decides as a first step he will ask Jessica whether she would like to have a coffee with him after class ends. Will develops the following verbal request for Jessica to have coffee, etc.: 'Jessica, would you like to have a coffee with me after class one day this week?' Will decides that his voice should be calm and clear. Regarding his body messages, Will decides he will make sure to sit next to her in class and smile pleasantly at her when he asks her to spend time with him.

Charlotte then suggests that Will rehearses asking Jessica the question, with her role playing Jessica. Before playing her part she finds out more about how Jessica communicates. At the first rehearsal, Will sounds very stilted and he fails to smile pleasantly at her and make her feel at ease. When Charlotte asks Will how he thought the rehearsal went, he replies that he felt that he came across very nervous. Charlotte suggests that he puts more emphasis into his voice and shows him how to do this. She also reminds him to smile. Will then rehearses with Charlotte again. Charlotte lets Will evaluate how he did and then acknowledges that she felt more comfortable this time with his question. Will has further rehearsals and gets more feedback until he performs competently in the session. Charlotte gets Will to write down his verbal, vocal and body messages and suggests that he practises on his own before asking Jessica.

18

Improving communication and actions

CHAPTER OUTCOMES

By studying and doing the activities in this chapter you should:
- gain insight into how to develop clients' monitoring skills;
- know something about timetabling activities;
- develop your setting progressive task skills; and
- help clients to use self-reward skills.

The previous chapter reviewed basic **skills** of coaching to help **clients** acquire **communication** and, to a lesser extent, **mind skills**. This chapter focuses on further ways that **counselling skills** students can assist clients to improve their **communication** and **action skills**.

Developing clients' monitoring skills

The following are examples of clients engaging in systematic monitoring of their communications and actions.

> Gary, 42, is receiving help for depression. Gary has a goal of increasing the number of times he engages in pleasant activities. He keeps a daily chart of each time he engages in a number of specific pleasant activities.
>
> Hannah, 62, has had heart problems and is on a weight loss programme. She keeps a chart listing her daily weight. Also, each time she eats between meals, she records the time, what happened immediately before, what she eats and with whom, and the consequences of her behaviour.

Systematic self-monitoring or self-observation enables clients to become more aware of their thoughts, **feelings**, and communications/actions. Here the main focus is on **monitoring** communications and actions. Systematic monitoring can be important at the start of, during and after interventions focused on developing specific communication skills. When commencing interventions, monitoring can establish baselines and increase **awareness**. During interventions, monitoring can act as a reminder, motivator and progress check. After an intervention, monitoring is relevant to maintaining gains, though clients may not collect **information** as systematically as during counselling. Monitoring is best thought of as an adjunct to other interventions. As an intervention on its own, the effects of monitoring often do not last (Kazdin, 1994).

Monitoring methods

The following are some methods whereby clients can monitor how they communicate and act.

- *Diaries and journals* Keeping a diary or journal is one way of monitoring communication/action skills. Clients can pay special attention to writing up critical incidents where skills have been used well or poorly. Although diaries and journals may be useful, some clients find this approach too easy to ignore and too unsystematic.
- *Frequency charts* Frequency charts focus on how many times clients enact a specific communication or action in a given time period, be it daily, weekly or monthly. For example, clients may tally up how many cigarettes they smoke in a day and then transfer this information to a monthly chart broken down by days.
- *Stimulus, response and consequences logs* To become more aware of their communication and its consequences, clients can fill in three-column stimulus, response, consequences logs.

Stimulus (What happened?)	Response (How I communicated)	Consequences (What resulted?)

For example, clients who work on managing anger skills might record each time they feel angry in the stimulus column, what they did in the response column, and the consequences for themselves and others in the consequences column.

- *Situation, thoughts and consequences (STC) logs* Filling in three-column situation, thoughts and consequences (STC) logs can help clients to see the connections between how they think and how they felt and communicated or acted.

Stimulus (What happened and when?)	Thoughts (What I thought?)	Consequences (How I felt and commmunicated/acted?)

- *Use of targeted skills logs* Counselling skills students and clients can go beyond monitoring communications to monitoring communication skills. During the intervention stage, clients can usefully monitor and evaluate use of targeted skills. For instance, a counselling skills student works with a teenager, Rajiv, on how assertively to stop a friend, Stephen, from borrowing money from him. Together, student and client agree on the following verbal, vocal and body message sub-skills for each time that Stephen makes such a request:

  - verbal messages make 'I' **statements** and say 'No'
  - vocal messages speak with a calm, yet firm voice

- body messages use good eye contact and avoid threatening gestures such as finger pointing.

   The student also asks Rajiv to complete a log that monitors how well he uses his assertion skills after each request from Stephen. In particular, the student asks Rajiv to record how he uses the sub-skills they have targeted.

Assisting clients to develop monitoring skills

Below are some ways that counselling skills students can assist clients to monitor themselves and to develop self-monitoring skills.

- *Offer reasons for monitoring* Clients are not in the **habit** of systematically recording observations about how they communicate and act. They may need to be motivated to do so. For instance, a counselling skills student can explain: 'Counting how many times you perform a behaviour daily not only indicates how severe your problem is, but also gives us a baseline against which to measure your progress in dealing with it', or 'Systematically writing down how you send verbal, voice and action messages after each time you go for an interview provides us with information to build your skills.'
- *Train clients in discrimination and recording* Clients are not naturally accurate self-observers. Consequently, counselling skills students need to train them in discriminating and recording specific communications and actions. Clients require clarity not only about what to **record**, but also about how to record it. In addition, clients require awareness of any tendencies they have to misperceive or selectively perceive what they do: for instance, being more inclined to notice weaknesses than **strengths**.
- *Design simple and clear recording logs* Counselling skills students should consider supplying recording logs yourselves. It may be best not to leave it to clients to make up their own logs. They may not do so in the first place and, if they do, they may get them wrong. Simple recording systems enhance comprehension and recording accuracy.
- *Use **reward skills*** You can reward clients with interest and praise when they fill in logs. This guideline is based on the basic behavioural principle that actions that are rewarding are more likely to be repeated. Furthermore, always reward clients for their efforts by debriefing them.
- *Encourage clients to evaluate monitoring information* When clients share monitoring logs, counselling skills students can help them to use this information for self-exploration and evaluation. Assist them to understand the meaning of the information they have collected, but do not do their work for them. When counselling and helping ends, students will not be around to assess the implications of clients' frequency counts and monitoring logs. Train them to do this for themselves.
- *Use other skills-building strategies* Clients should not be expected to develop communication and action skills on the basis of self-observation alone. They are likely to require other interventions, for example behaviour rehearsals and self-reward, to develop their skills. Furthermore, they require work and practise to acquire and maintain these skills.

Activity 18.1 Developing clients' monitoring skills

Role play a counselling/helping session with a partner as a client who has a goal of wanting to alter a specific communication skills deficiency. You decide that it would help both you and your client if she/he were to systematically observe the frequency of her/his communication skills deficiency over the next week. Within the context of a good counselling relationship, use the following skills:
- offer reasons for monitoring
- design a simple and clear recording log, and
- train the client in discrimination and recording.

Afterwards, discuss the activity with your partner and obtain feedback on your use of skills.

Then, reverse roles.

Timetabling activities

Counselling skills students can work with clients to timetable desired activities and to build clients' skills in this area. How to assist clients in timetabling activities varies according to their needs.

Areas for timetabling

The following are some areas in which timetabling may assist clients to perform desired activities and to build communication skills. Example 18.1 shows a blank weekly timetable that can serve numerous purposes.

- *Timetabling daily activities* Beck and his colleagues (Beck, Rush, Shaw and Emery, 1979; Beck and Weishaar, 2008) stress the usefulness of developing daily activity schedules for clients who are immobilized by depression and **anxiety**. **Counsellors** and clients collaborate to **plan** specific activities for one day at a time. These planned activities are recorded on a weekly timetable, with days represented by columns and hours represented by rows. As clients develop skills and confidence, they can do their own activity scheduling, with possibly the last activity for one day being the scheduling of the following day. It can ease pressure if clients are instructed to state what – rather than how much – they will accomplish and to realize that it is okay not to complete all activities; the important thing is to try.
- *Timetabling minimum* **goals** Some clients get extremely anxious over performing certain tasks and then engage in **avoidance** behaviour. For instance, Alex is a college student who is very distressed because he is not studying. He has lost all sense of control over his work. One approach to Alex is to assist him to timetable some minimum goals that he feels prepared to commit himself to keeping before the next session. His minimum goals may be as little as three half-hour study periods during the week. For each study period, Alex needs to write down time, task and place. This does not mean that he cannot spend more time studying if he wishes. With certain highly anxious clients, counselling skills students need to be

very sensitive to avoid becoming just another source of pressure. The idea of timetabling minimum goals is to show clients that they can be successful in achieving modest targets rather than to achieve large goals. Later on Alex may increase his study periods.

- *Timetabling to create personal space* Many clients require **timetabling skills** to prioritize and create personal space. Such clients include housewives trying to stop being at everyone's beck and call, stressed executives needing to create family and **relaxation** time, depressed people needing to timetable more pleasant activities, and students needing to **plan** their study time so that they know when they can say 'Yes' rather than 'No' to requests to go out. Counselling skills students can assist clients to define personal space goals and to allocate time accordingly.

- *Timetabling to keep contracts* Clients make commitments to themselves, to counsellors and to third parties, for instance their spouses, to perform certain activities. You can assist them to develop skills of keeping commitments if they timetable when they are going to carry out these activities. For instance, Max is a young man who has been resisting doing any of the household chores. He finally decides that sometimes he is prepared to wash up the dishes. Max may be more likely to keep this commitment if he timetables when he is going to perform this task.

Example 18.1 Weekly timetable							
Date							
Time	Monday	Tuesday	Wednesday	Thursday	Friday	Saturday	Sunday
6.00							
7.00							
8.00							
9.00							
10.00							
11.00							
12.00							
1.00							
2.00							
3.00							
4.00							
5.00							
6.00							
7.00							
8.00							
9.00							
10.00							
11.00							
12.00							

Some skills for timetabling

As shown above, many reasons exist why timetabling can be a part of counselling and helping. Below are some skills for counselling skills students in using timetabling when assisting clients to improve certain communication and action skills.

- *Provide timetables* Give clients timetables. Do not expect clients to have easy access to made-up timetables or to make the effort to develop their own.
- *Offer reasons for timetabling* For some clients the need to timetable activities and goals is obvious. Other clients require **explanations**. You can **challenge** certain clients with the negative consequences of their failure to timetable.
- *Be sensitive to anxieties and resistances* Timetabling can be very threatening to highly anxious clients – they feel failures if they do not do as agreed. Be very sensitive about how much pressure timetabling creates for vulnerable clients. Also, be aware that some clients play timetabling games – either consciously or unconsciously they have little intention of achieving goals.
- *Do not overdo timetabling* Even with less vulnerable clients, it is possible to overdo timetabling. Clients can spend too much time scheduling activities and too little time carrying them out.
- *Review progress* At the next session, check with clients on progress in adhering to timetabled activities and on any difficulties experienced.
- *Work with mind skills* Often, non-adherence to timetables reflects poor mind skills, for instance perfectionist rules about achievement. Identify and work with any relevant mind skills deficiencies.
- *Help clients to develop timetabling skills* Initially, counselling skills students should always work closely with clients regarding what goes in the timetable. However, you should aim to help clients develop their own timetabling skills so that you can 'fade' from assisting them.

Activity 18.2 Developing timetabling skills

Conduct a counselling/helping session with a partner as client. Your client has a communication skills deficiency for which together you decide that it will benefit her/him to use timetabling between sessions. Assist your partner to timetable using the following skills:
- offer reasons for timetabling
- provide the timetable, or at the very least generate it together
- be sensitive to anxieties and resistances, and
- ensure that your client knows how to fill out the timetable.

Afterwards, discuss the activity with your partner and obtain feedback on your use of skills.

Then, reverse roles.

Setting progressive tasks skills

Knowing how to assist clients to set progressive tasks is a useful skill for counselling skills students to have. Sometimes clients fail either to carry out a task or to succeed at it because they are trying to do too much too soon. **Setting progressive tasks** in conjunction with clients allows them gradually to build up their confidence and skills to attain communication and action goals. Sometimes progressive tasks are built into plans at the start of the changing stage. On other occasions, progressive tasks may be formulated to attain specific goals during the changing stage.

In very brief counselling and helping, there is limited opportunity for clients to build up desirable communications and actions by setting and implementing progressively difficult tasks over a period of time. All there may be time for is to assist clients to communicate or act better at relatively simple tasks. For example, a counselling student may help a client, whose goal is to become more honest, to make one or more relatively low **threat** disclosures to their partner. Another example is that of helping sales persons afraid of making cold calls to start cold calling with relatively non-threatening potential customers.

In setting progressively more difficult tasks, essentially what counselling skills students are doing is establishing a hierarchy of sub-goals clustered around a theme. Attaining sub-goals allows clients gradually to become more proficient in their targeted communication and action goals. However, even within specific situations, students can break tasks down and train clients progressively: for example, focusing first on verbal communication, then on **vocal communication**, then on **bodily communication** and then on putting all three together.

Counselling skills students should work closely with clients when listing progressive tasks. Start with small steps that clients think they can achieve. Achieving small first steps motivates clients to persist in attempting more difficult tasks. Be prepared to build in intermediate tasks if clients think the progression of tasks is too steep.

To avoid connotations of failure, counselling skills students can encourage clients to view attempting each progressively more difficult task as an experiment in which they gain valuable information about themselves. You can also use your **demonstration** and **rehearsing skills** to increase the chances of success in each progressive task. In addition, you can help clients to share feelings and thoughts about attempting graded tasks and train them in relevant mind skills, for instance how to use calming and coaching **self-talk**.

Usually, clients perform progressively more difficult tasks outside of counselling and helping. Wherever possible, encourage clients to report back on their progress. Use information about difficulties and setbacks to improve how clients perform in future. If a task on the list genuinely proves too difficult, either change the ordering of tasks or generate different and less difficult tasks to do next.

When clients succeed at tasks, counselling skills students can reward them with praise, encourage them to acknowledge their success, and help them to realize that succeeding results from willingness to take calculated risks, expending effort and changing how they communicate and act. Repeatedly succeeding with specific tasks consolidates clients' skills and confidence. Example 18.2 provides a brief illustration of progressive tasks negotiated by a counselling skills student to assist a client in changing how she communicates.

Example 18.2 Illustration of progressive tasks

Wendy is a 27-year-old social work student, who wants to be more assertive with her live-in boyfriend Roy, also 27.

Changing communication goals
Make a clear request for Roy to help to keep the flat tidy, have calm yet firm vocal communication, and make good eye contact.

Progressive tasks
1 Politely ask to have a chat with Roy.
2 Calmly state own opinions about Roy helping to tidy the flat and ask him if he will do so.
3 Do not tidy up any mess Roy makes, unless absolutely necessary.
4 If Roy persists in being very untidy, use a firmer voice and communicate more clearly that I want the flat kept tidy.

Activity 18.3 Setting progressive tasks skills

Work with a partner with one of you taking the role of counsellor/helper and one taking the role of client. For a specific communication that the client wants to improve, develop a hierarchy of at least five progressively more difficult tasks for the client to attain. Observe the following guidelines:
· work cooperatively with your client
· start with easy, small tasks
· have a gradual progression to more difficult tasks, and
· both counsellor/helper and client write down the hierarchy of tasks.
Afterwards, discuss the activity with your partner and obtain feedback on your use of skills.
    Then, reverse roles.

Assisting clients to reward themselves

Counselling skills students may choose to use reinforcement or reward to help clients to develop communication and action skills. Rewards you can use include praise, encouragement, smiles and head nods. Ultimately, clients have to learn to perform targeted communication and action skills independent of external rewards. Clients can influence and administer their own rewards.

Identify suitable rewards

In many instances, clients find that using targeted communication and action skills is both intrinsically rewarding and brings about rewards from others. For instance, clients developing appreciation skills may enjoy using paying compliments skills, give pleasure and also receive it. On other occasions clients may need to strengthen their motivation by self-administering rewards.

The basic idea in using self-reward to develop communication and action skills is that clients make the administration of rewards contingent upon occurrence of target behaviours. Rewards should be accessible and potent (Cormier and Nurius, 2002). Consequently, counselling skills students may need to assist clients in identifying suitable rewards. There are several ways of helping clients identify rewards, including asking them, getting them to monitor what they find rewarding, asking others who know them – though here you must be sensitive to confidentiality – observing them, and asking them to fill out reward questionnaires.

MacPhillamy and Lewinsohn's *Pleasant Events Schedule* is an example of an identifying rewards questionnaire (Lewinsohn, Munoz, Youngren and Zeiss, 1986; MacPhillamy and Lewinsohn, 1982). The questionnaire consists of 320 'pleasing events'. Respondents rate each item on three-point scales for frequency and pleasantness during the previous month. The authors believe that one way to combat clients' feelings of depression is to encourage them to participate in more rewarding activities. Illustrative pleasant events include being with happy people, thinking about friends, breathing clean air, **listening** to music, reading a good book, petting and necking, eating good meals, being seen as sexually attractive, seeing beautiful scenery, and visiting friends.

Assist clients to reward themselves

Counselling skills students can assist clients in knowing how to deliver positive self-rewards. There are two main categories of reward that clients can administer to themselves: external and internal.

- *External reward* External reward includes: (1) self-administration of new rewards that are outside the client's everyday life, such as a new item of clothing or a special event, and (2) initial **denial** of some pleasant everyday experience and later administration of it contingent upon a desired action. Wherever possible, a positive self-reward should be relevant to the target behaviour, for instance clients achieving weight loss goals might buy slimmer-fitting clothes.
- *Internal reward* Internal reward includes self-talk statements like 'That's great', 'I did it', or 'Well done' that clearly indicate the client's satisfaction at performing a sub-goal or goal. Clients can also use their imaginations to visualize significant others praising their efforts.

Counselling skills students can work with clients to determine the precise conditions for administering rewards to themselves. In making positive self-reward plans, several considerations may be pertinent: identification of rewards, sequencing of graded steps in developing communication and action skills, and clear connections between achievement and reward. Most often it is best for clients to reward themselves immediately after performing targeted skills or sub-skills.

Where appropriate, counselling skills students can encourage clients to draw up contracts that specify the relationship between rewarding themselves and developing targeted skills. Contracts should establish clear-cut criteria for achievement and specify the means whereby behaviour is observed, measured and recorded. Contracts can be unilateral or bilateral. In unilateral contracts clients obligate themselves to personal change programmes independent of contributions from others. Bilateral contracts, commonly used in relationship counselling, stipulate obligations and rewards for each of the parties. For example, partners can contract with one another to increase their exchange of caring behaviours for a specified time period.

Not all clients like self-reward plans or follow them. Some clients consider the use of self-reward too mechanical. There is a risk of introducing self-reward ideas too soon, before clients are sufficiently motivated to change. Counselling skills students can assess how well clients accept the idea of self-reward and their motivation for change. Often, you will need to intervene when clients' poor mind skills hinder change.

Activity 18.4 Assisting clients to reward themselves

Work with a partner who acts as client. Together design a plan for the client that uses self-reward to develop a specific communication skill. Your plan should contain the following elements:
- your overall goal
- a sequence of three to five graded steps to develop the communication skill
- what reward(s) you intend using
- how to observe, measure and record the rewards you intend using
- the precise conditions for self-administering reward(s)
- a time frame.

Afterwards, discuss the activity with your partner and obtain feedback on your use of skills.

Then, reverse roles.

19

Improving thinking

By studying and doing the activities in this chapter you should:
*   help clients to create preferential rather than demanding rules;
*   help clients to create perceptions that more closely fit the facts; and
*   help clients to create alerting, calming, coaching and affirming self-talk.

This chapter develops the changing specific communications and thoughts approach to stage three of the Relating–Understanding–Changing (RUC) **counselling and helping process model** by focusing on assisting **clients** to empower their **minds** so that they can deal with **problem situations** more effectively. In Chapter 3, six **mind skills** areas were outlined, namely creating **rules, perceptions, self-talk, visual images, explanations** and **expectations**. In that chapter the main focus was on helping counselling skills students see the application of these mind skills to yourselves.

The focus was changed to clients' thinking in the subsequent section in Chapter 12 on assessing unhelpful thinking. Towards that chapter's end the emphasis was in particular on three mind skills: rules, perceptions and self-talk. This chapter mainly reviews how counselling skills students can assist clients to empower their minds in these same three mind skills areas. Strategies for only three mind skills get focused on to provide a gradual introduction to a large and increasingly important approach to counselling and helping, the so-called **cognitive therapies**. The intention is to avoid encouraging introductory counselling skills students to attempt too much too soon.

Proceed with great caution when assisting clients to alter specific thoughts. I have witnessed a number of beginning students jump in with faulty analyses of thinking which clients have had neither the knowledge nor confidence to challenge. In addition, students may not understand the mind skills areas properly yourselves and therefore present them in a confused way to clients. Furthermore, sometimes students rush through learning sequences rather than train clients in them thoroughly. Remember that clients have usually built up and sustained their ways of faulty thinking over many years and, consequently, quick fixes are unlikely to succeed.

Assisting clients to create preferential rules

Unrealistic and demanding rules significantly contribute to many clients having difficulty managing problems and problem situations (Ellis, 2001, 2003, 2008). Demanding
rules can lay the foundation for creating negative self-talk and inaccurate perceptions.
Usually, demanding rules contain realistic as well as unrealistic parts. For example, it is
realistic for the counselling skills students to want to perform competently, but unrealistic to strive for perfection. Consequently, when assisting clients to alter their rules,
focus on discarding the 20-to-30 per cent of the rule that is irrational rather than
getting rid of it altogether.

How can clients be assisted to create preferential rules to replace their demanding
rules? In Chapter 12, some indicators or signals for demanding rules were reviewed.
Reading the signals, counselling skills students can assist clients to articulate or suggest
what might be one or more underlying demanding rules relevant to their problem situations. Then you can help clients to question and to challenge their demanding rules

and to restate them as preferential rules. Ellis observes: 'Most clients ... require a very
active-directive, questioning and **challenging** therapist, who works with them to use
a number of cognitive, emotive, and behavioral techniques, and who closely monitors
the homework assignments that they agree to take.' (Ellis, 2003: 93). Ellis is perhaps
more active-directive than many **counsellors** and therapists who follow his approach.

Questioning and challenging demanding rules

To keep matters simple when first learning to assist clients to alter their rules, counselling
students can restrict your focus to clients' use of the following four demanding rules:

- 'I must be liked by everyone'
- 'I must be perfectly competent'
- 'Other people must do what I want'
- 'Life must be fair'.

Ellis considers disputing to be the most typical and often-used method of his **rational
emotive behaviour therapy**. Three main ways that irrational beliefs or unrealistic
rules can be disputed and challenged are: realistic and empirical disputing, logical disputing, and practical disputing (Ellis, 2003). Realistic and empirical disputing is based
on the question 'Where is the evidence that I absolutely must ... ?', as
contrasted with it being preferable to do something. Logical disputing identifies flaws
in the client's logic. For instance 'Does it follow that, because it is highly desirable for
me to do well and be socially approved, this proves that I absolutely must be?', to
which the answer is 'Of course not'. Practical disputing looks at the practical consequences of holding demanding rules: for instance, 'Where will it get me if I insist that
I must do well and be socially approved?' Here the answers are likely to be negative.

Counselling skills students and clients can use reason, logic and facts to support, dis-

card or amend any rule considered to be potentially demanding. Example 19.1 provides examples of **questions** that you can use to challenge demanding rules. When
learning how to question clients' demanding rules, students are also encouraged to

elicit some questions from clients: for instance, 'How might you question or challenge that rule?' When students start asking questions, it can be done gently rather than forcefully and clients' answers can be responded to similarly. Furthermore, you can show restraint in the amount of questions you ask and remember to integrate **active listening** into the questioning and challenging process. Then, when more skilled and experienced, you may choose to challenge clients in a more active-directive fashion.

Creating preferential rule statements

Assisting clients to question and challenge their demanding rules should have the effect of loosening their effect on them. An added way of reducing the hold of demanding rules is to assist clients to restate them succinctly into preferential rules. Their challenges can be too many and varied to remember easily. Counselling skills students can help clients to create replacement statements that are easy to remember and recall. Sometimes, when time is very limited, students may eliminate time spent

---

Example 19.1 Illustration of questions that challenge a demanding rule

S = *Problem situation*
Janet, aged 18, is a college student who gets asked for a date by a young man, Bruce, aged 19.

T1 = *Janet's demanding rule*:
'I must be liked by everyone.'

C1 = *Janet's consequences if thinking is not altered*:
Feelings consequences: high **anxiety** will block out her pleasure on the date.
Communication and action consequences: says 'yes', but will not reveal much of herself on the date and this could make Bruce feel awkward.

Questions that Janet and her counsellor/helper can use to challenge this rule:
What evidence exists for the truth or falseness of this rule?
What are the positive and negative consequences of holding this rule?
Do I expect that the other young women in my class must be liked by every young man?
Does it follow that because it is highly desirable to be liked by Bruce that I absolutely must be?
Is it absolutely necessary for me to be liked by everyone to be successful in life or to find a close male friend?
If some young man does not want to spend more time with me why does this make me unlikeable?
Why is it awful if some young man does not want to spend more time with me?
What can't I stand about some young man not wanting to spend more time with me?

on questioning and challenging, and move straight into helping clients restate
a demanding rule as a preferential rule.

Counselling skills students and clients can alter characteristics of demanding rules
to become characteristics of preferential rules. An example is 'I'd PREFER to do very
well but I don't HAVE TO' (Sichel and Ellis, 1984: 1). Clients can replace rules about
mastery and perfection with rules incorporating **competence**, **coping** and 'doing
as well as I can under the circumstances'. Furthermore, students can assist clients
to refrain from rating their whole selves rather than evaluating how useful specific
communications and actions of theirs are.

In addition, students can help clients to avoid making out that the world is
absolutely awful by accepting that the world is imperfect and by refraining from exaggerating negative factors and possibilities. Students can also assist clients to eliminate
an 'I-can't-stand-it' attitude by encouraging them to tell themselves that they can stand
the anxiety and discomfort arising from themselves, others and the environment not
being as they would prefer them to be. Indeed, even in genuinely adverse circumstances, clients may have many **strengths** to rely on and supportive people to turn to.

When working on restating rules, counselling skills students should encourage
clients to participate in the process by sharing their ideas. Some students may want to
use a whiteboard and work together with clients to get the wording just right for
them to recall and use in future. Example 19.2 shows an example of restating a
demanding into a preferential rule.

Counselling skills students need to encourage clients to work and practise hard to
maintain their preferential rules. One approach is to make cassettes of clients' initial

---

Example 19.2 Restating a demanding into a preferential rule

S = Problem situation
Janet, aged 18, is a college student who gets asked for a date by a young man,
Bruce, aged 19.

T1 = Janet's demanding rule:
'I must be liked by everyone.'

C1 = Janet's consequences if thinking is not altered:
Feelings consequences: high anxiety will block out her pleasure on the date.
Communication and action consequences: says 'yes', but will not reveal much
of herself on date and this could make Bruce feel awkward.

T2 = Janet's preferential rule:
'I would prefer to be liked by almost everyone, but there are many fish in the
ocean and I can obtain a boyfriend if only some young men like me.'

C2 = Consequences of Janet's revised rule:
Feelings consequences: pleasure, but also some anxiety, which is likely to be
manageable at first and to dissipate as she and Bruce talk more on their date.
Communication and action consequences: says 'yes', thinks that on the date if
she makes an effort to help Bruce to enjoy the evening she will start feeling
more relaxed and enjoy herself too.

demanding rules, their challenges and their restatements. Clients can also post in prominent positions reminder cards stating their preferential rules. In addition, clients can use **visualized rehearsal** in which they imagine themselves in a specific situation experiencing the negative consequences arising from their demanding rule. Then they can imagine switching over to their preferential rule and visualize the positive consequences of doing so. Last, but not least, students should assist and encourage clients to change how they communicate and act in real life in line with their improved rules. Clients may need to forcefully direct themselves many times to use and act on their knowledge to change their behaviour.

Activity 19.1 Assisting clients to create preferential rules

Work with a partner who either uses a personal concern or role plays a client with a mind skills goal of creating one or more preferential rules to manage a problem situation better. Within the context of a good counselling/helping relationship and, possibly, using a whiteboard during the process:

- use **speaking skills** to describe the difference between demanding and preferential rules
- use **demonstration skills**
- cooperate with the client to identify any major demanding rules and put the main one into the **STC framework**

- use coaching skills to assist the client to question and challenge the main demanding rule
- use coaching skills to assist the client to create a preferential rule statement to replace the demanding rule
- use negotiating **between session activities** skills.

Afterwards, discuss and reverse roles. Playing back audio recordings or video recordings of rehearsal and practise sessions may assist learning.

Assisting clients to test the reality of perceptions

Clients, like everyone else, live in the world as they perceive it. Clients' perceptions about themselves, others and the environment are their subjective reality. However, when facts are taken into account, these perceptions are of varying degrees of accuracy. In longer-term counselling and helping, clients can be trained to become much more disciplined about not jumping to unwarranted conclusions but, instead, testing the reality of their perceptions (Beck and Weishaar, 2008). Even in brief helping for specific problem situations, counselling skills students can assist clients to identify potentially erroneous perceptions, assess their reality and, if necessary, replace them with more accurate perceptions.

Checking the accuracy of perceptions

When faced with problem situations, clients may make potentially erroneous statements about themselves, such as 'I'm no good at that', and about others, such as

'She or he always does ...' or 'She or he never does ...' Such statements or perceptions influence how they feel, and communicate and act. When helping clients check the accuracy of their perceptions, counselling skills students are asking them to distinguish between fact and inference, and to make their inferences fit the facts as closely as possible. In Chapter 3, the example was provided of 'All Aborigines walk in single file, at least the one I saw did' as being an illustration of how people can leap from fact, seeing one Aboriginal walking, to inference, stating that all Aborigines walk in single file. In Chapter 12, six mind tricks were identified, for instance black-and-white thinking, that can interfere with how accurately clients perceive.

Clients' perceptions may be thought of as propositions that, together, counselling skills students and clients can investigate to see how far they are supported by evidence. As shown in Example 19.3, counselling skills students can assist clients to check the accuracy of their perceptions in problem situations by asking three main questions:

- 'Where is the evidence for your perception?'
- 'Are there any other ways of perceiving the situation?'
- 'Which way of perceiving the situation best fits the available facts?'

In Example 19.3, the counsellor also helps the client go beyond checking existing perceptions to restate a leading perception to become more realistic.

Counselling skills students may need to assist clients to alter thoughts in more than one mind skills area. For instance, Maggie the client in Example 19.3 might also challenge and alter a demanding rule such as 'I must be liked by everyone'. Furthermore, Maggie could learn to use calming and coaching self-talk to guide her in communicating effectively when seeing clients. In addition, sometimes a good way to help clients challenge their thinking is to encourage them to experiment with communicating and acting differently. However, this is probably not necessary with Maggie, who just needs to acknowledge that her current rate of learning is satisfactory.

Example 19.3 Checking the accuracy of a perception

Problem situation
Maggie, 25, is a student who gets very anxious because she thinks that she is not performing well in the practical skills part of her counselling course.

Potentially erroneous perception
'I am not performing well in the practical skills part of my counselling course.'

Question 1 'Where is the evidence for your perception?'
When asked this question, Maggie says that she has little evidence. She reports that she does not appear to be learning as quickly as she would like, but that she is doing just as well as most of the other students.

Question 2 'Are there any other ways of perceiving the situation?'
Maggie and her counsellor/helper come up with the following different perceptions:
'Learning counselling skills takes time.'
'None of the students is particularly good.'

Example 19.3 Checking the accuracy of a perception – cont'd

'I have a tendency to expect that I will learn everything quickly and to put myself down if this is not the case.'
'The counselling skills trainer is too easy on the students.'
'I have received some good feedback from the trainer.'

Question 3 'Which way of perceiving the situation best fits the available facts?'
After some thought, Maggie decides that the most accurate perception is:
'I have a tendency to expect that I will learn everything quickly and to put myself down if this is not the case.'
Maggie also likes the perception:
'Learning counselling skills takes time.'

Restating a perception to be more realistic
Maggie's counsellor coaches her in challenging her need to learn everything quickly and together they come up with a more realistic perception:
'It's unrealistic for me to expect to learn counselling skills immediately, but I am doing all right so far even though I make mistakes at times.'

Activity 19.2 Assisting clients to test the reality of perceptions

Work with a partner who either uses a personal concern or role plays a client with a mind skills goal of creating one or more preferential rules to manage a problem situation better. Within the context of a good counselling/helping relationship and, possibly, using a whiteboard during the process:
- use speaking skills to describe the importance of testing the reality of perceptions rather than jumping to conclusions
- use demonstrating skills
- cooperate with the client to identify current inaccurate perceptions and their consequences
- use coaching skills to assist your client to reality test the existing evidence for a perception by addressing the questions:
  - 'Where is the evidence for your perception?'
  - 'Are there any other ways of perceiving the situation?'
  - 'Which way of perceiving the situation best fits the available facts?'
  - if appropriate, restate the perception that best fits the available facts to be more realistic, and
- use negotiating between session activities skills.
Afterwards, discuss and reverse roles. Playing back audio recordings or video recordings of rehearsal and practise sessions may assist learning.

Assisting clients to create coping self-talk

Despite being an experienced writer, before I started a new chapter for a book or a new journal article I almost always felt a minor episode of lack of confidence and well-being. As I became increasingly aware that this was the case, I learned to combat and control my pre-writing blues with self-talk like: 'Here we go again. These low feelings happen every time before I write something for publication. Calm down. I know from previous experience that I can cope with the situation by preparing adequately and then getting down to writing. Once I start writing I always get a greater sense of being in control and my usual feelings of optimism and well-being return.' Now my self-talk is always enough to manage my anxiety and help me to get started. Others, be they clients, students or academics, may talk to themselves much more negatively before writing than I do. If so, you may need to work much harder to correct your self-talk.

Dimensions of coping self-talk

In Chapter 3, I distinguished between negative and coping self-talk. Furthermore, I indicated that coping, or 'doing as well as I can', is preferable to mastery, or 'doing perfectly'. The following are some dimensions of coping self-talk.

- *Alerting self-talk* In the above example of my talking to myself before writing, I used the phrase 'Here we go again' to alert myself that I needed to use my coping self-talk to guide me into commencing writing. Clients may need to change gear from the buzz of their usual thinking into calmer and clearer states of **mind**. Counselling skills students can help clients to recognize danger signals in problem situations, for instance anxiety, anger or depression, and then consciously alert themselves to use coping self-talk. The basic alerting self-talk instruction is 'STOP ... THINK!' To be effective, train clients to give 'STOP ... THINK' self-instructions forcefully and possibly repeat them: for instance 'STOP ... THINK, STOP ... THINK!' After 'THINK' they can remind themselves to use their self-talk skills in their problem situations: for instance, 'STOP ... THINK ... My anxiety/anger is a signal for me to use my self-talk skills'. Clients can then engage in other forms of self-talk: for instance calming themselves down, coaching themselves in how best to communicate, and affirming their strengths and support factors.
- *Calming self-talk* Creating calming self-talk can assist clients to deal with problem situations in many ways. Before, during and after specific situations, they can calm their minds so that they can better handle unwanted feelings, such as harmful anxiety or excessive anger. In addition, clients may wish to calm and relax their mind as a way of managing extraneous stresses that then impact on how they handle problem situations. A third purpose for creating calming self-talk is to become more centred and focused when wanting to think or talk through how best to communicate or act in problem situations. Clients' use of calming self-talk helps them to clear a psychological space for getting in touch with their feelings and thinking more sharply and deeply.

  Counselling skills students may introduce calming self-talk to clients by talking about the concept and then providing an example of a calming self-instruction like 'Relax'. Then you can encourage clients to come up with some calming self-instructions of their own. Next, you might discuss which calming self-instructions the client prefers to use. In addition, students can tell, demonstrate and coach clients in how to use a calm and measured voice when giving calming self-instructions. Sometimes, the difference in self-talk may be highlighted by saying a phrase like 'Calm down' in a hurried and self-pressurizing way.

Cooling self-talk statements might be regarded as a sub-category of calming self-talk. You can train clients prone to angry outbursts in cooling self-talk statements. Example 19.4 provides examples of both calming and cooling self-talk statements.

- *Coaching self-talk* Coaching self-talk is no substitute for possessing the **communication skills** for achieving a task. The first step in coaching self-talk is to assist clients to break down tasks. Counselling skills students can work with clients to think through systematic approaches to attaining **goals** in problem situations, including how to handle setbacks. Once plans are clear, then clients require the ability to instruct themselves through the steps of implementing them. Students should remember to emphasize self-talk about vocal and bodily as well as verbal communication. Students can also assist clients to develop coaching self-talk statements to handle different ways other people in problem situations might respond.
- *Affirming self-talk* The notion of affirming self-talk is preferred here to that of positive self-talk. The danger of positive self-talk is that clients may tell themselves false positives that set them up for disappointment and failure. Affirming self-talk focuses on reminding yourself of realistic factors that count in your favour. The following are some aspects of affirming self-talk.

Example 19.4 Calming and cooling self–talk statements

Calming self-talk statements
'Keep calm'
'Slow down'
'Relax'
'Take it easy'
'Take a deep breath'
'Breathe slowly and regularly'
'I can manage'

Cooling self-talk statements
'Cool it'
'Count to ten'
'Be careful'
'Don't overreact'
'Don't let my pride get in the way'
'I can choose not to let myself get hooked'
'Problem solve'

First, clients can tell themselves that they can cope. Sample self-statements include: 'I can handle this situation', 'My anxiety is a signal for me to use my coping skills', and 'All I have to do is to cope'. In addition, once clients cope with situations better, they can acknowledge this: for example, 'I used my coping skills and they worked.'

Second, clients can acknowledge their strengths. Often when clients are anxious about difficult situations, they forget their strengths. For example, when asking for dates, clients may genuinely possess good points, though they do not have to boast about them. Also, they may have good conversational skills that they can acknowledge and use rather than thinking about what may go wrong. In addition, clients can think about any successful experiences they may have had in the past in situations similar to the one they face.

Third, clients may become more confident if they acknowledge supportive people to whom they have access. For instance, relatives, friends, spouses and counselling professionals might each be sources of support, though not necessarily so. Just realizing they have supportive people to whom they can turn may be sufficient to help some clients cope better with problem situations.

Putting it all together

Coping self-talk may be used before, during and after problem situations. Often alerting, calming, coaching and affirming statements are combined, though not necessarily all at the same time. Clients need to think through the combinations of self-instructions that work for them. Furthermore, counselling skills students can ensure that clients write down alerting, calming, coaching and affirming statements that they find useful.

Activity 19.3 Assisting clients to create coping self-talk

Work with a partner who either uses a personal concern or role plays a client with a mind skills goal of creating coping self-talk to manage a problem situation better. Within the context of a good counselling/helping relationship and, possibly, using a whiteboard during the process:
- use speaking skills to describe the difference between negative and coping self-talk
- assist the client to identify any current negative self-talk
- use coaching skills to help the client to formulate alerting, calming, coaching and affirming self-talk statements
- use negotiating between session activities skills.

Afterwards, discuss and reverse roles. Playing back audio recordings or video recordings of rehearsal and practise sessions may assist learning.

Remembering, rehearsing and practising

So far the chapter's main emphasis has been on counselling skills students assisting clients to change how they think. Here the focus is on how clients can help themselves when on their own.

Example 19.5 Illustration of coping self-talk

Bert, 45, runs a car repair garage and one of his problems is that of losing his temper with the staff. He agrees with his counsellor, Janice, that it would be helpful for him to develop some coping self-talk skills. Together he and Janice work on his self-talk and identify the following statements he can tell himself.

Alerting
STOP ... THINK ... potential trouble ahead!

Calming
Cool it.
Take some slow, deep breaths.

Coaching
Getting angry only makes things worse.
Think what I really want to achieve in the situation.
I can give clear instructions how I want things done.
I can calmly ask what seems to be the problem.

Affirming
I know I can handle this well.

Composite
STOP ... THINK. Calm down. Think what I really want to achieve in the situation. I know I can handle this well.

Remembering statements of preferential rules, statements of revised perceptions and coping self-talk statements is vital to implementing them in practice. Ways to enhance clients' memory include writing the statements down on A4 paper, making reminder cards and making cassettes. Clients can post written reminders in prominent places. In addition, clients can carry reminder cards with them to review immediately before difficult situations.

Counselling skills students can encourage clients to rehearse their revised thoughts, possibly using reminder cards and cassettes for rehearsal. In addition, students can encourage clients to practise hard at relinquishing unhelpful thoughts and replacing them with helpful thoughts in their actual problem situations. Clients can modify those revised thoughts that do not work for them.

Genuine learning rarely occurs without setbacks and difficulties. Clients can use coping self-talk to encourage themselves in handling these. In addition, they can challenge any demanding rules about having to be perfect learners. If clients find using their revised thoughts helps them to communicate and act more effectively, this should assist them in maintaining their revised thinking. Furthermore, if clients can acknowledge their successes, this also should help motivate them to persist.

20

Negotiating homework

CHAPTER OUTCOMES

By studying and doing the activities in this chapter you should:
*   understand the importance of homework;
*   have some skills at increasing clients' compliance with homework assignments;
*   know of some ways that clients can get support; and
*   know of some additional resources that might be used in conjunction with counselling and helping.

The theme of this chapter is that of how **clients** can use the time in-between **counselling** and helping sessions to best effect. The chapter reviews negotiating homework assignments and then goes on to look at ways of getting support and of using resources.

Negotiating homework

On many occasions counselling skills students may find it useful to discuss with clients homework activities that they might undertake before they meet again (Burns and Spangler, 2000). In formal counselling these would be **between session activities**. Here the term negotiating homework gets used because of the large variety of settings and ways in which counselling and helping takes place. Nevertheless, in some settings the word 'homework' might be considered stuffy or inappropriate because of its educational connotations. If so, students can use different terminology that works best for you and your clients. For the sake of simplicity, much of the following discussion on negotiating homework assumes formal counselling and helping sessions. Consequently, readers for whom this assumption is inaccurate should adapt the discussion to their special circumstances.

   In conjunction with presenting, demonstrating and coaching clients in improved ways of thinking and communicating/acting in the context of collaborative working relationships, counselling skills students can negotiate relevant homework assignments. Homework assignments include trying out changed behaviours in real life settings and filling out self-monitoring sheets and worksheets for developing **mind** **skills** that influence **feelings**, communications and actions. Other assignments can entail reading self-help books, **listening** to cassettes, watching videotapes and observing people with good **communication skills**.

Many reasons exist for suggesting to clients that they perform homework assignments. These reasons include speeding up the learning process and encouraging clients to monitor, rehearse and practise changed communications and actions. Furthermore, homework activities can help the transfer of behaviours worked on in counselling and helping to real life. Sometimes, when this happens, clients experience difficulties in applying their improved behaviours. Together you can address such difficulties when next meeting them. In addition, homework assignments can increase clients' sense of self-control and of **personal responsibility** for improving how they think, communicate and act.

One of the central problems in assigning homework activities is that of getting clients to do them. Often as a trainer I observed counselling skills students rush through negotiating homework assignments at the end of sessions in ways that virtually guaranteed client non-compliance. Common mistakes included not leaving enough time, inviting insufficient client participation, giving vague verbal instructions, and not checking whether clients clearly understood what they were meant to do.

The following are some guidelines for negotiating homework. These guidelines are influenced by the strategies for increasing client compliance recommended by prominent American cognitive therapists Christine Padesky and Dennis Greenberger (1995: 24–7).

- *Make homework assignments clearly relevant* Homework assignments must be client-centred in the sense that they are clearly seen by clients as being central to their problems and **problem situations** and to attaining their **goals**. It is a waste of time to set assignments unless clients are cooperative, see their relevance and, hence, are motivated to complete them. You can make judgments about whether to state client homework goals in terms of communication/**action skills** and **mind skills** in light of individual clients' circumstances.
- *Collaborate with clients in formulating assignments* Clients need to be involved in formulating homework assignments to perform outside of counselling and helping. They can make suggestions as to what specific communications, actions and thoughts they may change. Furthermore, once they understand the concepts of mind skills and communication/action skills, they can also suggest which ones they need work on and at what rate.
- *Keep assignments manageable* Homework assignments need to be manageable in a number of ways. They should be of a size that clients are likely to do them. Furthermore, they should be of a difficulty that clients can clearly understand what is required. Counselling skills students can discuss with clients what seems reasonable. Especially at first, small and simple may be the way to go.
- *Graduate the difficulty of homework assignments* With clients who are being seen for a number of sessions, counselling skills students can both set tasks within the clients' skill level at the same time as making them progressively more difficult. It is important that clients experience success in achieving assignments, so setting manageable, yet progressively difficult tasks needs to be taken very seriously. Sometimes, changing a way of thinking, communicating or acting requires clients to give up long-established habits. Here, it can be especially important for

students and clients not to agree on too difficult an activity too soon. Where possible, you should try to build in some early successes to encourage clients to persist in working on their skills.

- *Make sure that the client has a written summary of any instructions* Counselling skills students can protect clients if they are clear what they must do and that they have a record of what is required of them outside of time spent together. You can design your own homework assignment forms or write down tailor-made instructions as occasions arise. Example 20.1 presents four formats for homework forms based on the assumption of formal counselling and helping sessions. Where possible, either the counselling skills student or client should write down clear instructions for homework assignments on these forms. Writing instructions on scraps of paper is generally not good enough. Students should always check what clients write to make sure they have taken down the instructions correctly. If you want clients to fill out forms such as **monitoring** logs, you should provide these forms yourself. This practice ensures clear instructions and saves clients the extra effort of having to write out forms before filling them in.

- *Begin homework assignments during sessions* Where possible it can be important that clients begin homework assignments during sessions since it cannot be assumed that they understand them. Counselling skills students can check both the clarity of your instructions and how well clients understand the assignments.

Example 20.1 Formats for homework assignment forms

Format 1
Homework assignment form
In order to gain the most from your counselling session(s) you are encouraged to engage in the following between session activities.

Format 2
To follow up
In order to gain the most from your counselling session(s) you are encouraged to perform the following tasks.

Format 3
Take away sheet
Use this sheet for writing down (1) your main learnings from counselling and (2) any instructions for between session activities.

Format 4
Learning contract
I make a learning contract with myself to perform the following activities before the next counselling session.

Note: As appropriate, substitute the word helping for counselling.

For example, clients may require assistance in understanding a mind skill that they are going to work on during homework. Checking understanding saves time in the long run because otherwise clients may not do assignments properly, if at all. Further difficulties in understanding and doing assignments need to be dealt with as they occur.

- *Anticipate difficulties in completing homework assignments* When asked, clients often have a good idea of what might get in the way of their doing homework assignments. For example, some clients prefer to indicate definite times when they undertake to do tasks rather than leave them to chance. Clients inclined to forget homework tasks can put up reminder notices in prominent places. You can encourage clients, who on second thoughts think they may have taken on too much, to make their homework tasks briefer or easier.

  Counselling skills students can also help clients to deal with unsuccessful attempts at homework tasks. For example, after a seemingly negative attempt at performing a task, together you can explore how well they used specific targeted skills. If they did not do as well as they would have liked, options include trying to do the same task better in ways that either they or you have identified, or trying an easier task. Clients need to be helped to realize that it can take time to build good skills. In addition, you can assist clients to identify people who can support their efforts at change.

- *Emphasize learning* Counselling skills students can assist clients to view their attempts at homework as learning experiences. For example, some clients return to negative, if not downright hostile environments. If so, students may need to prepare these clients more thoroughly prior to suggesting that they implement their improved communication and actions outside their sessions. Such preparation may include devising strategies for dealing with negative feedback. You may also conduct role plays with clients who may face difficult people as they apply their changed skills.

  Clients can learn that there are numerous reasons that they might not get the results they want right away. For example, it can take time to learn a skill, so at first clients may not be as successful as they would like because they are still learners. Sometimes, clients may use good skills, but still not get positive results, so here it can be important to distinguish between process and outcome. You can also assist clients to learn even from tasks that they do not do properly or fail to do at all. For instance, a client may need further assistance in understanding how to implement skills like assertion or sharing intimacy. Where clients do not perform homework tasks, they can be assisted in understanding the feelings or other circumstances that they have allowed to interfere with progress. You can also check that the homework assignments were clear and appropriate for specific clients.

- *Show interest and follow up in the next appointment* Counselling skills students should signal a joint progress review by letting clients know that, when you next meet, you will ask them how they fared in their homework assignments. Clients who know that those assisting them are interested in and supportive of their attempts to complete homework assignments are more likely to be motivated to do so. However, this assumes that students avoid becoming controlling and judgmental.

Activity 20.1 Negotiating homework

Work as a **counsellor/helper** with a partner acting as client who selects a problem situation in which she or he wants to communicate better. Collaborate with your partner to identify some key verbal, vocal and body messages in need of improvement. Using coaching, demonstrating and rehearsing assist your partner to improve her/his skills. Then rehearse and practise how to negotiate one or more homework assignments so that your partner can use the time (assume a week) before you next meet to good effect. To increase your clients' chances of compliance, observe the following guidelines:

- make homework assignment(s) clearly relevant
- collaborate with the client in formulating the assignment(s)
- keep assignment(s) manageable
- graduate the difficulty of homework assignment(s)
- make sure that the client has a writing summary of any instructions
- begin homework assignment(s) during sessions
- anticipate difficulties in completing homework assignment(s)
- emphasize learning
- show interest and follow up in the next appointment (where possible).

Afterwards, hold a sharing and discussion session focused on the counsellor/helper's use of negotiating **homework skills**. If necessary, allow her/him to practise some more until she/he feels reasonably confident in negotiating homework assignments.

    Then, if feasible, reverse roles.

Assisting identification and use of supports and resources

Counselling skills students may need to raise some clients' **awareness** about the importance of identifying and using **supports** and of lessening contact with unsupportive people. Students can assist clients to identify people in their home environments who can support efforts to attain communication and action goals. For example, university students with **study skills** deficits can seek out sympathetic lecturers and tutors to help them attain action goals, for instance writing more polished essays or preparing well for examinations. Unemployed people can approach friends and relatives who may not only offer them emotional support, but may also be sources for job leads. Teachers who feel burned out can associate with colleagues relatively happy with their lot rather than those perpetually complaining. Furthermore, they can attain self-care goals by engaging in recreational activities with people unconnected with education.

    An inverse approach to support is for counseling skills students to assist clients in identifying unsympathetic or counter-productive people. Clients are then left with various choices: getting such people to accept, if not support, their efforts to change; seeing less of them; or stopping seeing them altogether. If these people are family members, avoiding them altogether may be difficult, especially if clients are financially dependent on them. Here, students and clients may discuss damage-control strategies. However, often clients can choose their friendship and membership groups. For example, if juvenile delinquents want to eliminate negative activities like stealing cars and taking drugs, they may need to change the company they keep.

Sometimes, counselling skills students can extend counselling and helping strategies into clients' home environments. You may use a variety of people as aides: teachers, parents, welfare workers, supervisors and friends. Some guidelines for using 'non-professional' third parties as helper aides include obtaining the permission of clients, identifying suitable people and, where necessary, training them in their roles. An example of using a third party as an aide is asking a teacher to help a shy and lonely pupil to participate more in class.

In addition, counselling skills students can assist clients to identify and use resources for helping them attain and maintain communication and action goals. Such resources include workshops and short courses; self-help books and manuals; instructional audiocassettes, videotapes and CD-ROMs; appropriate voluntary agencies; peer support groups and networks; telephone hot-lines and crisis **information** outlets; and computerized support and interaction (Goss and Anthony, 2003).

Counselling skills students should familiarize themselves with and establish contact with the human supports and educational and information resources of most relevance to the client populations with which you work. Access to suitable supports and resources may be of tremendous assistance to some clients as they take positive steps towards changing how they communicate and act in problem situations.

Activity 20.2 Identifying supports and resources

Part A   Identifying supports

For a population of clients either with whom you work now or are likely to work with in future:
1 identify as many categories of people as you can who might support clients in dealing with their problems
2 where possible, provide one or more specific examples of clients who are confronting problems either being supported or who might be supported by relevant others.

Part B   Identifying resources

For a population of clients either with whom you work now or are likely to work with in future:
1 identify educational and informational resources that might help clients in dealing with their problems
2 where possible, provide one or more specific examples of clients who either are being assisted or who might be assisted by using educational and informational resources as they confront their problems.

21

Conducting middle sessions

CHAPTER OUTCOMES

By studying and doing the activities in this chapter you should:
- understand the importance of using both heart and head;
- possess some basic skills for the preparing phase of counselling/helping sessions;
- possess some basic skills for the starting phase;
- possess some skills for the working phase;
- possess some skills for the ending phase; and
- understand some issues about length, frequency and number of sessions.

This chapter addresses what to do after conducting an initial session. In the change stage of the Relating–Understanding–Changing (RUC) **counselling and helping process model**, students need to be careful not to become 'the horror of the dehumanized **helper** who goes around with a package of **skills** but no warmth and no presence' (Brain Thorne, personal communication, 20 December 1998). It is possible to get so wrapped up in trying to help **clients** by doing things to and for them that the critical importance of maintaining a client-focused, humane and **compassionate** relationship gets lost. Person-centred **counsellors** like Carl Rogers viewed the relationship as the core element in assisting clients to change. Even leading behavioural counsellors like Joseph Wolpe asserted that, to a large degree, clients change because of 'non-specific relationship factors' (Wolpe, 1990).

Counselling skills students can strive to help clients by using both their hearts and their heads. In his book of sermons entitled *Strength to Love*, the late American civil rights leader Martin Luther King encouraged readers to develop 'a tough **mind** and a tender heart' (King, 1963). A tender and compassionate heart will enable students to see more deeply and lovingly behind the facades that clients present, thus enabling them to be treated with respect and non-possessive warmth. Behind the disfigurement sometimes caused by clients' mental pain and **anxiety**, it is possible to glimpse and prize their potential. In addition, you can acknowledge your shared humanity and capacity for human frailty. A tough mind will enable counselling skills students to look behind and work on your own facades so that you can be more present to clients. Furthermore, a tough mind will help you to develop the technical skills required for delivering different interventions for change.

It can be difficult for counselling skills students to keep hold of your humanity when interviewing. So many things can be going on in your head at once. You want to help your clients. You are trying to stay tuned into them and observe and listen carefully to their various verbal, **vocal** and **bodily communications**. You are thinking about what interventions to adopt and how to deliver them. In addition, both you and your clients may be mindful of being video-recorded or cassette-recorded for **supervision** purposes.

Counselling skills students can try not to add to your difficulties by burdening yourself with needing to appear as an expert. Being helped by a concerned and caring human being is much more important to most clients than being helped by a technical expert. As in any relationship, clients will pick up whether students are really interested and concerned about them. In addition, as in any relationship, if the concern gets transmitted, clients will help students to relate to them. In an atmosphere of mutual liking and often with clients' assistance, you can retrieve many of your mistakes. Furthermore, if you are honest about being counselling skills students, clients will make allowances for your lack of professional technical expertise. However, clients are much less likely to make allowances for students' deficiencies as concerned human beings. Remember that many clients have suffered from the phoniness of significant others in their pasts and have a keen sense of smell in sniffing out counsellor and helper phoniness.

Conducting sessions

This chapter is relevant to counselling skills students who either use or are likely to use your counselling skills in settings where it is possible to conduct a series of formal sessions. Nevertheless, it is hoped that those of you who use counselling skills in either informal helping contacts or as part of other primary roles can also find something of value from it. The focus here is on middle sessions, those that take place after the initial session and before the last session. If anything, the following review focuses more on conducting sessions in the improving **communication/action skills** and **mind skills** approach than the helping to solve problems approach to the changing stage of the RUC helping model. However, many points are relevant to both approaches.

Counselling and helping sessions have four phases: preparing, starting, middle, and ending. In Box 21.1, based on the assumption that contact will continue for at least one more session, some relevant skills are listed for each phase.

The preparing phase

In Chapter 9, I mentioned that preparation skills were important before starting counselling and helping. These skills included trying to ensure that clients' pre-session contact with the helping service was positive. Other points stressed included arriving early for sessions, making sure the room was in order, checking any recording equipment to be used and, if necessary, relaxing yourself. Furthermore, I suggested that you do not allow clients into the interview room before you are ready to devote full attention to them. Most of the above considerations are just as relevant to preparing for second and subsequent sessions as for initial ones.

Box 21.1 The four phases of counselling and helping sessions

1 The preparing phase
Illustrative skills
- Reflecting on previous and next session(s)
- Consulting with trainers, supervisors and peers
- Understanding how to improve the targeted communication/action skills and mind skills
- Arriving on time
- Setting up the room
- Relaxing oneself

2 The starting phase
Illustrative skills
- Meeting, greeting and seating
- Re-establishing the collaborative working relationship
- Reviewing **homework**
- Establishing **session agendas**

3 The middle phase
Illustrative skills
- Actively involving clients in the change process
- Coaching, demonstrating and rehearsing
- Checking clients' understanding
- Refining session agendas
- Keeping sessions moving

4 The ending phase
Illustrative skills
- **Structuring** to allow time for ending
- Reviewing sessions
- Negotiating homework
- Arranging subsequent contact

On introductory counselling skills training courses, students' practice sessions are mainly with peers and, sometimes, with volunteer 'clients'. In many instances, these sessions are recorded for later reviewing by students themselves, trainers, supervisors and peers. Students can perform many **between session activities**. One such activity is to play back any tape of the previous session and review your use of **counselling skills**, how the client responded, what progress she or he made, and the usefulness of the **communication patterns** established between you and the client. Some introductory courses may require students to make such observations in written logs as a prelude to keeping 'professional logs' recording details of each supervised placement session.

Trainers and peers can also help students to review the previous session to gain insights into how you might approach the next one. In addition, you can revise interventions you intend using to understand their content thoroughly. Furthermore, you can practise delivering the interventions. Students can also use between session time to ensure that any written material, such as handouts and between session activity sheets, are readily available. However, you should be careful not to be too rigid in how you **plan** to approach the next session. Remember that it is vital that you consult with clients as part of establishing a strong **working alliance** rather than impose your ideas.

The starting phase

The starting phase has three main tasks: re-establishing the relationship and working alliance, reviewing between session activities, and establishing a session agenda. The meeting, greeting and seating skills for subsequent counselling and helping sessions are similar to those required for initial sessions. Possibly students have already obtained permission for recording sessions.

Once clients are comfortably seated, sometimes they will start talking of their own accord. However, on most occasions, counselling skills students need to make an opening statement. Sample **opening statements** are provided in Example 21.1. A 'softly, softly' approach that starts by checking 'where the client' is at is advocated rather than moving directly into intervening. Such an approach allows clients the psychological safety and space to bring students up to date with **information** that they select as important. By not pushing an agenda, you can avoid taking over the session or suppressing significant information that clients may wish to share with you, for instance a death in the family or a car crash. You can use **active listening** skills to help clients know that you are still interested and concerned in how they see the world and their **problem situations**.

Once counselling skills students have allowed client's airtime, you may still require further information to help you to assess how they have progressed in any between session activities that were negotiated in the previous session. Example 21.1 provides some statements that you might make if you have not already reviewed progress in-between session activities. As appropriate, you can ask additional **questions** that clarify and expand your own and clients' understanding of progress.

Counselling skills students can encourage clients to acknowledge their agency in bringing about positive changes. For example, Jack, a client prone to being too compliant, has acted assertively in a recurring problem situation with his partner Alan and says 'Things are going better in our relationship'. A student could help Jack to acknowledge that by changing his behaviour, for instance by replacing negative with coaching **self-talk**, he has helped to bring about the improvement. Jack might now say to himself 'If I use my self-talk skills, then I can be more assertive and improve my relationship with Alan'.

Near the start of each session in the change stage, students should consider consulting with clients to establish session agendas. Such agendas may be for all or part of sessions. For example, together you may decide where you will work first and then, later, make another decision regarding where to work next. Alternatively, as part of your initial agenda-setting discussion, you may target one area to start on and then agree to move on to another area. However, you need to remain flexible once session agendas get established so that you can respond to developments during sessions.

> **Example 21.1 Some starting phase statements**
>
> **Opening statements**
> · 'How's your week been?'
> · 'How have you been getting on?'
> · 'Where would you like to start today?'
>
> **Reviewing between session activities statements**
> · 'What progress did you make with your activities?'
> · 'What happened when you tried out your changed thoughts/communications?'
> · 'Things didn't just happen, you made them happen by changing [specify what].'
>
> **Establishing a session agenda**
> 'In our first session we stated two mind skills **goals** for developing your inter-view skills, using **coping** rather than negative self-talk and **challenging** and then replacing your demanding rule about giving perfect answers. We also stated some goals for developing aspects of your verbal, vocal and bodily communication. Where would you like to work first?'

When establishing session agendas, I favour paying considerable attention to clients' wishes, since I want to encourage their motivation and involvement. If I thought there was some important reason for starting with a particular mind skills or communication skills goal, I would share this observation with clients. However, I would still be inclined to allow clients the final say in where we worked. Example 21.1 illustrates the kind of agenda setting statements that counsellors and helpers might make near the start of a second session. Session agendas for later sessions tend to be heavily influenced by work done in and between session activities negotiated in the previous session.

Activity 21.1 Starting middle counselling and helping sessions

Part A   Formulating statements

Using Example 21.1 as a guide, formulate at least one additional starting phase statement in each of the following categories:
· opening statements
· reviewing between session activities statements
· establishing a session agenda.

Part B   Practising the starting phase

One student acts as counsellor/helper, another as client, with possibly a third student acting as observer. The client chooses a problem situation of relevance to her/him. Assume that an initial session, in which the first two stages of the Relating–Understanding–Changing counselling and helping process model have

(Continued)

Activity 21.1 Starting middle counselling and helping sessions – cont'd

been completed, has already been performed. Furthermore, assume that you and your client have identified at least one communication/action skill and at least one mind skill to be altered during the changing stage, which may last for at least one more session after this one. If this is not a real second session, you will need to discuss how each participant can best get into their role. Then conduct the starting phase of a second helping session up to and including the establishment of a session agenda.

Afterwards, hold a sharing and feedback discussion. Then, if appropriate, change roles and repeat this activity.

Using audiocassette or videotape recording and playback may add value to the activity.

The middle phase

Once session agendas are established, however informally, counselling skills students can implement interventions to assist clients to attain one or more goals. One way of viewing this middle phase is that it is the working phase of the session. However, the term working phase is not used here because it may detract from valuing work performed in the preparing, starting and ending phases.

Already, the importance of **client–centred coaching** has been emphasized when delivering interventions and some strategies for developing mind skills and communication/action skills have been reviewed. You need to be sensitive to the communication patterns or interaction processes that you establish with clients. For example, some students may have a tendency to establish communication patterns that are insufficiently client-focused. If so, you can become aware from clients' reactions to clues indicating that they are doing most of the talking or taking most of the responsibility for session content.

In the middle phase counselling skills students can involve clients in choices that take place while delivering particular interventions, for instance how many rehearsals they require to develop a targeted communication goal. Furthermore, you can involve clients in choices about moving on to different items in the session agenda and refining agendas as appropriate. Together, student and client may make trade-offs and compromises regarding spending session time: for instance, curtailing time spent in one mind skills or communication skills area so that time becomes available for another.

Counselling skills students need to keep middle sessions moving at an appropriate pace, neither too fast nor too slow. There are risks in both directions. On the one hand, you may rush through delivering interventions in ways that confuse clients and leave them little to take away after sessions end. Furthermore, you may put too much pressure on clients to reveal themselves and to work at an uncongenial pace.

On the other hand, students may allow 'session drift' – sessions that drift along rather aimlessly with little tangible being achieved. Sometimes session drift occurs because students are poor at balancing relationship and task considerations, at the expense of the latter. You may need to develop assertion skills to curtail long and unproductive conversations. Furthermore, you require a repertoire of checking out and moving on statements. Example 21.2 provides illustrations of such statements.

Though the responsibility should be shared, ultimately it is the students' responsibility as counsellor or helper to see that session time is allocated productively. Be careful not to make moving on statements that allow insufficient time to deal with the next agenda items properly. Generally, it is best to avoid getting into new areas towards the end of sessions rather than to start working on them in rushed and hurried ways.

The ending phase

There are various tasks involved in skilfully ending sessions in the changing stage of the RUC counselling and helping model. Counselling skills students need to bring closure to any work on a targeted skill in process during the middle phase. You may want either to review progress yourself or suggest that clients review the session. If clients have not done so already, this may be an opportunity for them to write down their main learnings. In addition, you should leave sufficient time to negotiate and clarify any between session activities clients will undertake. Furthermore, you and your clients should discuss and be clear about arrangements for the next session.

To allow time to perform the tasks of the ending phase properly, often it is a good idea to make an early **structuring** statement that allows for a smooth transition from the middle to the ending phase of the session. Such a statement might be made about 5-to-10 minutes before the end of a 40-to-50 minute session. The first two ending phase statements in Example 21.2 are illustrations of how to do this.

Example 21.2 Illustrations of statements for the middle and ending phases

Middle phase statements
- 'Do you want to spend more time now working in this area or are you ready to move on?'
- 'I sense that we've taken working on changing your ___ skills [specify] as far as we can for now, what do you think?'
- 'Do you want another rehearsal for communicating better in that situation or do you think you can manage all right?'

Ending phase statements
- 'I notice that we have to end in about ten minutes … and, assuming you want to meet again, perhaps we should spend some of this time **summarizing** and looking at what you might do between sessions to build your skills.'
- 'Before we end it might be a good idea to review what we've done today and see how you can build upon it before we next meet.'
- 'Is there anything you would like to bring up before we end?'

Sometimes, reviewing a session may help clients clarify and consolidate what they have learned during a session. However, reviews of sessions are not always necessary, especially if you have been thorough in how you have worked during the session. Furthermore, when negotiating between session activities, some of the same ground may get covered anyway.

The previous chapter mentioned some ways of increasing clients' compliance in performing homework or between session activities. At risk of repetition, these ways include making homework assignments clearly relevant, collaborating with clients in formulating assignments, keeping assignments manageable, graduating the difficulty of assignments, making sure that clients have written summaries of any instructions, beginning assignments during sessions, anticipating difficulties in completing assignments, emphasizing learning, and showing interest and following up in the next appointment.

When ending sessions, counselling skills students may also check whether clients have any **unfinished business**, queries or outstanding items that they would like to mention. In addition, you can check how clients have experienced the session and whether they have any feedback they would like to share. Lastly, you can make sure that you negotiate clear agreements with clients about whether and when you are next going to meet. Maintain boundaries and be careful at the end of sessions not to let working relationships slide into social relationships. Though generally not the case on introductory counselling skills courses, students may want to tell vulnerable 'at risk' clients under what circumstances and how they can contact you between sessions.

Length, frequency and number of sessions

Perhaps it is most common for individual counselling and helping sessions to be around 45 to 50 minutes long, the so-called '50-minute hour', with the remaining 10 minutes being left for writing up notes, resting and preparing for the next client. However, there are no hard and fast **rules**. Many considerations determine the length of sessions, including the counsellor or helper's workload, what is a financially viable length of time to see clients who are fee-paying or paid for by third parties, and the purposes of the session. Some counselling skills students may conduct initial sessions longer than 45 to 50 minutes because you are trying to complete the relating and understanding stages of the RUC counselling and helping process model thoroughly. Sometimes subsequent sessions can be shorter than 45 to 50 minutes because students are focusing on delivering specific interventions.

When counselling students state that a session is going to be a certain length, you should try to adhere to this limit. Reasons for so doing include encouraging clients to speak out within their allotted time, having a break between clients, and not keeping subsequent clients waiting. In informal settings, the length of helping contacts varies according to what seems possible and appropriate to both parties at the time.

Frequency of sessions can range from daily, to weekly, to fortnightly, to monthly or to ad hoc arrangements when clients come to see counsellors only when in special need. Students working in informal sessions may have regular unstructured contact with clients depending on the nature of the service, for example nurses' contacts with hospital patients or prison officers' contacts with juvenile delinquents in residential units.

Most often, counselling and helping interviews are conducted on a weekly basis. However, counselling skills students need to keep the time frames of clients' problem situations in mind. For instance, a secondary school student highly anxious about an important exam in two weeks' time or a spouse who has to attend a potentially acrimonious child custody hearing in ten days' time might require more frequent meetings than once weekly.

In counselling and helping focused on handling specific problem situations, the number of sessions may range from one to about six. Though generally outside the scope of introductory counselling skills courses, counselling focused on helping clients manage broader problems and the underlying **problematic skills** that sustain them can last from a few to 30 or more sessions. Counselling and **helping relationships** with severely emotionally deprived clients may last longer, sometimes over a year or more. In addition, some clients may return for counselling and helping on an ad hoc basic when they have **crises**, decisions and problems that it is important for them to handle skilfully.

Activity 21.2 Conducting middle counselling and helping sessions

Part A   Formulating statements

Using Example 21.2 as a guide, formulate at least one additional statement in each of the following categories:
- middle phase statements
- ending phase statements.

Part B   Practising conducting middle sessions

One student acts as counsellor/helper, another as client, with possibly a third student acting as observer. Using the same assumptions, either for the problem situation worked on in Activity 21.1 or for another problem situation, conduct a counselling/helping session consisting of the following four phases:
- preparing phase (this may include addressing issues connected with your respective roles)
- starting phase
- middle phase
- ending phase.

Afterwards, hold a sharing and feedback discussion. Then, if appropriate, change roles and repeat this activity.

Using audiocassette or videotape recording and playback may add value to the activity.

22

Terminating counselling and helping

By studying and doing the activities in this chapter you should:
- have some idea about when to terminate;
- know about some formats for terminating;
- understand about reviewing progress and summarizing learnings;
- have some further ideas for maintaining change; and
- know about how clients can use mind skills for self-helping.

This chapter deals with issues connected with terminating final sessions and with how **clients** can help themselves afterwards. As with the previous chapter it is mainly based on the assumption that **counselling skills** students have the opportunity to work with clients over a series of sessions, say three or more. Again, it is hoped that those readers for whom this assumption does not hold because of the different nature of your client contacts are able to gain something of value from the discussion.

When to terminate

Within the Relating–Understanding–Changing (RUC) counselling and helping model, when does the process get terminated? Sometimes clients may terminate of their own accord before counselling skills students think they are ready. Though this may be either because of a mismatch or because insufficient skill has been shown, this is not necessarily the case. Clients may have found their session or sessions of value, but think they can continue on their own. Sometimes, external circumstances such as a change of job or illness may prevent them continuing. In addition, some clients just resist the ideas of having to change and of being helped.

Many **problem situations** have their own time frames. When assisting clients handle specific future events, clients may only wish to continue up until that event. In informal helping, contact may end when clients leave settings, such as hospitals and residential units for juvenile delinquents. On other occasions, contact may end when clients have made sufficient progress in either the helping to solve problems or the improving **communication/action skills** and **mind skills** approaches to the third stage of the **RUC model**.

The following are four main sources of **information** that **counsellors**, **helpers** and clients can use in reviewing when to terminate contact. First, there is information from what clients report about their **feelings** and progress. Are they happy with progress and do they feel they can cope better? Second, there are counsellors and helpers' own observations about clients' progress. Third, there is feedback from significant others in clients' lives, for instance spouses, bosses or peers. Sometimes this feedback goes direct to clients and then gets relayed to those helping them. Lastly, **termination** may be based on evidence of attaining measurable **goals**. An example might be that of a single mother and teenaged son, previously in conflict, who report having ten minutes of 'happy talk' each day for a week, the son mowed the lawn as agreed during the week, and the mother expressed love and appreciation at least once each day.

Premature and prolonged termination

Sometimes, with or without warning, clients do not come to their next appointment. However, counselling skills students should be careful about automatically interpreting a missed appointment as a wish to terminate. When clients build up track **records** of good attendance, missed appointments are almost invariably for sound reasons. Where sufficient evidence has yet to be amassed to interpret missed appointments accurately, after waiting for an appropriate period for clients to make contact, one option is to enquire tactfully if they wish to schedule another appointment.

Premature termination may take place where there is a mismatch between the kind of counselling relationship offered and that which clients expect. Counselling skills students who clumsily handle clients' doubts about and **resistances** to counselling increase the likelihood of premature termination. Further reasons why clients leave prematurely include pressure from significant others, laziness, defensiveness, lack of money and fear of being trapped by students unwilling to 'let go' or who have personal agendas, such as mixing religious proselytizing with counselling.

Sometimes clients reveal their decision to terminate to counselling skills students who are of the opinion that this is not the wise thing to do. For example, students may consider it premature if clients leave counselling feeling able to cope with immediate problems, but having insufficiently consolidated the relevant mind and communication/action skills for dealing with future problems. Dryden and Feltham (1992) assert that counsellors should respect the right of clients who wish to terminate abruptly to do so and avoid trying to persuade or coerce them to change their minds. When students have developed good collaborative working relationships, you can calmly discuss the advantages and disadvantages of terminating now and still leave the final decision entirely to clients.

There are many 'shadow' reasons why counselling skills students may consciously or unconsciously prolong their contact. Such reasons include appreciative and admiring clients who feed the student's narcissism, and being erotically attracted to clients. Sometimes students and clients establish and maintain patterns of communication that can lengthen the process, for example powerful students breeding passive clients or both parties becoming friends rather than engaging in a professional relationship.

Formats for terminating helping

Often, counselling skills students and clients have limited choice over when to termi-nate. Frequently your contact is deliberately set up to be brief. Other instances where you may not have much choice include when clients leave town, when terms end, and when helping address specific forthcoming situations, such as important examinations or a divorce hearing. On other occasions, students and clients can have more choice about when to terminate. The following are some possible formats for terminating counselling and helping.

- *Fixed termination* Counselling skills students and clients may have contracts that you work for, say, four sessions in one or more problem or **problematic skills** areas. Advantages of fixed termination include lessening the chance of **dependency** and motivating clients to use time to best effect. Potential disadvantages include restricting coverage of problems and insufficient thoroughness in training clients to improve specific skills.
- *Open termination when goals are attained* With open terminations, contact con-cludes when students and clients agree that clients have made sufficient progress in attaining their main goals. Such goals include managing specific problems better and developing improved skills to address current and future problems.
- *Faded termination* Here the **withdrawal** of assistance is gradual. For example, instead of meeting weekly, the final sessions could be at fortnightly or monthly intervals.
- *Terminating with booster session(s)* Booster sessions, say after three months, are not to teach new skills, but to check clients' progress in consolidating skills, moti-vate them, and help them work through difficulties in taking away and using trained skills in their home environments.
- *Scheduling follow-up contact after ending* Counselling skills students can schedule follow-up phone calls or postal and e-mail correspondence with clients. Such phone calls and correspondence perform some of the same functions as booster sessions.

Assisting maintaining change

Issues surrounding maintaining changes in problem situations should not be left to final sessions. Counselling skills students can assist clients to maintain changes during the counselling and helping process by identifying the key mind and communication skills clients need to develop, training thoroughly, and negotiating relevant homework that helps clients to transfer what they have learned inside sessions to problem situations outside.

During counselling and helping, counselling skills students may make statements indicating its finiteness: for instance, comments about the usefulness of homework for developing improved skills for use when contact ends. Such comments may encour-age clients to make the most of their regular sessions and the time between them. You can also introduce the topic of termination with one or more **transition statements** that clearly signal that formal contact is coming to an end. Example 22.1 provides examples of such transition statements.

Example 22.1 Transition statements for terminating counselling and helping

- 'We only have a few more sessions left. Perhaps we should not only discuss an agenda for this session, but think about how best we can spend our remaining time together.'

- 'Our next session is the final session. Would it be all right with you if we spent some time discussing how to help you retain and build on your improved skills for managing your problem?'
- 'Perhaps the agenda for this final session should mainly be how to help you use the skills you've learned here for afterwards. For instance, we can review how much you've changed, where there is still room for improvement, how you might go about it, and **plan** how to deal with any difficult situations you anticipate.'

The main task in terminating is to assist clients to consolidate what they have learned so that they may continue to help themselves afterwards. One method of enhancing consolidation is for either the counselling skills student or client to summarize the main points learned for dealing with problem situations in future. In addition, students and clients can spend time anticipating difficulties and setbacks and develop strategies for dealing with them. Some of these strategies may be focused on communication: for instance, how to seek support during attempts to handle a difficult problem situation better.

Counselling skills students can **stress** the importance of clients understanding that often they can retrieve mistakes and always they can learn from them. Together, students and clients can develop appropriate **self-talk** statements for retrieving lapses and possibly get them written down on reminder cards. Furthermore, you can prevent discouragement by distinguishing between a process success and an outcome success: even though clients have used good skills in a problem situation (a process success), they may not get what they want (an outcome success). Not getting what they want does not negate the fact that they still performed competently and can do so again in future.

In addition, where appropriate, counselling skills students can challenge clients' demanding **rules** that 'change must be easy' and 'maintaining change must be effortless'. You should encourage clients to replace such rules with more **preferential rules** stressing that changing and maintaining change can involve effort, practise and overcoming obstacles. You can also emphasize clients' assuming **personal responsibility** for continuing to cope with their problem situations to the best of their ability.

Self-support is the main way in which clients can receive continuing support. Nevertheless, sometimes it is appropriate for counselling skills students to explore with clients some arrangements for ongoing support. The following are some options.

- *Further contact with the counselling skills students* Possibilities for further contact with students include scheduled booster sessions, follow-up sessions at clients' request, and either scheduled or unscheduled phone calls and e-mails. Students can discuss with clients how they view further contact with you.

- *Referral for further individual counselling* Though clients may have made considerable progress with the problems and problematic skills for which they came for assistance, they may still require further professional assistance. For many reasons counselling skills students may decide to refer such clients to other counsellors: for instance, your time may be limited or another counsellor has special expertise in an emerging problem area.

- *Using outside* **supports** Counselling skills students can encourage clients to view identifying and using supports as a useful **self-helping** skill. One way of using others as support is to encourage them to give honest feedback in non-threatening ways. Such feedback can be either confirmatory, indicating that former clients are on track in using their improved skills, or corrective, informing them that they have wandered off course and need to get back on track (Egan, 2007). Open acknowledgment by others of positive behaviour changes can motivate clients to keep improving their skills.

- *Continued support from aides* During the termination phase, counselling skills students can contact any aides that you have used to receive assessments of clients' progress. You can also work with aides to identify ways in which they can continue supporting clients once counselling or helping ends. Sometimes three-way meetings between students, clients and aides are desirable. For example, at the end of a series of sessions designed to help an elementary school child become more outgoing, teacher, child and counselling skills student might together plan how the teacher could continue supporting the child.

- *Group counselling and training* Some clients might gain from joining groups in which they can practise and develop targeted skills. Peer self-help groups provide an alternative to professionally led groups. Counselling skills students can also discuss opportunities for clients to participate in appropriate courses or workshops.

- *Further reading and audiovisual material* Some clients appreciate the support provided by further reading. Clients can also listen to and watch self-help audiocassettes and videotapes. On your own initiative or by request, counselling skills students can suggest appropriate books, training manuals, audiocassettes and videotapes.

Activity 22.1 Issues in terminating counselling and helping

1 Critically discuss the importance and validity of each of the following considerations for when counselling/helping should terminate:
   - client self-report
   - counsellor/**helper** observations
   - third party feedback
   - attainment of measurable goals
   - other factors not mentioned above.
2 Critically discuss the merits of each of the following formats for terminating counselling/helping:
   - fixed ending decided in the initial session
   - open ending negotiated between client and counsellor/helper.

(Continued)

Activity 22.1 Issues in terminating counselling and helping – cont'd

3 Critically discuss the value of each of the following ways of assisting clients to maintain their improved behaviours:
   · **summarizing** the main learnings
   · anticipating difficulties and setbacks and developing strategies for dealing with them
   · focusing on how clients can think effectively afterwards
   · exploring arrangements for continuing support
   · other ways not mentioned above.

Further termination tasks and skills

In addition to the major task of consolidating improved behaviours, there are other tasks when terminating counselling and helping. How counselling skills students handle them varies with length of contact, the nature of problem(s) and problematic skills, and the counsellor–client relationship.

Dealing with feelings

Clients' feelings when terminating fall into two main categories: feelings about how they are going to fare without counselling skills students and feelings toward students and being helped. Clients may have feelings of ambivalence about how they will cope afterwards. On the one hand, they may feel more competent, yet on the other hand they may still have doubts about their abilities to implement skills. You can facilitate open discussion of clients' feelings about the future. Looking at how best to maintain skills also addresses the issue of clients' lingering doubts. Other clients feel confident that they can cope now on their own, which is hopefully a sign of work well done.

Counselling skills students should allow clients the opportunity to share feelings about their contact with you. You may obtain valuable feedback about both how you come across and clients' reactions to different aspects of the counselling process. You can also humanize terminating by sharing some of your feelings with clients: for instance, 'I enjoyed working with you', or 'I admire the courage with which you face your situation', or 'I'm delighted with your progress.'

Terminating ethically

Counselling skills students should aim to say goodbye in a business-like, yet friendly way, appropriate to professional rather than personal relationships. By ending helping sloppily, you may undo some of your influence in helping clients to maintain their skills.

There are a number of important **ethical issues** surrounding termination. For example, students need to think through their responsibilities to clients afterwards.

Too much support may engender dependency, too little is a failure to carry out professional obligations. Each case must be judged on its merits. Another ethical issue is what you should do when you think clients have other problems on which they need to work. One option is tactfully to bring such views to clients' attention.

A further set of ethical issues surrounds the boundaries between personal and professional relationships. Most professional associations have **ethical codes** about providing counselling and helping services. Counselling skills students who allow personal and professional wires to get crossed when terminating are not only acting unethically, but can make it more difficult for clients to be assisted by either you or conceivably by others, if future need arises.

Evaluating counselling skills

With each client, counselling skills students have many sources of information for evaluating their counselling skills. These sources of information include attendance, intentional and unintentional feedback from clients, **perceptions** of client progress, session notes, possibly videotapes or audiocassettes of sessions, clients' compliance and success in carrying out homework, and feedback from third parties such as supervisors.

Counselling skills students can make a final evaluation of your work with each client soon after terminating regular contact. **Questions** you can ask yourself include: 'To what extent did the client manage her/his problem(s) better and improve her/his skills?', and 'How well did I use the skills for each stage of the Relating–Understanding–Changing model?' If you defer performing such an evaluation for too long, you risk forgetting valuable information. When evaluating your counselling skills you should beware of your characteristic perceiving errors: for example, you may be too hard or too easy on yourself. What you seek is a balanced appraisal of your good and poor skills to guide your work with future clients.

Client self-helping

Where counselling and helping has focused on improving mind skills and communication/action skills to manage current and future problems more successfully, clients should have a reasonable grasp of how to keep using their improved skills, monitor their progress, retrieve lapses and, where possible, integrate their improved skills into their daily lives. The process of consolidating skills in the middle and terminating sessions of counselling can continue when clients are on their own. Since this process is much more likely to continue if clients use good mind skills, some pertinent skills are briefly reviewed.

- *Creating rules* Former clients are more likely to keep using their improved mind and communication/action skills if they can challenge any demanding rules that may weaken their resolve and restate them into preferential rules. In particular, those clients who have worked with counselling skills students on demanding rules are in a strong position to do so. Example 22.2 provides two examples of restating demanding into preferential rules about maintaining improved skills.

Example 22.2 Creating preferential rules about maintaining improved skills

Demanding rule 'Maintaining my improved skills must be easy.'
Preferential rule 'There is no such thing as cure. I need to keep practising my improved skills so that using them may then become easier.'
Demanding rule 'After terminating counselling, I must never go backwards.'
Preferential rule 'Maintaining any skill can involve mistakes, uncertainty, and setbacks. All I can do is to learn from and retrieve mistakes and cope with setbacks as best as possible.'

- *Creating perceptions* Counselling skills students should help clients to perceive their good and poor skills accurately. Clients can discourage themselves if they pay disproportionate attention to setbacks rather than to successes. When lapses occur, former clients can try to avoid the perceiving error of over-generalizing them into relapses: 'Since I have gone back to my old behaviour once, I have permanently relapsed and can do nothing about it.' Lapses should stimulate using retrieval or 'getting back on the track' skills rather than giving up.

- *Creating self-talk* Former clients can use **coping self-talk** to deal with 'hot' thinking connected with temptations such as food, alcohol, drugs, or high-risk sex. As former clients become aware of high-risk situations they can say 'Stop ... think ... calm down' and then instruct themselves on what to do. Further instructions include telling themselves that cravings will pass, engaging in distracting activities or thoughts, and reminding themselves of the benefits of resisting temptation and the costs of giving in.

  When former clients do have lapses they can say to themselves: 'Now is the time for me to use my retrieval skills'. For instance, a former client of mine, who became extremely anxious about performing his golf down-swing correctly, learned to replace his **anxiety** engendering self-talk when his golf ball ended up in awkward situations by telling himself 'No upheaval, just retrieval.' Former clients can also use affirming self-talk to maintain their improved skills. They can encourage themselves with internal rewards like 'Well done', 'I hung in there and made it', and 'I'm happy that I'm maintaining my skills'.

Activity 22.2 Terminating a series of counselling and helping sessions

Work with the same partner with whom you performed Activity 21.2. Again, one student acts as counsellor/helper, another as client, with possibly a third student acting as observer. For the problem situation worked on in Activity 21.2, assume that you are now in your third and final session. Conduct all or part of this final session in which you focus on:

(Continued)

Activity 22.2 Terminating a series of counselling and helping sessions – cont'd

· assisting your client to maintain changes
· terminating counselling/helping smoothly
· saying goodbye.

Afterwards, hold a sharing and feedback discussion. Then, if appropriate, change roles and repeat this activity.

Using audiocassette or videotape recording and playback may add value to the activity.

PART FIVE

FURTHER CONSIDERATIONS

MAIN TASK: To start establishing a collaborative working relationship.

Part Five presents some further considerations. Chapter 23 focuses on relaxation and meditation, while Chapter 24 discusses ways of helping clients to manage crises. Chapter 25 looks at different characteristics that counsellors or helpers and clients may possess, for instance culture and race. Chapter 26 examines some ethical issues and dilemmas, both of counselling and helping and of being a student. Chapter 27 makes some suggestions for running and participating in training groups and supervision. Chapter 28 looks at the main theoretical schools and approaches to counselling and then reviews some research issues. The final chapter gives you some ideas about where to go next in developing your counselling and helping skills and in becoming more human.

23

Relaxation interventions

Counsellors and helpers can train **clients** in muscular and **mental relaxation** skills. Clients may use **relaxation** skills both for managing **feelings** like anger and **anxiety** and for dealing with problems such as **tension** headaches, hypertension and insomnia. Relaxation skills may be used alone or as part of more complex procedures such as systematic desensitization, a helping strategy described in my book *Practical Counselling and Helping Skills* (Nelson-Jones, 2005).

Progressive muscular relaxation

The physical setting where counselling students train should be conducive to relaxation. This involves absence of disruptive noise, interior decoration that is restful, and lighting which may be dimmed. You may teach clients to relax in recliner chairs, or on mattresses or, at the very least, in comfortable upright chairs with headrests.

From the start, counselling students can teach relaxation as a useful skill for daily life. Furthermore, clients should understand that success at learning relaxation, just like success at learning any other skill, requires practise and that they will require relaxation homework. Before starting relaxation, you can suggest that clients wear loose–fitting, comfortable clothing both during interviews and when doing relaxation homework. Furthermore, it is helpful to remove items such as glasses and shoes.

In training muscular relaxation there is a succession of instructions for each muscle group. **Counselling** students can demonstrate how clients should go through a five step tension–relax cycle for each muscle group. These steps are:

1   *Focus* – focus attention on a particular muscle group
2   *Tense* – tense the muscle group
3   *Hold* – maintain the tension for five to seven seconds

4   *Release* – release the tension in the muscle group
5   *Relax* – spend 20 to 30 seconds focusing on letting go of tension and further relax-
    ing the muscle groups.

Clients need to learn this *focus–tense–hold–release–relax* cycle so that they may apply it
in their homework.

Having explained the basic tension–relax cycle, counselling students may then
demonstrate it by going through the cycle in relation to your own right hand and
forearm and at each stage asking clients to do the same. Thus, 'I'm focusing all my
attention on my right hand and forearm and I'd like you to do the same', progresses
to 'I'm clenching my right fist and tensing the muscles in my lower arm ...', then on to
'I'm holding my right fist clenched and keeping the muscles in my lower arm tensed ... ',
followed by 'I'm now releasing as quickly as I can the tension from my right fist and
lower arm ...', ending with 'I'm relaxing my right hand and forearm, letting the tension
go further and further and letting these muscles become more and more relaxed...'.
The final relaxation phase tends to last from 30-to-60 seconds, frequently accompanied
by relaxation 'patter' about letting the tension go and acknowledging and experiencing
feelings of deeper and deeper relaxation as they occur. Having been through the
tension–relax cycle once, especially in the initial sessions you may instruct the client
to go through it again, thus tensing and relaxing each muscle grouping twice.

Counselling students are then likely to take clients through the muscle groups,
demonstrating them as necessary. Box 23.1 shows 16 muscle groups and suggested
tensing instructions. The arms tend to come at the beginning, since they are easy to
demonstrate. For most clients relaxing parts of the face is particularly important
because the most marked anxiety-inhibiting effects are often obtained there.

Box 23.1 Relaxation training muscle groups and tensing instructions

Muscle group	Tensing instructions*
Right hand and forearm	Clench your right fist and tense the muscles in your lower arm.
Right biceps	Bend your right arm at the elbow and flex your biceps by tensing the muscles of your upper right arm.
Left hand and forearm	Clench your left fist and tense the muscles in your lower arm.
Left biceps	Bend your left arm at the elbow and flex your biceps by tensing the muscles of your upper left arm.
Forehead	Lift your eyebrows as high as possible.
Eyes, nose and upper cheeks	Squeeze your eyes tightly shut and wrinkle your nose.
Jaw and lower cheeks	Clench your teeth and pull the corners of your mouth firmly back.

Box 23.1 Relaxation training muscle groups and tensing instructions – cont'd

Muscle group	Tensing instructions*
Neck and throat	Pull your chin down hard towards your chest yet resist having it touch your chest.
Chest and shoulders	Pull your shoulder blades together and take a deep breath.
Stomach	Tighten the muscles in your stomach as though someone was about to hit you there.
Right thigh	Tense the muscles of the right upper leg by pressing the upper muscle down and the lower muscles up.
Right calf	Stretch your right leg and pull your toes towards your head.
Right foot	Point and curl the toes of your right foot and turn it inwards.
Left thigh	Tense the muscles of the left upper leg by pressing the upper muscle down and the lower muscles up.
Left calf	Stretch your left leg and pull your toes towards your head.
Left foot	Point and curl the toes of your left foot and turn it inwards.

* With left-handed people, tensing instructions for the left side of the body should come before those for the right.

Once clients have learned how to tense the various muscle groups, counselling students can instruct them to keep their eyes closed during relaxation training and practice. Towards the end of relaxation sessions, you may ask clients for a summary of their relaxation, along the lines of 'Well, how was your relaxation today?' and discuss any issues that arise. Terminating relaxation sessions may be achieved by your counting from five down to one and when at one, asking your clients to wake up pleasantly relaxed as though from a peaceful sleep.

At the end of the initial relaxation session counselling students can stress the importance of practicing muscular relaxation. You can give clients the homework assignment of practising muscular relaxation for one or two 15–minute periods a day. Ask clients whether they anticipate any obstacles to practising, such as finding a quiet place, and help them to devise strategies for ensuring good homework. You can also either make up cassettes of relaxation instructions that clients can take away for homework purposes or recommend existing relaxation training cassettes. There is some evidence that clients who record details of their relaxation practice are much more likely to continue doing it. Consequently, it may be helpful to give clients logs for **monitoring** their relaxation homework.

Brief muscular relaxation

Brief muscular relaxation skills aim to induce deep relaxation with less time and effort than the 16-muscle group relaxation procedure. When clients are proficient in full **progressive muscular relaxation**, counselling students can introduce such skills. Brief relaxation skills are useful both in counselling and helping sessions and in daily life. The following are two examples.

Sequential brief relaxation

Here, counselling students can first instruct clients and then get them to give themselves the following instructions focused on tensing and relaxing in turn four composite muscle groupings.

> 'I'm going to count to ten in units of two. After each unit of two I will instruct you to tense and relax a muscle grouping. One, two... focus on your leg and feet muscles... tense and hold the tension in these muscles for five seconds... release... relax and enjoy the sensations of the tension flowing from your legs and feet. Three, four... take a deep breath and focus on your chest, shoulder and stomach muscles... tense and hold the tension in these muscles for five seconds... release... relax and enjoy the sensations of the tension flowing from your chest, shoulders and stomach. Five, six... focus on your face, neck and head muscles... tense and hold the tension in these muscles for five seconds... release... relax and enjoy the sensations of the tension flowing from your face, neck and head. Seven, eight... focus on your arm and hand muscles... tense and hold the tension in these muscles for five seconds... release... relax and enjoy the sensations of the tension flowing from your arms and hands. Nine, ten... focus on all the muscles in your body... tense all the muscles in your body together and hold for five seconds... release... relax and enjoy the sensations of the tension leaving your whole body as your relaxation gets deeper and deeper... deeper and deeper... deeper and deeper.'

Simultaneous brief relaxation

As at the end of the previous example, counselling students can instruct clients to tense all muscle groupings simultaneously. You can say:

> 'When I give the signal, I would like you to close your eyes very tightly, take a deep breath and simultaneously tense your arm muscles, your face, neck and throat muscles, your chest, shoulder and stomach muscles, and your leg and foot muscles. Now take a deep breath and tense all your muscles... hold for five seconds... now release and relax as quickly and deeply as you can.'

Mental relaxation

Counselling students can assist clients to identify one or more favourite scenes conducive to feeling relaxed. Often clients visualize such restful scenes at the end of progressive muscular relaxation. The following is an example of instructing a client to mentally relax.

'You're lying on an empty beach on a pleasant, sunny day, enjoying the sensations of warmth on your body. There is a gentle breeze. You can hear the peaceful noise of the sea steadily lapping against the nearby shore. You haven't a care in the world, and you enjoy your feelings of peace and calm, peace and calm, peace and calm and your feelings of relaxation and well-being.'

Clients can visualize mental relaxation scenes independent of muscular relaxation. In addition, clients can use the 'counting to ten in groups of two' as a mental relaxation rather than as a muscular relaxation procedure. For example: 'One, two … focus on your leg and feet muscles … relax and enjoy the sensations of the tension flowing from your legs and feet.' As a mental relaxation procedure, clients edit out the tense, hold and release instructions.

Using coaching, demonstrating and rehearsing, counselling students can train clients to develop mental relaxation procedures as **self-helping** skills. Clients may wish to record their self-instructions for playback outside of helping sessions.

Mindfulness of breathing

Increasingly in Western **psychology**, there is a growing emphasis on meditation practices (Walsh and Shapiro, 2006). The Buddhist tradition has over the past 2500 years concerned itself with cultivating positive states of mental well-being as well as with treating problems of the **mind** (Wallace and Shapiro, 2006). Focusing attention on breathing is possibly the most universal of meditative practices in the world and is also the starting point of Buddhist mind training (Thitavanno, 2002).

Some counsellors and helpers may wish to train clients in **mindfulness of breathing**. In Eastern countries, the lotus posture with fully crossed legs is most commonly adopted for breathing meditation. Westerners not wanting to use this position can sit upright in a relatively comfortable chair with their legs slightly apart and feet firmly placed on the floor. The hands of those meditating are usually cupped on their laps, most usually with the left hand being placed palm up below the right, which is also palm up. Alternatively, the hands may be placed face down on the knees. When attending to their breathing, clients may close their eyes to prevent the mind being distracted by what is seen. Some people, however, when focusing on breathing for extended periods of time prefer to keep their eyes slightly open to avoid drowsiness. One option here is to focus on the tip of your nose and attempt to be oblivious to all other things.

Counselling students can teach clients that the main task in mindfulness of breathing is to concentrate on the natural flow of the breath – breathing in, breathing out, breathing in, breathing out and so on – to establish concentrated **awareness**. The nose is the starting point of the in-breath, the chest the middle, and the abdomen the end. While breathing out, the reverse is the case. Those engaging in mindfulness of breathing can follow the process of their breaths through these stages of breathing in and breathing out. Either after or instead of doing this, clients can establish a check point, with the nose-tip being most recommended, and fix their attention there where the breaths are sure to pass in and out. One variation on mindfulness of breathing is to accompany each out-breath by gently and sub-vocally saying 'calm' to yourself. Another variation is to accompany successive in-breaths by quietly and sub-vocally counting from one to nine, then down to one, then up again to nine, and so on.

When starting to learn mindfulness of breathing and even when more experienced in it, people's minds meander into extraneous thoughts or fantasies, be they past, present or future. On such occasions, counselling students can teach clients gently to bring their minds back to focusing on their next breath. They should not worry if they repeatedly have to bring themselves back to being aware of their breathing. Analogies that are sometimes used for training in mindfulness of breathing are those of training a puppy or a calf. At the end of a mindfulness of breathing session, clients who have closed their eyes should gently reopen them.

Relaxation training considerations

Counsellors and helpers differ in the number of sessions they use for relaxation training. Furthermore, clients differ in the speed with which they attain a capacity to relax. The late Dr Joseph Wolpe, a noted pioneer of **behaviour therapy**, taught progressive muscular relaxation in about six lessons and asked his patients to practise at home for two 15-minute sessions per day (Wolpe, 1990). He considered that it was crucial for clients to realize that the aim of relaxation training was not muscle control per se, but emotional calmness. Counselling students may vary training in a relaxation timetable according to clients' needs and your own workload. Nevertheless, it is important that clients have sufficient sessions to learn relaxation adequately. Furthermore, clients need to practise their relaxation skills diligently and review progress with those helping them. In addition, many clients can gain from integrating relaxation skills into their daily lives.

Activity 23.1 Training a client in relaxation

Conduct a helping session in which partner A's task is to train partner B, who acts as a client in progressive muscular relaxation skills. During the session partner A:
(a) offers reasons for using progressive muscular relaxation;
(b) provides a live demonstration of tensing and relaxing the first muscle grouping in Box 23.1;
(c) makes up a progressive muscular relaxation cassette as she or he relaxes partner B using the five step tension–relax;
(d) presents a mental relaxation scene at the end of the muscular relaxation;
(e) checks how relaxed the client became and provides further relaxation instructions for any muscle group where she or he still feels tense
(f) negotiates a progressive muscular and mental relaxation homework practice assignment with the client.
Afterwards, both partners hold a sharing and discussion session and, if feasible, reverse roles.

24

Managing crises

CHAPTER OUTCOMES

By studying and doing the activity in this chapter you should:
- know when clients are in crisis; and
- possess some skills for managing clients in crisis.

Though **counselling** and helping students should not at first be faced with **clients** in crisis, this cannot be guaranteed. Often the fact that clients are in crisis becomes apparent at the start of initial sessions, but this is not always the case. In crisis counselling and helping, you are faced with making immediate choices to help clients get through their sense of being overwhelmed. Some of these choices may also help clients to manage better any underlying problems contributing to the crisis.

Defining crises

Crises may be defined as situations of excessive **stress**. Stress tends to have a negative connotation in our culture. This is unjustified if you think of stress in terms of challenges in life. Each person has an optimum stress level or a particular level of stimulation at which they feel comfortable. At this level they may experience what Selye terms 'stress without distress' (Selye, 1974). Beneath this level they may feel insufficiently stimulated and bored. Above this level they are likely to experience physiological and psychological distress. If the heightened stress is prolonged or perceived as extremely severe, clients may feel that their **coping** resources are inadequate to meet the demands being made upon them. In such circumstances they are in situations of excessive stress or are in states of crisis.

This section, on handling crises, relates mainly to clients who are in fairly acute states of distress. At this juncture clients may be experiencing heightened or maladaptive reactions in a number of different, though interrelated, areas.

Physical reactions

Physical reactions may include hypertension and proneness to such things as heart attacks and gastric ulcers. The weakest parts of different clients' bodies tend to be most adversely affected by stress.

Feelings

The **feelings** associated with excessive stress include shock, depression, frustration, anger, **anxiety**, disorientation and fears of nervous breakdown or insanity.

Thoughts

Some of the main thoughts associated with excessive stress are that clients are powerless to make a positive impact on their situations, that things are getting out of control, and thoughts associated with despair and lack of hope for the future. The notion of excessive stress can imply that clients' thought processes have become somewhat irrational. They think ineffectively: for example, with **tunnel vision** involving focusing on only a few factors in a situation.

Communication/actions

Avoidance and over-activity are two of the main ways in which clients handle excessive stress. Their behaviour may range from giving up and not making an effort to rigid, repetitive and frenetic attempts to deal with their problems. Violence, turned either outwards or self-inflicted, is more likely at times of excessive stress than when clients' stress levels are lower.

It is very important that counselling and helping students realize that crises, however large or small they may appear from outsiders' frames of reference, tend to seem overwhelming from insiders' frames of reference. Some crises simmer in the background for a long time and suddenly erupt, whereas others are more clearly a reaction to an immediate precipitating event, for instance a bereavement or loss of a job. Perhaps many stressful situations only really turn into psychological crises at the point where clients feel that their efforts to adapt and cope are totally insufficient. There are numerous situations which may cause clients to feel that they are at the limit of their coping resources, though there are wide differences in people's abilities to tolerate these various stressors. Resilience in the face of stress depends partly on personal resources and **skills**. However, it may also be heavily influenced by the amount of family, social and community support available.

Guidelines for crisis counselling and helping

Crises for clients can be crises for counselling and helping students too. You may feel under great pressure to relieve clients' distress at the same time as being threatened by the strength of their emotions. Below are suggested some guidelines for crisis counselling and helping.

Be prepared

Counselling and helping students responsible for clients can relieve much of stress if it is realized that, since these events are likely to be part of any **counsellor** or

helper's life, it is best to be prepared. One means of preparing is to ensure that you can quickly mobilize a good support system: for example, a competent physician or a bed in a psychiatric hospital. You can also prepare for crises by being clear about the limit of your responsibility for clients.

Act calmly

Even though it may seem a limitation on being genuine, it is important that counselling and helping students act calmly. You should not add your anxieties to clients' agitation and distress. Responding in warm yet firm and measured ways may both give clients the security of feeling helped by a strong person and also calm their heightened emotions.

Listen and observe

A main reason that stressful situations become crises for many clients is that they feel that they have no one to whom they can turn who will listen to and understand their difficulties. Clients may become calmer and feel less isolated and despairing simply by being able to share their problems and air the related emotions with you. Catharsis is another word for this process of letting out pent-up feelings. **Listening**, observing and empathic responding can help you to understand clients' worlds as well as contributing to their feelings of being heard and accepted.

Assess severity and risk of damage to self and to others

One area of assessing severity concerns the degree to which clients are in contact with reality. Assessing risk may also mean assessing the damage clients may do to other people. However, it is more likely to involve assessing the damage that clients may do to themselves, including committing suicide. A high proportion of suicidal people talk about the possibility before making any attempt. Counselling and helping students need to be sensitive at picking up cries for help and not allowing anxiety to interfere with listening skills. Suicidal people are often ambivalent about doing it. A caring question about whether or not they are suicidal may be very appropriate. Avoidance or dealing with the topic indirectly may sometimes increase rather than diminish risk.

Assess clients' strengths and coping skills

Counselling and helping students can both assess and help clients to explore and assess their **strengths** and coping skills. Often in crises clients are so overwhelmed by negative thinking that they allow themselves to forget their strengths. While not advocating superficial reassurance, the following remarks may be helpful to certain clients in some situations: 'Well, we've explored your problems in some detail. I'm now wondering whether you feel that you have any strengths or resources for dealing with them?', 'You've been telling me a lot about negative aspects of your life. Can you tell me if there are any positive aspects as well?' and 'As you talk you seem to be facing your problems very much on your own. I'm wondering whether there are any friends, relatives or other people who might be available to offer you some support.'

Assist exploration and clarification of problem(s)

Clients in crises have often lost perspective on themselves and their problems. One reason for this is that crises involve very intense feelings. Until some progress is made in dealing with relieving the intensity of feelings, clients may have insufficient ability to be rational about the factors generating their strong emotions. Skills that you can use during the work of exploring and clarifying problems are likely to include empathic responding, use of **questions**, **summarizing**, and **challenging** any distortions in clients' thinking that make their lives seem hopeless.

Assist problem-management and planning

A primary emphasis in crisis counselling is to help clients regain some sense of control over their lives. For some clients the opportunity to talk with an understanding person may give them enough confidence in their ability to cope with life to move out of the danger zone. With other clients, a counselling and helping student's role will include helping them to develop strategies for coping with their immediate distress and, where appropriate, initiating ways and skills for dealing with their longer-term problems. If clients are at any risk, **plans** for coping with immediate situations should be formulated as specifically as possible. For example: 'We have agreed that you will stay at your sister's tonight and that we will meet at 11 am tomorrow. Do you think there is any reason why you cannot do this?'

Assisting problem-management and planning may involve mobilizing additional resources, who may be either professional helpers, such as doctors and priests, or friends and relatives. In some instances it is best for clients to take responsibility for making contact, but not invariably. You always need to assess what is in clients' best interests and, at highly vulnerable times in their lives, act accordingly.

Be specific about availability

Part of a crisis management plan with certain clients may be to give them the security of another appointment with you in the near future. In addition, attention needs to be paid to the matter of between-session contact. If such contact seems appropriate, a counselling and helping student can say something along the lines of 'If you feel you need me in an emergency, please don't hesitate to get in touch with me either here or on my mobile phone. The numbers are_____.' In most instances clients will not get in touch until the next session. However, your willingness to be contacted can reassure distressed clients.

Apparently the Chinese use two symbols for the concept of crisis: one for danger and another for opportunity. Crises can be the impetus for certain clients to work hard on problems that have been simmering in the past, yet which have to date not been properly confronted. At best, crises can give both counselling and helping student and client the opportunity to form an effective relationship. Such relationships can provide the basis for clients to develop confidence and skills either to prevent or to cope better with future crises.

Activity 24.1 Crisis counselling and helping skills

1 Identify, with regard to your present or future counselling and helping work, the kinds of stressors that bring or may in future bring clients in crisis to see you.
2 Counsel or help a partner, who role plays a client in crisis. Inasmuch as possible, keep in mind the following guidelines:
  · act calmly
  · listen and observe
  · assess severity and risk of damage to self and others
  · assess client strengths and coping skills
  · assist exploring and clarifying problems
  · assist problem-management and planning
  · be specific about your availability.
Afterwards, discuss and reverse roles.

25

Diversity in counselling and helping

CHAPTER OUTCOMES

By studying and doing the activities in this chapter you should:
- know about some of the many personal characteristics of counselling and helping skills students and clients; and
- get some idea of how counselling and helping may be affected by these characteristics.

Counselling and helping **skills** students and **clients** bring numerous personal characteristics into contact with one another. For example, each of you has a life history of varying degrees of happiness and suffering. In addition, each of you has differing levels of poor and good **mind skills** and **communication/action** skills for **coping** with the problems and opportunities in their lives.

Over the past 60 years, there has been a growing interest in **diversity**-sensitive counselling and helping (Moodley, 2007). All students and clients possess and bring a mixture of different characteristics to the counselling and **helping relationships**. You also possess **perceptions** and evaluations of these different characteristics in yourselves and others. There is no such thing as perfect counsellor–client matching, though there may be important and often desirable similarities, for example regarding culture or race. Box 25.1 indicates just some of the many areas of diversity in the practice of counselling and helping. Each of these areas is now discussed in turn.

Box 25.1 Eleven areas of diversity in counselling and helping

1 *Culture* Ancestral origins in either the mainstream or in a minority group culture and, if the latter, one's degree of acculturation.
2 *Race* Possessing distinctive physical characteristics according to a racial sub-grouping or being of mixed race.
3 *Social class* Differences attached to such matters as income, educational attainment or occupational status.
4 *Biological sex* Female or male.
5 *Gender-role identity* Differences in **feelings**, thoughts and behaviour according to the social classification of attributes as 'feminine' or 'masculine'.

(Continued)

Box 25.1 Eleven areas of diversity in counselling and helping – cont'd

6 *Marital status* Single, cohabiting, married, separated, divorced, remarried, or widowed.

7 *Sexual and affectionate orientation* Heterosexual, lesbian, **gay** or bisexual.

8 *Physical disability* A deficiency in the structure or functioning of some part of the body.

9 *Age* Childhood, adolescence, young adulthood, middle age, late middle age, old age.

10 *Values* Principles that guide one's life: for instance, survival, love, friendship and achievement.

11 *Religion or philosophy* Christian, Hindu, Muslim, Buddhist or some other religious or secular belief system.

Culture

Culture can be defined as a patterned system of tradition-derived norms influencing behaviour. Cultural norms are processes in a constant state of flux. Furthermore, there can be numerous sub-cultures within an overall mainstream culture. Culture encompasses thoughts, communications, actions, customs, beliefs, values and institutions. A colloquial definition of culture is 'the way we do things here.'

Some indication of the importance of culture to contemporary counselling and helping can be found in the demographic statistics of various countries. Demography is the study of population sizes, movements and trends, including those concerning ethnic minorities. In June 2005 the total population of the United Kingdom numbered 60.2 million people (Thurman, 2006). In 1999/2000, Caucasians formed 93.3 per cent of the total population. The overall ethnic minority population, comprising both those born abroad and those born in the UK, was estimated to have been 6.7 per cent or about 1 in 15 of the total population, up from 5.8 per cent or about 1 in 18 in 1995/96. In 1999/2000, the four largest ethnic minority groups were Indian, 1.7 per cent, Pakistani, 1.2 per cent, Black-Caribbean, 0.9 per cent, and Black African, 0.7 per cent (Tyrrell, 2001).

Australia is one of the most multicultural and, increasingly, multiracial countries in the world. Australia's population has grown more than five-fold since the beginning of the twentieth century, from 3.77 million to 20.6 million in 2006 (Australian Bureau of Statistics, 2006). Since the end of World War II, the proportion of the population born overseas increased from 10 to 24 per cent. Of the migrants from different countries of origin who settled in Australia between 1947 and 1999, 29 per cent were from Britain and Ireland, 22 per cent were from Eastern and Southern Europe, and 21 per cent were from Asia (Price, 2000). There has been a shift in migration patterns in favour of Asia: for example, in 1995–96, nearly 40 per cent of arrivals were Asian born (Department of Immigration and Multicultural Affairs, 1997). In the 1996 Australian census, 352,970 people identified themselves as of Aboriginal and Torres Strait Islander descent.

The United States of America has a long history of multicultural diversity. The 2000 Census showed that the United States population was 281.4 million (US Census Bureau, 2001/2002). Though the majority of the population is still white, these white people have their ancestry in numerous countries. Of the United States population, 12.9 per cent reported themselves as Black or African American, of whom 12.3 per cent reported themselves as only Black. There were 12.5 per cent reporting as Hispanic, of whom over 7 per cent were of Mexican origin, between 1 and 2 per cent were Puerto Rican and under 1 per cent Cuban. The Asian population was 4.2 per cent, with 3.6 per cent reporting themselves as only Asian. The American Indian and Alaska Native population was 1.5 per cent, with less than half this number claiming that they were exclusively American Indian or Alaska Native. The Native Hawaiian and other Pacific Islander population was 0.3 per cent, again with less than half these people claiming that they were only Native Hawaiian or Pacific Islander. Currently, people of colour constitute over 30 per cent of the US population. Projections indicate that they will constitute a numerical majority sometime between 2030 and 2050 (Sue and Sue, 2003).

Sometimes in the literature the **goals** of multicultural counselling and helping are simplified to that of how best to assist minority group members when faced with a hostile majority group culture. In reality, multicultural counselling and helping is a much more complex and varied endeavour. Box 25.2 presents some goals, which may overlap, for working with clients for whom cultural issues play an important part.

Box 25.2 Ten goals for multicultural counselling and helping

1 *Support* Providing culture-sensitive support when migrants first arrive in their new home countries.

2 *Dealing with post-traumatic* **stress** Offering specialized counselling for migrants suffering from post-traumatic stress disorders caused by their previous home country and refugee experiences.

3 *Acculturation and assimilation* Assisting clients to deal with the practical and psychological challenges of adjusting to a new country and culture.

4 *Coping with racism* Providing clients with support and skills to deal with the inner wounds and outer circumstances of racism.

5 *Handling cross-cultural relationships* Assisting clients with intergenerational and cross-cultural difficulties, for example value conflicts between migrant parents and their children and negotiating differences in cross-cultural intimate relationships.

6 *Minority group consciousness raising and liberation* Assisting clients to take pride in their culture and race and to liberate themselves from internalized negative stereotypes.

7 *Majority group consciousness raising and liberation* Assisting mainstream culture clients to relinquish negative aspects of their enculturation, such as a false sense of cultural and racial superiority.

(Continued)

Box 25.2 Ten goals for multicultural counselling and helping – cont'd

8 *Avoiding further marginalization* Resisting colluding when some minority group clients further marginalize themselves by unfairly 'demonizing' their host cultures at the same time as doing little positive to change their situations.

9 *Attaining higher levels of development* Assisting clients to grow psychologically beyond the average for their culture. Visions of higher levels of development can differ by culture and also transcend culture in that they espouse universal values.

10 *Creating the good society* Developing formal and informal norms within societies that are synergistic rather than antagonistic to developing the full human potential of all their members.

Counselling and helping skills students and clients can come from different cultures and be at differing levels of assimilation to the mainstream culture. Even if you both come from the mainstream culture you may have differing levels of adaptation or rejection of its main **rules** and conventions. Students and clients who are native-born of migrant parents may experience split loyalties between the pull of parental cultures and personal wishes to assimilate into mainstream culture.

Counselling and helping students and clients who are migrants may experience differing levels of repulsion and attraction both to your previous and new home cultures. Migrants always carry around part of their previous cultures in their hearts and heads. Some migrants are never really happy in their host countries. However, migrants idealizing previous cultures can get a rude awakening when they go home for the first time.

In addition to the cultures that students and clients bring, you each have differing experiences of how accepted you have been within your own and other cultures. Some will have been fortunate enough to have cultural differences accepted and cherished, while others will have received feedback that your cultures are inferior.

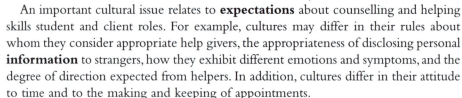

An important cultural issue relates to **expectations** about counselling and helping skills student and client roles. For example, cultures may differ in their rules about whom they consider appropriate help givers, the appropriateness of disclosing personal **information** to strangers, how they exhibit different emotions and symptoms, and the degree of direction expected from helpers. In addition, cultures differ in their attitude to time and to the making and keeping of appointments.

Race

As shown in Box 25.2, racism and multiculturalism can overlap. Counselling and helping skills students and clients may come from different races: for instance, you may be Caucasian, Aboriginal, Asian, Polynesean, African or of mixed race. Whereas cultural differences can be subtle, racial differences are readily observable. Both students and clients may have experienced or be experiencing racial discrimination in relation to the majority white host culture. Furthermore, sometimes those from majority cultures can feel suspicion and hostility when venturing into minority cultures. The idea of racially matching counsellors and clients (Black with Black, Asian with Asian etc.) is not universally supported. However, many relationships between students and clients who are of different races involve **working through** and moving beyond racial stereo-types. In multiracial societies, it is important that counselling and helping skills students possess race-sensitive as well as culture-sensitive **counselling skills**: for instance, clients may appreciate permission to share their views on the role of race in their lives and in the counselling and helping relationship.

Social class

Despite increasing flexibility, social class is still a big issue in Britain and, to a lesser extent, in Australia and the United States. Income, educational attainment and occupational status are currently three of the main measures of social class in Western countries. Other indicators include schooling, accent, clothing, manners, nature of social networks, and type and location of housing.

Counselling and helping skills students and clients bring social class into relationships. You also bring your sensitivity to the effects of others' social class on you and your social class on others. If insufficiently skilled, social class considerations may create unnecessary barriers to establishing effective **counselling relationships**. If you possess feelings of either inferiority or superiority on account of your social class, you should strive to eliminate them. Furthermore, you should attempt to use language appropriate to your client group. Being effective is difficult enough without the intrusion of avoidable social class agendas.

Biological sex

Counselling and helping skills students and clients bring biological sex to relation-ships. In most formal counselling settings, women outnumber men both as helpers and clients. This may be less the case in settings where counselling skills get used as part of other primary roles. In such instances the sex ratio of helpers and clients may more reflect that of the working context, be it educational, health or business. Whether the counselling or helping relationship exists between people of the same sex or of different sexes is likely to influence the quantity and quality of the communication within it, but this may be for better or worse depending on those involved.

Gender-role identity

As well as sometimes referring to biological sex, gender also refers to the social and cultural classification of attributes and behaviours as 'masculine' and 'feminine'. Counselling and helping skills students and clients bring gender or sex-role identities to the relationship – how you view yourselves and one another on the dimensions of 'masculinity' and 'femininity' and the importance that you attach to these constructs. You and your clients can be categorized according to the importance you attach to gender issues: for instance, to what extent and in what ways you are advocates for women's or men's issues.

Gender-role expectations can permeate counselling and helping in a number of ways. Clients may be assessed differently according to whether they fit into traditional gender roles. Counselling and helping skills students may possess inflexible and sexist assumptions for appropriate behaviour in dating, marital and partner relationships, and parenting. Your attitudes to sexual harassment, rape and domestic psychological and physical violence may be sexist. You may also possess unexamined sexist assumptions about the place of males and females in the home or workforce and about jobs and careers appropriate for each sex. In addition, you may engage in simplistic over-generalizations about the characteristics of males and females and insufficiently acknowledge within-group differences.

Marital status

Though especially among younger people, there is a trend towards people cohabiting outside of marriage, by far the most adults in Western countries still get married. In 2004, the number of marriages in England and Wales rose for the fourth year running to 271,000, an increase of 2 per cent compared with 2003 (Gask, 2006). People appear to be marrying older. For instance in England and Wales, only 16 per cent of single men who married in 2000 were aged under 25, compared with 38 percent in 1990, with the corresponding proportions for single women being 30 and 57 per cent respectively (Office for National Statistics, 2002). In many instances where counselling and helping skills students use counselling skills as parts of other primary roles, your marital status is likely to be considered irrelevant by yourselves and by your clients. However, when students assist clients in improving their intimate relationships, marital status is an issue for some clients. In 2004 the proportion of divorced people in England and Wales was 8.9 per cent of the adult population (i.e., those aged 16 or over) compared with 6.5 per cent in 1991 (Gask, 2006).

Also related to marital status and divorce is the number of one-parent families and dependent children living in them. For example, the number of one-parent families in Great Britain in 2000 was provisionally estimated at 1 in 4 of all families with dependent children, up from 1 in 7 in 1986, and from 1 in 5 in 1991. In 2000, 23 per cent of all dependent children lived in one-parent families. Children in single lone mother families where the mother had never married formed 1 in 11 of all dependent children (Haskey, 2002).

Sexual and affectionate orientation

Counselling and helping skills students and clients bring sexual orientation to relationships, whether you are heterosexual, lesbian, **gay** or bisexual. The term 'sexual orientation' gets preferred here to sexual preference. Many, if not most, predominantly lesbian and gay people's sexual orientation is a fact of life, based on genetics and significant learning experiences, rather than a preference, based on free choice. Sometimes the term 'affectionate orientation' is now used as a way of acknowledging that in same sex relationships, as in opposite sex ones, there are many other aspects than the sexual.

Students and clients not only bring sexual and affectionate orientation to counselling and helping relationships, you bring your thoughts and feelings about your own and other people's sexual orientation too. Lesbian, gay and bisexual counsellors and clients may be at varying levels of acceptance of your own and other people's homosexuality. You may have to deal with the issues that affect heterosexuals as well as need to cope with stigmatization, family rejection, oppression, sexual identity issues, and internalized societal homophobia (Goldfried, 2001). In addition, lesbian and gay clients may wonder about the sexual orientation and attitudes of counselling and helping skills students and have fears about being accepted.

Probably few counselling and helping skills students are openly homophobic, but many may in varying degrees be heterosexist. By heterosexist, it is meant that either knowingly or unknowingly such students assume the superiority of demonstrating affection towards members of the opposite sex. On the other hand, some lesbian and gay students may have difficulty working with repressed heterosexuality or the openly heterosexual components of bisexual clients. Wittingly or unwittingly, such students may seek to influence such clients into lesbian and gay moulds.

Physical disability

Either the counselling and helping skills student or the client or both may be physically disabled in some way. Many people have mobility, hearing, sight and other impairments. Sometimes these impairments are genetic and on other occasions result from life events, such as industrial or car accidents or military service. Students and clients are likely to have thoughts and feelings about your own and one another's disabilities. Furthermore, some students may rightly feel inadequately skilled to work with certain physically disabled clients.

Being a physically disabled counselling and helping skills student raises numerous issues, many of which depend on the nature of the disability. All physically disabled people have to deal with their physical restrictions. Many physically disabled counsellors have become calmer and stronger people when they have successfully navigated the emotional ramifications of their disabilities. Often, physically disabled people can be very effective counsellors with the non-physically disabled. In addition, they may have added insights into the challenges faced by physically disabled clients.

Sometimes counselling and helping skills students, whether physically disabled or not, may be under pressure to change the nature of the relationship because of other agendas connected with disabled clients: for example, pressure from insurers or workers compensation boards for brief helping or to write reports about clients. Though very much a minority, some disabled clients may allow financial claim considerations to sabotage the integrity of their counselling relationships.

Age

One aspect of age that is changing is that of life expectancy. For example, in Australia boys and girls born at the beginning of the twentieth century could be expected to live for 55 and 59 years respectively, while those born a hundred years later can expect to live to 76 and 82 years respectively. However, life expectancy for indigenous Australians is around 20 years lower than for the total population. During the twentieth century, the age at which over half the people were older increased by over 12 years, from 22.6 to 35.2 years and the Australian Bureau of Statistics suggests that by the year 2051 this 'median' age will increase by another 8 to 11 years. The age profile of the country no longer represents a pyramid, with progressively less people at middle ages. This trend is likely to continue to include a higher proportion of older people as well (Weston, Qu and Soriano, 2001). Life expectancy is also increasing in the United Kingdom and the United States. This change has many challenges for counselling and helping, including paying more attention to the needs of older people.

Immediately counselling and helping skills students and clients meet for the first time assumptions are made about and connected with one another's age. **Assessment** of age can be a starting point for other thoughts and feelings about yourselves and one another. For example, young students may perceive yourselves as being out of your depth with older clients due to insufficient life experience. Young clients may fear that older students will be unable to understand them on account of the generation or, possibly, generations gap.

Age is partly a physical concept, but it is also an attitude of **mind**. Older people can be psychologically alive and vibrant, whereas some young people are mentally rigid. In addition, how counselling and helping skills students and clients communicate can reinforce or dispel assumptions based on physical age. For example, youthful students can communicate in calm and comfortable ways that reassure older clients, while older students can show understanding of young clients' culture and aspirations.

Values

Values are principles that guide your life. Values influence how counselling and helping skills students and clients work with each other. Furthermore, students may be subject to value conflicts both within your own and between your clients' values.

A prominent measure of Western values is the Rokeach value survey (Rokeach, 1967). Rokeach saw values as conceptions of the desirable means and ends of action. The Rokeach value survey distinguishes between terminal values, or the ultimate end goals of existence, and instrumental values, or the behavioural means for achieving such end goals. Between 1968 and 1981, American terminal values were highly stable. In 1981 the six most highly ranked terminal values were: a world at peace, family security, freedom, happiness, self-esteem and wisdom. Rokeach last surveyed American instrumental values in 1971, when the six most highly ranked values were of being: honest, ambitious, responsible, forgiving, broad-minded and courageous (Rokeach and Ball-Rokeach, 1989).

Schwartz is another prominent researcher in the area of values (Schwartz, 1992; Schwartz and Bilsky, 1990). Schwartz classified values into 10 types: power, achievement, hedonism, stimulation, self-direction, universalism, benevolence, tradition, conformity and security. Based on information from 20 countries in six continents, Schwartz (1992) confirmed each of the 10 values was found in at least 90 per cent of the countries he surveyed, suggesting that his value types are near universal.

Using the Schwartz Universal Values Questionnaire (Schwartz, 1992), Kelly (1995) surveyed a national sample of nearly 500 American counsellors. Items were rated on a nine-point scale from –1 (opposed to my values) to 7 (of extreme importance), with the middle score of 3 (important). The average scores of the value items within each type were: benevolence, 5.3; self-direction, 5.1; universalism, 4.9; achievement, 4.6, hedonism, 4.1; security, 4.1; conformity, 4.1; stimulation, 3.6; tradition, 3.2; and power, 2.1. Similar information is not available for British and Australian counsellors.

Counselling and helping skills students can view yourselves as possessing a profile of values or guiding principles for your lives. This profile is composed of your values and the importance that you attach to each. Students also bring your value conflicts to counselling and helping. For instance, you may feel conflicted about wanting to help others and at the same time charging fees. Furthermore, you can experience many value conflicts similar to those of clients: for instance between home and career and between religious teachings and liberal-pragmatic values, for example regarding abortion.

The values that students bring to counselling and helping may put you in conflict with clients. Sexual behaviour constitutes a potential area of value conflict. For instance, student and client may have different attitudes toward pre-marital sex, extra-marital sex, casual sex, group sex, teenage sex, and homosexuality. For Catholic students, issues of contraception, abortion, divorce and intentional single parenting can create value conflicts. Value conflicts are not restricted to personal counselling. For instance, in academic counselling, how might a student feel about clients consciously choosing not trying to work hard when their parents sacrifice to keep them in college? In vocational counselling, how might a student feel about clients drawing unemployment benefits for as long as possible?

Religion or philosophy

Counselling and helping skills students bring religious beliefs, spiritual yearnings and **explanations** of the meaning of life to relationships. Such beliefs can be sources of strength. For example, in Western cultures, many students are strongly motivated by the Christian concept of *agape* or unselfish love. Furthermore, sharing the same religious beliefs as clients can strengthen a collaborative working relationship.

Students vary in ability to develop relationships with clients whose attitudes towards religion and spirituality differ from their own. An issue for religious students is the extent to which the explicit values and teachings of your church influence how you work. For instance, Roman Catholic counselling skills students may face value conflicts with clients in areas such as divorce, contraception, abortion and pre-marital or lesbian and gay sex.

Eleven key characteristics that counselling and helping skills students and clients bring to contacts and relationships have been reviewed. Student and client personal characteristics come in different permutations and combinations. No counselling relationship exists in a vacuum. You require sensitivity to the effect that your own and your clients' personal characteristics have on how you communicate and on how you can best develop your counselling and helping relationships. You also need to be realistic about your limitations and be prepared to refer clients to others who might understand their special circumstances better.

Activity 25.1 Influences of diversity

To what extent and in what ways do you think that each of the following characteristics may influence how you work as a counsellor/helper?

Culture
a) clients similar to me
b) clients different from me

Sexual and affectionate orientation
a) clients similar to me
b) clients different from me

Race
a) clients similar to me
b) clients different from me

Physical disability
a) clients similar to me
b) clients different from me

Social class
a) clients similar to me
b) clients different from me

Age
a) clients similar to me
b) clients different from me

Biological sex
a) clients similar to me
b) clients different from me

Values
a) clients similar to me
b) clients different from me

Gender-role identity
a) clients similar to me
b) clients different from me

Religion or philosophy
a) clients similar to me
b) clients different from me

Marital status
a) clients similar to me
b) clients different from me

Other characteristics (specify)
a) clients similar to me
b) clients different from me

Summarize what are the most important issues of diversity that either influence or are likely to influence how you work as a counsellor/helper.

Activity 25.2 Experiencing diversity in relationships for good or ill

Look at the list of diversity characteristics in Activity 25.1.
1 For at least one of the characteristics, give an example from your experience of the good use of power or influence in either a counselling relationship or another kind of helping relationship involving the characteristic.
2 For at least one of the characteristics, give an example from your experience of the misuse of power or influence in either a counselling relationship or another kind of helping relationship involving the characteristic.

26

Ethical issues and dilemmas

CHAPTER OUTCOMES

By studying and doing the activities in this chapter you should:
- know about some key ethical issues in counselling and helping;
- possess some basic knowledge about codes of ethics and practice;
- possess insight into the process of decision making for ethical dilemmas; and
- understand some ethical issues and dilemmas for students on introductory counselling and helping skills training courses.

Ethics are **rules** of conduct or systems of moral standards for different situations. They address considerations of right and wrong behaviour. All **counsellors**, **helpers** and **counselling** and helping skills students develop implicit and explicit personal systems of ethics about using **counselling skills**. Furthermore, the different groups to which you belong are likely to have developed codes of conduct and guidelines for ethical practice.

Ethics differ from **values**, which are the underlying principles upon which people and groups develop **ethical codes** and behaviour. Ethics also differ from laws, which are rules of behaviour set by the legislature and the courts to establish standards that help society function in an orderly fashion.

Sometimes it is obvious when there has been an ethical lapse, for instance engaging in sexual relations with **clients**. However, in the complexities of practice, **ethical issues** often are unclear. Consequently, counselling and helping skills students are faced with **ethical dilemmas** involving choices about how best to act.

This chapter mainly focuses on ethical issues and dilemmas connected with using counselling and helping skills with individuals. Many counsellors and helpers consider it insufficient to deal with ethical issues only when working with individuals. Instead, such practitioners use community, organizational, and political change agent skills to create environments in which clients and others can develop more of their human potential. For example, those striving for greater multicultural and racial understanding and legislative support fall into this category.

Ethics in practice

Ethical issues and dilemmas permeate counselling and helping practice. To use legal language, counselling and helping skills students always have a duty of care to their clients.

Virtually everything you do can be performed ethically or unethically. Here ethical issues and dilemmas connected with enacting this duty of care are introduced in four, albeit overlapping, main areas:

- **competence**
- client autonomy
- **confidentiality**
- **client protection.**

Competence

With so many approaches to counselling and helping, the issue arises as to what is competence. A useful distinction exists between relationship competence, offering a good relationship, and technical competence, the ability to assess clients and to deliver interventions. There is far greater agreement between the different counselling approaches on the ingredients of relationship competence, such as respect and support for clients as persons and accurately **listening** to and understanding their worldviews, than there is for technical competence. Suffice it for now to say that technical competence is what leading practitioners in a given approach would agree to be competent performance of the technical aspects of that approach.

Another helpful distinction related to competence is that between readiness to practice and fitness to practice. Readiness to practice means that counsellors and helpers require appropriate training and practise before being ready to see clients and use counselling skills competently. Fitness to practice assumes that you have satisfactory counselling skills in your repertoire and it only becomes an ethical problem when you are precluded in some way from using these skills competently. An example of readiness to practice as an ethical problem is if you were to take on a case referred to you, for example an anorexic client, that was beyond your level of training and competence. An example of fitness to practice as an ethical problem is if you were to drink alcohol at work and so fail to maintain competence.

Counselling and helping skills students can avoid ethical issues concerning readiness to practice if you are prepared to refer certain clients to others more qualified to help them. Furthermore, where you do not possess the requisite competence to help some categories of clients, you can discourage people from referring such people to you. However, you have to start somewhere and hence it is important that your competence is aided by good **supervision** and consultative support. You have a responsibility to current and future clients to keep **monitoring** your performance and developing your counselling skills. You always need to evaluate and reflect upon what you do.

Client autonomy

Respect for the client's right to make the choices that work best for them in their lives is the principle underlying client autonomy. Counselling and helping skills students should seek to support clients' control over and ability to assume **personal responsibility** for their lives. If, for example, you provide inaccurate pre-helping **information** or make false statements about your professional qualifications and competencies you are stopping potential and actual clients from making informed choices about whether to commence and/or continue in helping with you.

Most often it is unnecessary and unrealistic for you to provide lengthy **explanations** to clients about what you do. Nevertheless, before and during counselling and helping, you can make accurate statements concerning the process and about your respective roles. Furthermore, you can answer clients' queries about what you are trying to do honestly and with respect.

Students should also make realistic statements about the outcomes of counselling and helping and avoid making claims that might be disputed both outside and inside of law courts. Throughout, clients should be treated as intelligent participants who have a right to explanations about why you suggest interventions and what is entailed in implementing them.

An issue in client autonomy is where the values and backgrounds of clients may differ from those of counselling and helping skills students, for instance as a result of cultural or religious influences. You should not impose your values on clients and, where appropriate, you should be prepared to refer clients on to others who may more readily understand their concerns. It is highly unethical to assess and treat clients as pathological on the basis of judgments determined by culture, race, sex or sexual orientation, among other characteristics.

Confidentiality

Sometimes it is said that all people have three lives: a public life, a private life, and a secret life. Since frequently counselling and helping deals with material from clients' secret lives, normally their trust that their confidences will be kept is vital. However, as the Geldards observe 'Absolute confidentiality is not always possible and may be unethical' (Geldard and Geldard, 2005). There may be reasons connected with matters such as agency policy and sometimes the law why counselling and helping skills students cannot guarantee confidentiality. For example, when you are working with minors, there are many ethical and legal issues surrounding the boundaries of confidentiality and obligations to parents, teachers and significant others.

Counselling and helping skills students should try to communicate pertinent limitations on confidentiality to clients in advance. Furthermore, other than in exceptional circumstances, you should seek clients' permission for any **communication** to third parties. Having said this, the issue of whether or not to disclose to third parties is at the forefront of ethical dilemmas for counsellors and helpers, especially where risks to children are involved. In a study, published in 1999, by British psychologists Lindsay and Clarkson the answers of a sample of psychotherapists' reporting ethically troubling incidents concerning confidentiality fell into the following four areas:

*   risk to third parties – sexual abuse
*   risk to the client – threatened suicide
*   disclosure of information to others – particularly to medical agencies, other colleagues, the client's close friends, relatives
*   careless/inappropriate disclosure – by the psychotherapist or others.

Confidentiality assumes that clients have the right to control the disclosure of their personal information. In instances where counselling and helping skills students require tapes for supervision purposes, you should refrain from putting pressure on clients to be recorded. Most clients will understand a tactful request to record and, provided they are assured of the security of the tapes, will give their permission. In cases where clients have reservations, they are often reassured if told that they may stop the recording any time they wish.

Clients' **records**, whether they are case notes, cassettes or videotapes, need to be held securely at all times. A final word about confidentiality is that counselling and helping skills students, when talking socially with colleagues, relatives or friends, should learn to keep your mouths shut about details of clients' problems and lives. Unfortunately, a few students are tempted to break confidentiality for the sake of a good story.

Client protection

The category of client protection encompasses looking after clients as persons. Counselling and helping skills students require sufficient detachment to act in clients' best interests. **Dual relationships** are those where, in addition to the counselling relationship, counsellors and helpers may already be in, or consider entering, or enter other kinds of relationships with clients: for instance, friend, lover, colleague, trainer, supervisor among others. In certain rural and cultural communities dual relationships may be normative, for instance in some smaller communities the client may be the only mechanic in town (Kocet, 2006). Furthermore, dual relationships are often part of the fabric of **helping relationships** where helpers perform other primary roles, for example nurse–patient. Therefore whether a dual relationship is ethical, unethical or presents an ethical dilemma depends on its circumstances.

Sexual contact with clients is always unethical. Instead of or as well as sexual exploitation, clients may also be subject to emotional and financial exploitation. Emotional exploitation can take many forms, but has the underlying theme of using clients in some way for counselling and helping skills students' personal agendas, for example encouraging dependent and admiring clients rather than fostering autonomy. Financial exploitation is unlikely to be a problem on counselling skills training courses, but outside of them it may take many forms, including counsellors and helpers charging for services they are unqualified to provide, overcharging, and prolonging helping unnecessarily.

Counselling and helping skills students can protect clients and the public image of the profession if steps are taken to address the detrimental behaviour of other students. Where you suspect misconduct by others, you can be mindful of your professional association's codes of ethics and practice. For instance, if a student suspects misconduct by another student, first you may try to resolve or remedy it through discussion with the person concerned. If still dissatisfied, you can bring the issue to the attention of your trainers and supervisors. Outside of training settings, counsellors and helpers can implement any complaints procedures provided by their professional associations, doing so without breaches of confidentiality other than those being necessary for investigating the complaint. However, again they should try first to address their concerns informally and directly with the person concerned, otherwise they may be acting unethically themselves (Kocet, 2006).

Ethical codes and guidelines

When counselling and helping skills students develop personal systems of ethics, monitor practice, and deal with ethical dilemmas, where should you turn? Bond (2000) suggests six sources of counselling ethics:

1   personal ethics
2   ethics and values implicit in therapeutic models
3   agency policy
4   professional codes and guidelines
5   moral philosophy
6   law.

Students on introductory counselling and helping skills courses should be introduced to the ethical codes and guidelines pertinent to current and subsequent use of counselling skills. Box 26.1 lists some illustrative ethical codes and guidelines for counselling, **psychology** and **psychotherapy**. In addition, different areas such as nursing, social work and human resource management have their own ethical codes and guidelines. Since ethical codes and guidelines tend to get updated, find out about and use the most recent versions.

Box 26.1 Illustrative British and Australian ethical codes and guidelines

Britain

British Association for Counselling and Psychotherapy (BACP)
Ethical Framework for Good Practice in Counselling and Psychotherapy

British Psychological Society (BPS)
Professional Practice Guidelines: Division of Counselling Psychology
Guidelines on Confidentiality and Record Keeping, Division of Counselling Psychology

United Kingdom Council for Psychotherapy (UKCP)
Ethical Requirements for Member Organizations

Australia

Australian Psychological Society (APS)
APS Code of Ethics
APS Guidelines for Therapeutic Practice with Female Clients

Psychotherapy & Counselling Association of Australia
Introduction to PACFA, A Definition of Psychotherapy and Counselling, Ethical Guidelines, Professional Training Standards

---

Ethical codes and guidelines are designed to protect clients and those helping them. Such codes and guidelines are statements of what is an acceptable level of conduct and what is not. As such, these codes and guidelines lay down standards of accountability to which counsellors, helpers and counselling skills students can be held responsible. However, many areas of ethical practice are grey rather than black and white. Nevertheless, ethical codes can provide a useful framework that suggests acceptable norms when making ethical decisions in light of the individual circumstances of each unique client.

Ethical codes protect clients by stating guidelines for counsellors, helpers and counselling skills students behaving responsibly towards them. Ethical codes also protect those adhering to them by offering group guidelines rather than leaving a vacuum regarding what constitutes ethical practice. Furthermore, those complying leave themselves less open to complaints and malpractice litigation than those who do not.

Some ethical statements are pertinent to counselling skills training and supervision, but they have the limitation of being geared more to trainers and supervisors than to students. A case exists for developing student ethical guidelines, especially since all practitioners, trainers and supervisors start as students. Furthermore, discussion of ethical issues during counselling skills and counsellor and helping training may have more relevance if focused on students' current rather than future practice.

Making decisions about ethical issues and dilemmas

American counselling writers Marianne and Gerald Corey (2003) observe that, along with codes of ethics of relevant organizations, possessing a systematic way of approaching difficult ethical dilemmas increases counsellors' chances of making sound ethical decisions. Bond (2000) states that he has grown more aware of the need to encourage ethical mindfulness rather than an unquestioning adherence to ethical principles. Being ethically mindful consists both of wrestling with the issues involved in ethical decisions and dilemmas in a systematic and considered way and assuming personal responsibility for acting ethically. Example 26.1 presents two models for ethical decision making: first, Bond's ethical problem-solving model (Bond 2000; 2006); and second, the Corey's ethical decision-making model (Corey and Corey, 2003).

Example 26.1 Decision making models for ethical issues and dilemmas

Bond's ethical problem-solving model
1 Produce a brief description of the problem or dilemma
2 Consider who holds responsibility for resolving the problem
3 Consider all the relevant ethical and legal guidance
4 Identify all possible courses of action
5 Select the best course of action
6 Evaluate the outcome.

> **Example 26.1 Decision making models for ethical issues and dilemmas – cont'd**
>
> **Corey and Corey's ethical decision-making model**
> 1 Identify the problem
> 2 Apply the ethical guidelines
> 3 Determine the nature and dimensions of the dilemma and seek consultation
> 4 Generate possible courses of action
> 5 Consider the possible consequences of all options and determine a course of action
> 6 Evaluate the selected course of action
> 7 Implement the course of action.

Perhaps rather more than is justified, both the Bond and the Corey models seem to imply that making ethical decisions is a rational process. As the saying goes: 'Whoever said that humans were rational?' Counsellors, helpers and students tend to bring different decision-making styles to ethical decisions: for example, some avoid making them for as long as possible, others rush into making them, still others worry over every detail. In addition, even when you make decisions, you differ in your commitment to them and in your ability to implement them skilfully.

Furthermore, both experienced practitioners and students – like clients – differ in **mind skills strengths** and weaknesses. Here, some examples are provided of how poor skills can interfere with making decisions rationally. You may use negative **self-talk** that increases your **anxiety** about making and implementing decisions on ethical issues: for instance, if you suspect serious misconduct on the part of another student. Accompanying your negative self-talk may be unhelpful **visual images** about the processes and outcomes of acting ethically. Furthermore, you may have rules that interfere with ethical action: for instance, a demanding rule like 'I must be approved of all the time' may get in the way of openly discussing an ethically ambiguous situation such as being strongly sexually attracted to a client. Areas for ethical dilemmas are fertile breeding grounds for creating false **perceptions**. For instance, controlling students may possess little insight into your ethical lapses in the areas of client autonomy, undue pressure and informed consent. If you are blind to the existence of your ethical lapses, you are scarcely in the position to embark on an ethical decision-making process about the issues and dilemmas associated with your behaviour.

Counselling and helping skills students always need to be alert for how turning what is outwardly a rational decision-making process into one that is less than completely rational might occur because of your own needs and anxieties. Furthermore, the more you can successfully work on your own **mental development** both as a person and as a helper, the more likely you are to work your way rationally through ethical dilemmas.

Activity 26.1 Making decisions about ethical issues and dilemmas

1 Critically discuss the strengths and weaknesses of:
   · Bond's ethical problem-solving model
   · Corey and Corey's ethical decision-making model.
2 What factors do you think might interfere with your rationally making decisions about ethical dilemmas:
   2.1 your current style of making decisions (please specify)
   2.2 poor mind skills in one or more of the following areas:
      · creating self-talk
      · creating rules
      · creating perceptions
      · other mind skills (please specify)
   2.3 any other factors (please specify).
3 What can you do to improve your ability to make decisions wisely when faced with ethical issues and dilemmas in future?

Ethical issues in introductory counselling skills courses

Many of the ethical issues and dilemmas connected with counselling and helping practice are present in introductory counselling and helping skills courses. Three ethical areas relevant to all introductory counselling and helping skills courses – competence, confidentiality, and dual relationships – are now briefly reviewed.

Competence

The gaining of basic competence is the main goal of introductory counselling and helping skills courses. Most students work hard at this and some make huge sacrifices to attend courses and develop skills. However, for various reasons, some other students' motivation to gain competence may not be as strong as desirable. Example 26.2 provides an illustration of an ethical lapse and an ethical dilemma in the area of gaining competence.

Example 26.2 Competence: Illustrations of ethical lapses and dilemmas

Ethical lapse
Martha intentionally does just enough work to achieve the minimum standards for passing an introductory counselling skills course. She frequently comes to skills classes very late and misses other classes without contacting the trainer in advance. Martha rarely practises her skills.

> ### Example 26.2 Competence: Illustrations of ethical lapses and dilemmas – cont'd
>
> #### Ethical dilemma
> Ron is taking an introductory counselling skills course as part of a larger helping services course. The culture of the department in which the course is held values academic work and research more highly than professional competence. Ron feels under considerable pressure to pay more attention to the academic rather than the practical dimensions of his course.

If, by any chance, readers are students either tempted or under pressure to reduce their commitment to their introductory counselling and helping skills courses, the following are some points for your consideration. If the course has minimum attendance requirements, for instance attending 9 out of 12 sessions, you will be failed for insufficient attendance. In addition to what you perceive as your interests, any decision to short change the course affects the interests of many others. You are making it more difficult for trainers to achieve their **goals** for the group and you may also create less productive learning environments for fellow students. Furthermore, introductory counselling and helping skills courses are not ends in themselves, but the means by which students can offer better services to clients. By paying insufficient attention to the course, you jeopardize the interests of future clients. In addition, if an introductory skills course is a prelude to having a counselling skills placement, you place yourself and your trainers in an invidious position regarding readiness to see clients.

Confidentiality

Some students on counselling and helping skills courses do not take the issue of confidentiality sufficiently seriously. Probably most problems of confidentiality on introductory skills courses fall more into the category of ethical lapses than ethical dilemmas. Since students tend to be counselling one another rather than real clients, many situations that make confidentiality a central ethical dilemma for counsellors and helpers do not occur: for instance, the rights of parents when their children are clients. Example 26.3 provides two illustrations of ethical lapses in which another student's disclosures have been insufficiently protected: one involving verbal leakage and another involving the potential for pictorial as well as verbal identification.

> ### Example 26.3 Confidentiality: Illustrations of ethical lapses
>
> Ellie has been using counselling skills in a practice session with fellow student Will as client. Will discusses a problem in his relationship with his partner. When Ellie gets home she talks about contents of the session to her husband.

(Continued)

> **Example 26.3 Confidentiality: Illustrations of ethical lapses – cont'd**
>
> In a counselling skills class, Claire records a videotape in which she counsels Jessica who discusses a problem situation in her life. Claire leaves the videotape lying around in the classroom, with the door unlocked, when the training group goes out for a coffee break.

Within the framework of relevant ethical codes, trainers and students on counselling and helping skills courses can develop rules about confidentiality for your particular groups. Sometimes these rules get formalized into group contractual agreements signed by all concerned. In addition, where students record counselling sessions with 'volunteer clients', clients must be informed in advance of any limitations of confidentiality connected with the training process. Furthermore, trainers and students have an ethical obligation to protect confidentiality in how 'volunteer client' recordings are used, stored and disposed of.

Dual relationships

Some counselling and helping skills trainers may have a pattern of exploiting students to meet their own needs. However, other trainers may be vulnerable only in special circumstances, for instance if lonely after a recent separation or divorce. The majority of students enrolled in introductory counselling skills courses are of mature age. Students also have a responsibility not to engage in trainer–student relationships that may have negative consequences for fellow students, trainers and possibly for yourself. Some students may seek special treatment on assessments by becoming friendly with trainers. Others may genuinely possess strong **feelings** of sexual and emotional attraction to trainers rather than seek to influence the **assessment** processes of the course in any way. In some instances it may be appropriate to express these feelings, so long as it is not done seductively or in a way that manipulates the trainer to respond in kind.

Counselling and helping skills students may receive messages from trainers that the training relationship might be accompanied by an emotional or sexual relationship. Mostly students should use assertion skills to nip such advances in the bud. In rare instances, you might suggest to the trainer that the possibility of engaging in a personal relationship be put on hold, pending the end of the course. If sexually harassed, students can go to people like heads of departments, students' rights officers, counselling services, and consider using institutional sexual harassment procedures, assuming they exist.

Not all cases of dual relationships are clear-cut. For example, a student and a trainer may have known one another before the start of the course. Furthermore, some trainers and students may have genuine common interests, for instance football or drama, that provide a shared bond. Both students and trainers need the freedom to express humanity at the same time as guarding against the danger of exploiting and being exploited by each other.

Activity 26.2 Ethical issues on introductory counselling and helping skills courses

1 Critically discuss the ethical issues and dilemmas for introductory counselling and helping skills students in each of the following areas:
- competence
- confidentiality
- dual relationships.
2 What other areas for ethical issues and dilemmas are important and why?

27

Training groups, supervision and support

CHAPTER OUTCOMES

By studying and doing the activities in this chapter you should:
* understand some distinctive features of learning counselling skills;
* know about the importance of cohesive group environments;
* identify some skills for getting the best from trainers;
* know about some goals and formats for supervision;
* know about different ways of presenting material in and making use of supervision; and
* know about getting support.

This chapter starts by showing some ways that counselling skills students can make the most of training groups. It then discusses some issues for those whose counselling skills groups are accompanied by **supervision** and concludes by discussing support, whether or not students receive supervision.

Training groups

Many factors contribute to creating a happy and productive environment for learning counselling skills. The professional **competence** and personal qualities of the trainer or trainers are crucial. The size of the training group makes a difference. For instance, Dryden, Horton and Mearns (1995) recommend a maximum staff–student ratio of one trainer to twelve students. In addition, the physical resources allocated to training are important. In both academic settings where I trained **counsellors**, the University of Aston in Birmingham and the Royal Melbourne Institute of Technology, we were fortunate enough to have both a suitably furnished large group room and two smaller interview rooms available for training. Suitably furnished means that the space was flexible and students could sit in circles, horseshoes, or sub-groups. Counselling skills training is further enhanced by easy access to audiovisual aids, for instance video recording and playback facilities. Students may also learn more if supported by good counselling skills library facilities: including books, journals, cassettes and videotapes.

Counselling skills training is different

Let's look at a few of the ways in which learning counselling skills may differ from the types of learning students have experienced before. Strange as it may sound, much of counselling skills training is about unlearning rather than learning. Many of the ways students have learned to listen and interact in everyday life differ from how skilled counsellors and **helpers** work. For example, social conversations, emphasizing meeting both parties' needs, differ from counselling conversations, emphasizing mainly meeting **clients**' needs. As students learn counselling skills, a **tension** exists between the pull of the past and the requirements for present and future skilled work. For some students a further tension exists between the pull of the counselling approach adopted in your training group and that of approaches that you have been or are being exposed to elsewhere.

Another difference in applied counselling skills training is that students are not learning academic knowledge but practical skills. It is insufficient to know and be able to talk about what to do, you have to be able to do it as well. Furthermore, trainers need to adapt their teaching styles to incorporate a focus on the transmission of practical 'how to' knowledge and skills.

Counselling skills training also differs in that learning counselling skills involves students as persons and, as such, is more than the application of techniques. In Chapter 3 some ways were reviewed showing that students' mental processes might influence ability both to learn and to use counselling skills. Students may need to work through personal agendas before able to be fully present to clients. Many counselling skills students can gain from both a broadening and deepening of life experience. Students who have led sheltered lives may perform more effectively once gaining insight and experience of other lifestyles: for instance different social classes, cultures, and problems. Furthermore, you may need to work on deepening your humanity and on getting more in touch with your potential for compassion and **inner strength**.

A cohesive group environment

Skilled trainers recognize that much counselling skills training involves student self-appraisal and student-to-student rather than trainer-to-student feedback. Consequently, it is critical to attend to processes that make for cohesive working groups. Many students make big sacrifices to come to counselling skills training groups and you should enjoy coming. The group is likely to be more fun if you can get to know one another as persons. Time spent at the beginning on ice-breaking exercises and, possibly, an introductory social event can get the group off to a good start. In these beginning sessions, students should circulate and try to know and be known to as many members of the group as possible. Programming breaks for coffee, tea or meals in training groups is another way that you can get to feel comfortable with one another.

In any group, **rules** develop about appropriate ways of thinking, feeling and behaving in the group. Also, there are issues of trust, power and control. Box 27.1 lists possible group rules or norms that make for cohesive and effective counselling skills training groups. Such a list of norms can be openly discussed with students as the basis for a learning contract.

Box 27.1 Illustrative rules for counselling skills training groups

- Though the trainer or trainers have ultimate control of the direction of the group, students participate in decisions about how the group is run.
- Students are expected to focus on their mental processes as well as their external counselling skills.
- Each student accepts responsibility for their own learning.
- The expectation of the group is that students will attend all sessions and come on time.
- Students accept responsibility for participating in the group's training activities to the best of their ability, including carrying out homework assignments.
- Trainers and students accept responsibility for helping one another learn counselling skills.
- Trainers and students treat one another with respect and support and challenge one another as appropriate.
- No student in the training group should feel under pressure to reveal any personal **information** about which they are uncomfortable.
- No telling tales out of school – students have a right to **confidentiality** from one another and their trainer(s).
- Students do not expect the trainer(s) to act as a personal counsellor or to participate in a therapy group.
- All students adhere to guidelines about conducting and handing in assignments and do not seek special treatment for themselves.

Getting the best from a training group

Introductory counselling skills students can reframe the question 'What can I get from my training group?' to become 'What can I give to my training group?' Paradoxically, a giving attitude may get you more of what you want than a demanding attitude. Below are a few suggestions for how to get the most from skills training.

Use time management and study skills

All introductory counselling skills students require good time management skills. However, some of you sabotage your learning through poor skills. The time demands on students are real enough. You may be trying to juggle partner, parenting, home maintenance, recreational, work, and academic study commitments. However, enrolling in an introductory counselling skills class implies an implicit, if not explicit, contract that you are willing to devote sufficient time and energy to learn and practise the skills. It may be a good idea to develop weekly timetables in which times are blocked out for training group sessions, practising skills and completing assignments.

Some counselling skills students need to attend to improving academic **study skills**: for example, reading skills and meeting deadline skills. For instance, procrastinating students who address their problem can become more effective at studying and therefore have more time to learn counselling skills. Students requiring study skills counselling should not hesitate to get it. As a counsellor trainer, I referred many students to the local student counselling service for this purpose.

Develop giving and receiving feedback skills

Ralph Waldo Emerson once observed: 'I pay the schoolmaster, but 'tis the schoolboys that educate my son.' For good or ill, students learn a tremendous amount from one another. Skilled trainers can rely on and use the wisdom and experience of the group. Students in cohesive counselling skills training groups are likely to have developed good skills of tactfully commenting on one another's work. It becomes much easier to receive feedback, when trainers and students are good at giving feedback. Example 27.1 summarizes some guidelines for giving and receiving feedback, though you should vary which guidelines you follow according to circumstances.

Example 27.1 Guidelines for giving and receiving feedback

Giving feedback
Use 'I' messages rather than 'You' messages
'You' message
'You did...'
'I' message
'I thought you ...'
Be specific and, where possible, state feedback in the positive
Non specific and negative
'You interviewed poorly.'
Specific and positive
'I thought you could use more eye contact and speak in a louder voice.'
Use confirmatory as well as corrective feedback
'I thought your use of eye contact was good, but that you could still speak in a louder voice.'
Consider emotional as well as behavioural feedback
'When you made very direct eye contact and spoke in a loud voice, I felt overpowered by you.'
Consider demonstrating your feedback
'I would like to show you how your eye contact came over to me ... [then demonstrate]'
Consider cultural sensitivity feedback
'I wonder whether there wasn't a cultural issue [specify which] operating in the helping session.'
Provide an opportunity for the receiver to respond to your feedback
'Would you like to respond to my [or the group's] feedback?'

Receiving feedback
· Where appropriate, consider requesting feedback.
· Listen carefully and, unless absolutely necessary, avoid interrupting.

> **Example 27.1 Guidelines for giving and receiving feedback – cont'd**
>
> - If necessary, check the accuracy of your understanding.
> - If you consider the feedback helpful, consider thanking the provider.
> - Be assertive in stopping any feedback that you consider is being given destructively.
> - You can choose either to respond to feedback at the time or to keep silent about it and process it in your own time.

Use empathy and assertion skills to get the best from the trainer(s)

Counselling skills students have both rights and responsibilities in relation to trainers. Rights and responsibilities intertwine and both trainers and students need to exercise rights responsibly. Here two student skills, **empathy** and assertion, that can make for good working relationships with trainers are examined.

Students can show empathy to trainers. The training relationship is a person-to-person relationship that goes both ways. Some counselling skills students are excellent at taking the perspective of trainers. However, a minority make unrealistic demands for **unconditional positive regard** and empathic understanding from trainers at the same time as showing little empathy themselves.

If working in an educational institution, trainers are likely to be in a position of trying to fulfill multiple roles: administrator, teacher, researcher, skills trainer and professional counsellor. On top of this, students are seeking certification or some form of official acknowledgment that you have successfully completed an introductory counselling skills training group. Thus, trainers face the further role conflict of both training and evaluating students. In addition, very possibly trainers are working in the wider context of an academic research culture that undervalues professional training. Furthermore, in all academic departments and institutions there is competition for resources. Almost certainly, the counselling skills staff has to justify the extra expenses attached to practical skills training over traditional classroom teaching. On the one hand the student contact provided by counselling skills training is very rewarding. On the other hand, partly due to contextual factors, being a counselling skills trainer can be very stressful. Trainers appreciate students who understand this.

Students can be assertive about getting the best from your training. Even with suitably qualified and conscientious trainers, during the course of a training group situations may emerge requiring improvement. One example might be that of a relatively new trainer who is not doing enough demonstrating. This may be more a matter of insufficient confidence and teaching experience than incompetence. Here students can use feedback skills to bring to the trainer's attention that more demonstration would be appreciated. If the trainer then makes an effort to fulfill the request, this change is more likely to be maintained if you show your appreciation.

Another situation might be that of inadequate training facilities: for instance poor, but not terrible, accommodation. Students are quite within their rights to request a room change. However, whether the change gets made may be outside the control of skills trainers who probably also want better accommodation. You will maintain better working relationships with trainers if making such requests assertively rather than aggressively and if accepting realistic limitations on what trainers can do.

Activity 27.1 Developing counselling skills training group rules

1 What good or bad experiences of counselling skills training have you had?
2 Look at the illustrative rules for counselling skills training groups listed in Box 27.1.
    a) How applicable are the rules to your introductory skills training group?
    b) Develop a list of rules for your introductory skills training group.
3 What are your hopes/anxieties/anticipations related to your counselling skills training group?

Supervision

Many introductory counselling skills students may not have access to supervision. However, it is hoped that even so, some of you gain something of value from the following discussion. Counselling and helping students require competent supervision to develop counselling skills well. Supervision literally means overseeing. Students discuss your use of counselling skills with experienced practitioners who can assist you to develop effectiveness in working with clients.

Goals and formats for supervision

The overriding goal of supervision is to assist those supervised to think and communicate as effective counsellors and helpers and, in so doing, to become your own *internal* supervisors. Early on supervisors may have to do some 'hand holding' as they assist counselling skills students in breaking the ice with real clients. In addition, you can receive help from supervisors to assist you to examine and address poor **mind skills** contributing to performance **anxiety**. Throughout supervision, students should receive emotional support in ways that encourage self-reliance and honest self-appraisal rather than dependence and a need for supervisor approval.

Supervisions can take place either one-to-one, or with two or more students. Resources permitting, it is probably best, especially when students start seeing clients, to have individual supervision. Advantages of individual supervision include providing students with adequate time to be supervised thoroughly and the fact that many of you are more likely to discuss sensitive issues regarding clients and yourselves than if supervised with others.

Small group supervision also has some advantages. For example, members may get exposure to a greater range of clients and develop skills of discussing and receiving feedback on your work from peers as well as from the supervisor. Furthermore, you may be more self-disclosing in the context of other supervisees' honest appraisals of your performance.

A combination of participating in individual supervision and in counselling skills training groups has much to recommend it. Students can learn **assessment** skills and different interventions in training groups. Furthermore, in such groups you can share your experiences of working with clients in ways that may be beneficial for all concerned.

To some extent the supervision process parallels the counselling and helping process, in that supervisors should develop good collaborative working relationships with students to provide fertile contexts in which to monitor and improve skills. In supervision, however, the emphasis is on improving the mind skills and the **communication** skills required for effective counselling and helping rather than on managing personal problems. In a British study, both supervisees and supervisors rated creating a learning relationship as the most important of seven tasks of counselling supervision (Fortune and Watts, 2000).

The supervision literature is full of references to **counter-transference**, the process by which counsellors distort how they perceive and behave towards clients to meet their own needs. For instance, supervisees and even experienced counsellors too may, at varying levels of **awareness**, be encouraging **dependency**, sexual interest or even distance in some clients. Effective supervision assists students to identify, explore and address such distortions, at least insofar as they affect their work with clients. Supervisors should also identify and address their own counter-transference distortions towards those whom they supervise (Ladany et al., 2000).

Presenting material in supervision

The following are some methods whereby students can present counselling and helping session content in supervision sessions. Some of these methods can be used in combination to add to the validity of understanding what actually transpired.

- *Verbal report* Verbal reporting on its own relies entirely on memory, which will certainly be incomplete and will almost certainly be highly selective. The greater the period of time between sessions and supervision, the more invalid memory may become. Furthermore, if students are seeing other clients, it becomes difficult to remember exactly what happened with whom.
- *Process notes* Process notes, if written up immediately after counselling and helping sessions and using a structured format, do not rely so heavily on memory. Such notes can act as an aid to memory during supervisions. The combination of process notes and verbal report, while still open to a high degree of invalidity, is probably more valid than relying on verbal report alone.
- *Audiotaping* Audiotaping means that there is a valid record of all the verbal and vocal content of sessions. Another advantage of audiotaping is that either students can choose or supervisors can request specific segments on which to focus. Audiotaping can be relatively unobtrusive when only a small microphone is visible to clients.
- *Videotaping* Videotaping has the great advantage over audiotaping that there is a valid record of bodily as well as verbal and vocal session content. Viewing video-tapes of sessions is my preferred way of conducting supervisions. However, some placements may not be set up for videotaping, in which case audiotaping is the next best choice. A possible disadvantage of videotaping is that the machinery tends to be much more obtrusive than that required for audiotaping.

- **Role playing** Where videotaping is not available, role playing can provide a way of finding out how students actually communicate with clients. The student can orient the supervisor to the client's role and then counsel the supervisor as 'client' in a way that resembles part of the actual session.
- *Client feedback* Clients can provide feedback relevant to understanding what happened in counselling and helping sessions in a number of ways. Counselling skills supervisors and students should take note of and try to understand the reasons for single session clients and for missed appointments. Towards the end of sessions, students can ask clients to provide feedback about the relationship and procedures. Clients can also fill out brief post-session questionnaires asking them for similar feedback.

Making use of supervision

Supervision sessions can be broken down into three stages: preparation, the supervision session itself, and follow-up. In the preparation stage, students can do such things as write up and reflect on your session notes and go through audiocassettes or videotapes selecting excerpts for presentation of their use of good and poor counselling skills. In addition, you can read up on possible interventions to use with clients, think about issues connected with differences between yourself and your clients, ponder **ethical issues**, and in other ways reflect upon how you can make the most of your supervision time.

Early in sessions, students and supervisors can establish **session agendas**. Sometimes, students only get one supervision hour for five or eight hours of client contact. If taping is used, important decisions can be which tapes to present and, for those tapes chosen, which excerpts to review. When observing videotapes, a risk is that so much time is spent watching the first few minutes of a session that later work in sessions either receives none or insufficient attention.

In Chapter 17, mention was made of the importance of counselling skills students using **client–centred coaching** skills with clients. Students may gain from similar skills being employed by supervisors during the time together. Sometimes supervisors may wish to stop tapes to point something out. However, on many occasions, students should be the ones to choose which excerpts to present and when to stop tapes for discussion. Supervisors can facilitate the process by asking **questions** such as 'What was going on there?', 'What were you trying to do?', 'What were you feeling?' and 'What skills were you using and how well were you using them?' Within the context of good collaborative relationships, supervisors develop students' skills of thinking systematically about your counselling work so that you may become your own internal supervisor. Towards the end of supervision sessions both participants can review the main points and negotiate any specific homework assignments.

The follow-up stage of a supervision session has two main **goals**. One goal is that of you using in your next sessions with clients the improved skills that you discussed and worked on in supervision. Another goal is that of carrying out specific homework assignments. For instance, student and supervisor may agree that the student should practise a specific counselling intervention before using it in a session. A further assignment might be reading some specific references relevant to particular clients' problems. Supervision homework can also focus on improving students' own mind skills and not just on those of clients. For example, students can agree to spend time **challenging** and restating any demanding rule or rules that contribute to performance anxiety.

Counselling skills students vary in ability to make the most out of supervision. Some are not prepared to work hard at achieving competence. Others have personal problems of such magnitude that possibly they should not be counselling clients at all until their own life is in better shape. It is particularly hard to supervise students who are defensive and possess little insight into how poor mind and communication skills interfere with using counselling skills. Some students are difficult to supervise because, in varying degrees, you know it all already. A minority of students either initiate and/or engage in unethical behaviour, be it with either clients or supervisors.

Activity 27.2 Being supervised

1 What good or bad experiences of having your counselling skills supervised have you had?
2 Assuming that there is some form of supervision attached to your introductory skills training course:
   2.1 What are the goals of the supervision?
   2.2 What format does the supervision take?
   2.3 How do you prepare for your supervisions?
   2.4 How is material presented in supervisions and what are the advantages and disadvantages of presenting material this way?
   2.5 What sort of follow-up is required after supervision sessions?
   2.6 What are the strengths of the supervision you are receiving and how might it be improved?
   2.7 Are there any things you could be doing to make your supervisions more useful?
3 What are your hopes/anxieties/anticipations related to your counselling skills supervision?

Getting support

There are many reasons why students may not have access to formal supervision arrangements to build introductory counselling skills. One reason is that the introductory counselling skills courses do not allow students to see real clients. Another reason is that many students are using counselling skills as part of other primary roles, for instance teaching, nursing, or offering financial advice. In such situations resources for staff support and development may focus on your primary tasks rather than on your counselling activities. The provision of supervision to monitor and build employees' counselling skills can be expensive and time-consuming and employers may neither have nor perceive that they have sufficient funds for this purpose. Furthermore, some institutions and agencies attach a low priority to the use of counselling skills by their employees, instead preferring more directive approaches.

In work and voluntary agency settings, apart from formal supervision, there are a number of ways in which students can gain valuable support and assistance in building your counselling skills. You may be assigned to bosses or mentors with whom you review your work on a regular basis or seek help when you feel you need it. You may also be part of teams that meet on a regular basis in staff meetings and case conferences to discuss how to deal with clients. In such instances, students may have access to skilled team leaders who can both teach you how to improve your basic counselling skills and also draw on the experience of the other group members to provide enriched learning environments. In addition, work settings or voluntary agencies may run special workshops or short courses to assist students to develop specific skills for dealing with special clienteles. Furthermore, the settings in which students use counselling skills may have their own support systems of competent professionals with whom individual clients can be discussed.

In instances of inadequate provision of support from institutions and agencies, counselling skills students can identify more experienced colleagues to act as informal mentors. In addition, you can consider forming your own peer support groups. On occasion, students may be forced to look outside employing institutions or agencies to obtain suitable professional advice, for instance from trusted counselling professionals or psychiatrists. However, in such instances, you need to be guided by the best interests of clients and be very sensitive to protecting their rights to confidentiality.

Activity 27.3 Getting support

1 What good or bad experiences of getting support for learning counselling skills have you had?
2 Are you satisfied with the amount of support you are receiving as you learn introductory counselling skills?
3 If not completely satisfied, what additional sources of support would you like?
4 If wanted and possible, make an effort to obtain at least one additional source of support.

28

Counselling theory and research

CHAPTER OUTCOMES

By studying and doing the activity in this chapter you should:
- gain some understanding about theoretical schools of counselling;
- gain some understanding about theoretical approaches to counselling;
- gain some understanding about different modes of working with clients; and
- know about the importance of counselling research.

Counselling theory

This chapter draws your attention to the theoretical and research literature about different approaches to **counselling** and **psychotherapy**. Understanding theory can also be relevant to **helpers** who, while not conducting formal counselling, neverthe- less seek reasoned **explanations** for **clients'** and their own behaviour. Theories of coun- selling are conceptual frameworks that allow practitioners to think systematically about human development and the counselling and helping process. To varying degrees, such theories of counselling are formulated on the basis of research and then tested by research into the results of their practical application.

Counselling theories may be viewed as possessing four main dimensions if they are to be stated adequately:

1 a statement of the basic concepts or assumptions underlying the theory
2 an explanation of the acquisition of helpful and unhelpful behaviour
3 an explanation of the maintenance of helpful and unhelpful behaviour
4 an explanation of how to help clients change their behaviour and consolidate their gains when counselling ends.

The first three of the above dimensions may be viewed as a theory's model of human development, whereas the final dimension is its model of practice. A theory's model of human development is relevant to whether people engage in either formal counselling or less formal helping contacts. A theory's model of practice is invariably stated by its originators in respect of formal counselling and psychotherapy and, in varying degrees, requires modifying for less formal helping.

Schools and approaches to counselling

A useful distinction exists between *schools* of counselling and psychotherapy and *approaches* to counselling and psychotherapy. A theoretical approach presents a single position regarding the theory and practice of counselling. A school of counselling is a grouping of different theoretical approaches that are similar to one another in terms of certain important characteristics that distinguish them from theoretical approaches in other **counselling schools**.

Probably the three main schools that influence contemporary counselling and psychotherapy practice are the psychodynamic school, the humanistic school, and the cognitive-behavioural school. Sometimes the humanistic school can incorporate existential therapeutic approaches and then gets the broader title of being the humanistic-existential school. You should be careful not to exaggerate the differences between counselling and therapy schools, since there are similarities as well as differences among them. Box 28.1 briefly describes some distinguishing features of the psychodynamic, humanistic and cognitive-behavioural schools.

Box 28.2 presents what are probably the two main theoretical approaches from each of the three main counselling and psychotherapy schools: classical **psychoanalysis** and analytical therapy from the psychodynamic school; **person–centred therapy** and **gestalt therapy** from the humanistic school; and **rational emotive behaviour**

Box 28.1 Three counselling and psychotherapy schools

The psychodynamic school
The term psychodynamic refers to the transfer of psychic or mental energy between the different structures and levels of consciousness within people's minds. Psychodynamic approaches emphasize the importance of unconscious influences on how people function. Counselling aims to increase clients' abilities to exercise greater conscious control over their lives. Analysis of dreams or **dream interpretation** can be a central part of counselling.

The humanistic school
The humanistic school is based on humanism, a system of values and beliefs that emphasizes the better qualities of humankind and people's abilities to develop their human potential. Humanistic counsellors emphasize enhancing clients' abilities to experience their feelings and think and act in harmony with their underlying tendencies to actualize themselves as unique individuals.

The cognitive-behavioural school
Traditional behavioural counselling focuses mainly on changing observable behaviours by means of providing different or rewarding consequences. The cognitive-behavioural school broadens behavioural counselling to incorporate the contribution of how people think to creating, sustaining and changing their problems. In cognitive-behavioural approaches, counsellors assess clients and then intervene to help them to change specific ways of thinking and behaving that sustain problems.

therapy and **cognitive therapy** from the cognitive-behavioural school. In addition, there are numerous other approaches of varying degrees of originality and importance in each school. So that you can obtain a sense of the history of the development of ideas within counselling, the dates of the originators of each approach have been included. Those wishing to pursue a study of counselling theory are referred to the following books: my introductory *Theory and Practice of Counselling and Therapy* (2006), *Dryden's Handbook of Individual Therapy* (2007) and Corsini and Wedding's *Current Psychotherapies* (2008). The descriptions provided in Box 28.2 reflect the stance of the originators of the different positions, rather than developments within a theoretical approach stimulated by others.

Box 28.2 Six counselling and psychotherapy approaches

Psychodynamic school
Classical psychoanalysis *Originator: Sigmund Freud (1956–1939)*
Pays great attention to unconscious factors related to infantile sexuality in the development of neuroses. Psychoanalysis, which may last for many years, emphasizes **working through** the **transference**, in which clients perceive their therapists as reincarnations of important figures from their childhoods, and the interpretation of dreams.

Analytical therapy *Originator: Carl Jung (1875–1961)*
Divides the unconscious into the personal unconscious and the collective unconscious, the latter being a storehouse of universal archetypes and primordial images. Therapy includes analysis of the transference, active imagination and dream analysis. Jung was particularly interested in working with clients in the second half of life.

Humanistic school
Person-centred therapy *Originator: Carl Rogers (1902–1987)*
Lays great stress on the primacy of subjective experience and how clients can become out of touch with their actualizing tendency through introjecting others' evaluations and treating them as if their own. Counselling emphasizes a relationship characterized by accurate **empathy**, respect and non-possessive warmth.

Gestalt therapy *Originator: Fritz Perls (1893–1970)*
Individuals become neurotic by losing touch with their senses and interfering with their capacity to make strong contact with their environments. Counselling emphasizes increasing clients' **awareness** and vitality through awareness techniques, **experiments**, sympathy and frustration, and dream work.

Cognitive-behavioural school
Rational emotive behaviour therapy *Originator: Albert Ellis (1913–2007)*
Emphasizes clients re-indoctrinating themselves with irrational beliefs that lead to unwanted feelings and self-defeating actions. Counselling involves disputing clients' irrational beliefs and replacing them with more rational beliefs. Elegant or profound counselling entails changing clients' philosophies of life.

(Continued)

Box 28.2 Six counselling and psychotherapy approaches – cont'd

Cognitive therapy *Originator: Aaron Beck (1921–)*
Clients become distressed because they are faulty processors of **information** with a tendency to jump to unwarranted conclusions. Therapy consists of educating clients in how to test the reality of their thinking by interventions such as Socratic questioning and conducting real-life experiments.

So far, the different schools and theoretical approaches have been presented as though they are separate. In reality, many counsellors regard themselves as working in either eclectic or integrative ways. A detailed discussion of **eclecticism** and integration is beyond the scope of this practical book. Suffice it for now to say that eclecticism is the practice of drawing from different counselling schools in formulating client problems and implementing treatment interventions. Integration refers to attempting to blend together theoretical concepts and/or practical interventions drawn from different counselling approaches into coherent and integrated wholes. To a large extent the **counselling skills** presented in this book are drawn from the humanistic and cognitive-behavioural schools and approaches.

Modes of using counselling skills

Another way of looking at counselling and helping theory, practice and research is in terms of different modes or ways of using counselling skills with clients. Unlike **counsellors** and psychotherapists, helpers often use their counselling skills within each of these modes in informal rather than in formal contexts. By far the most common mode is that of one-to-one or individual counselling and helping. Another mode is that of couples work, in which counsellors and helpers work with partners or marital spouses. In some counselling and helping settings, such as schools and offices, couples work may be extended to working with problems between two teachers, students or workers. A further mode is that of **family counselling** and helping, in which families and their component parts are the target of using counselling skills. An example of using counselling skills in a family mode would be that of school counsellors working with families to help unsuccessful and often unhappy pupils to perform better.

Still another mode for using counselling skills is that of **group counselling** and helping. In formal group counselling, an optimum size for a group is often thought to be around 6-to-8 members so as to allow for **diversity**, yet not become so large that individual members receive insufficient attention. Counsellors and helpers may use counselling skills when working with groups of different sizes and with different agendas, for instance supervisors in work groups or youth workers with groups of young people. Sometimes groups focus on the relationships between participants and on other occasions they can have more of a focus in the training of specific skills, for instance health maintenance skills, job-seeking skills or **study skills**. In both kinds of groups, counsellors and helpers can use counselling skills.

While the focus of this book is primarily on individual work, the basic counselling skills covered in it are relevant to other modes of working with clients. Modes of using counselling skills and theoretical approaches to counselling interact in at least two important ways. First, most leading theoretical approaches to counselling can be adapted from working in the individual mode to working in couples, family or group modes. For example, person-centred practitioners can work in individual, couples, family and group modes. Second, there may be special theoretical underpinnings that apply to the different modes. For example, there are many different theoretical approaches to family counselling and helping. Counsellors and helpers who work in other modes beyond working with individuals must recognize that they will almost certainly require further counselling skills to be maximally effective in each additional mode.

Research and counselling

Does counselling and psychotherapy work? If so what types of clients' problems does it work for and what skills do the counsellors and therapists require for treating these problems effectively? Furthermore, what research skills should counsellors receive training in and what is the best way to teach it? The term 'research' refers to the process of careful and systematic study or investigation into a field to establish facts, to refine hypotheses where necessary, and to reach valid conclusions. Counselling and psychotherapy research seeks to illuminate the processes and outcomes of therapy, thereby leading to better practice. Numerous methods exist for conducting **counselling research** that fall into two main categories, quantitative and qualitative. Qualitative approaches include detailed case descriptions and open-ended interviews. Quantitative approaches emphasize the systematic collection and analysis of quantitative information: for example by comparing interventions for groups of clients or by the detailed analysis of the treatment of single clients. To date, training in research skills seems to have been more a feature of counselling and clinical psychologists than of counselling. However, there are increasing calls for counsellors to be able to evaluate work scientifically and to be informed consumers of the counselling research literature (Dryden, Mearns and Thorne, 2000; McLeod, 2003).

The application of research findings to counselling and psychotherapy is complicated by the fact that there are so many different approaches to it. Furthermore, many clients have problems that do not fit neatly into research categories. Nevertheless, for over 50 years there has been a considerable effort made by psychologists, psychiatrists and others in the helping professions to try to put counselling and psychotherapy on to a sound research footing. Possibly leading the way, the American Psychological Society's Division of Clinical Psychology has promulgated 'empirically supported therapies' for various problems. However, the APA's Division of Counseling Psychology's special task group on empirically supported interventions 'found itself attracted to enunciating principles that would guide the collection and presentation of research as well as scientifically informed practice rather than stipulating criteria and ordaining constricted interventions' (Wampold, Lichtenberg and Waehler, 2002: 204). Consequently, the Division endorsed seven principles to aid in the review of evidence to support interventions rather than endorsing specific interventions: for instance the first principle was that level of specificity should be considered when evaluating outcomes.

In Britain, the Department of Health has published a document making recommendations about research into psychological therapies and counselling (Department of Health, 2001). Its most highly weighted recommendations were that: (1) post-traumatic stress symptoms may be helped by psychological therapy, with most evidence for cognitive behavioural methods; (2) depression may be treated effectively with cognitive therapy or interpersonal therapy, though a number of other brief structured therapies, such as psychodynamic therapy, may also be of benefit; and (3) **anxiety** disorders with marked symptomatic anxiety – such as panic disorder, agoraphobia, social phobia, obsessive–compulsive disorders, generalized anxiety disorders – are likely to benefit from cognitive behaviour therapy. A clear assumption of the document was that the different treatment interventions would be administered competently.

There are really three broad models for viewing the role of research in counselling practice: the **reflective practitioner** model, the scientist-professional model, and the practitioner-researcher model (Nelson-Jones, 2001). Prominent in the thinking of the British Association for Counselling and Psychotherapy has been the idea of helping students to develop as reflective practitioners. This model takes your own practice as its starting point with practitioners being researchers continually engaged in a process of making and evaluating hypotheses in how you respond to, relate to, assess and intervene with your clients. Criteria for the effectiveness of reflective practitioners include the adequacy of your hypotheses, how systematically you observe and collect data, and how assiduous you are in keeping sources of invalidity out of the way you interpret these data.

The scientist-practitioner model tends to characterize the training of clinical and counselling psychologists rather than of counsellors and psychotherapists. Both academic and practitioner values are preeminent in that the model assumes that practitioners require the skills of conducting as well as consuming research. Thus, in addition to such subjects as counselling and psychotherapy theory and skills, there is a great emphasis on students learning statistical, computer programming, research design and conducting and evaluating research project skills. Perhaps the heavy emphasis on conducting experimental research has more to do with power politics in academic institutions and psychological societies than with the practical task of educating skilled and humane counsellors and therapists. Though counselling and psychotherapy need some students trained as scientist practitioners, the reality is that most students, even those trained in psychology departments, are going to become practitioners.

A third model for linking research to counselling and psychotherapy practice is that of the practitioner-researcher. Here the main emphasis is on research as a guide to practice rather than on conducting experimental research studies. Counsellors and psychotherapists as practitioner-researchers require the skills and motivation to evaluate systematically their practice, be it with individuals, couples or groups. Where appropriate, small self-evaluative studies can be designed to this effect. In addition, practitioner-researchers require skills in order to access competently the professional and research literature regarding therapeutic processes and outcomes. However, even in those areas where empirically supported treatments exist, there may be still better ways of treating clients. In addition, empirically supported treatments do not succeed with all clients who participate in the controlled studies. Furthermore, the concerns of many clients do not fall into prescribed problem areas and the unavoidable messiness of much counselling practice does not easily lend itself to empirical research studies.

What are the training implications of the practitioner-researcher model? Two core areas in which students require research training are in how to evaluate your own work and in how to be an intelligent consumer of the counselling and psychotherapy process and outcome research literature. Another possible research training area is that of how to evaluate service delivery programmes in the interests of accountability and of making strong cases for funding. An inevitable issue is the extent to which students require statistics, computer programming and research design skills. Considerations here include the extent to which students understand this material – especially the more advanced it gets, the extent to which you will use it after your initial training, the length of training, and what gets left out of the course if more research-related content is included. Arguably, it is preferable to teach students relatively simple single case design and programme evaluation skills than train you in more advanced skills that only a small minority of students are ever likely to use afterwards. Professional associations and experts can help practitioner-researchers by providing practitioner-friendly summaries and overviews of research studies about treatments of choice for various problems, including – where necessary – treatment manuals.

Because of the mounting pressures to control the costs of providing counselling and helping services, a growing and interesting area of research is the extent to which helpers can provide competent services for particular problems more cheaply than accredited counsellors and psychotherapists. For example, nurses with thorough training and supervision in addressing specific health care problems may provide counselling help for these problems that compares favourably with that offered by accredited counsellors and psychotherapists. One reason for this is that nurses may possess years of prior experience in working with certain kinds of patients.

Activity 28.1 Counselling theory and research

1 What school(s) and approach(es) are represented in the introductory counselling skills training course that you are taking? Are you happy with this selection?
2 What do you think of each of the following approaches to incorporating research into counsellor training and counselling:
   · reflective practitioner
   · scientist-professional
   · practitioner-researcher.
3 Do you think that as either a counsellor or a helper you need to be trained in either conducting and/or consuming research? If so, what kinds of research skills should you be taught?

29

Becoming more skilled and human

CHAPTER OUTCOMES

By studying and doing the activities in this chapter you should:
- know about the importance of monitoring your counselling and helping skills;
- gain some ideas about self-help methods for maintaining and developing your skills;
- gain information about training paths for developing counselling skills;
- know more about books and journals relevant to counselling skills; and
- gain some ideas about how to develop and maintain your humanity.

Once as a counselling skills student you acquire some introductory **counselling skills**, you are challenged to become even more skilled. However, readers work in numerous contexts and roles, have widely disparate backgrounds and experience, and also differ in motivation to improve **skills**. Consequently, any suggestions for becoming more skilled need be taken in the context of individual students' evaluations of current counselling skills and also of personal agendas, work requirements and career aspirations.

Monitoring skills

The term '**reflective practitioner**' is used to describe **counsellors** and **helpers** who monitor, evaluate and think deeply about their counselling work, often with the aid of others such as supervisors and trusted colleagues. The end of an introductory counselling skills course is a good place for a participant to reflect about future practice by taking stock about where you are at present. You will have developed some ideas about how well you are getting on and which counselling skills you need to develop.

In a sense, the term introductory counselling skills is inaccurate. Possibly, it is better to think of them as fundamental skills that provide the basic toolkit for a student's helping work, especially if you **plan** to become a qualified counsellor. There is no shame in thinking about needing to improve fundamental skills: quite the contrary. High levels of **competence** can only be attained and maintained by those realistic about how hard it is to become good practitioners. Students who do not properly monitor skills, fail to realize limitations and then rush out to practice well beyond **strengths** are dangers who give counselling and helping a bad name.

Activity 29.1 asks you to evaluate your present level of competence at using the introductory counselling skills described in this book for each stage of the **Relating–Understanding–Changing (RUC) counselling and helping process model**. Depending on the length and **goals** of your introductory course, some of you will have covered more ground than others. Just as with **clients**, change for counselling skills students involves taking responsibility for developing skills, being honest about strengths and limitations, and pinpointing where change is needed. Complete the activity as best you can.

Activity 29.1 Monitoring my counselling and helping skills

Monitor your good and poor skills at using each stage of the Relating–Understanding–Changing (RUC) counselling and helping process model. For each skills area, focus on both your **mind skills** and your **communication/action skills**. In addition, when focusing on your communication/action skills, remember to assess vocal and bodily as well as verbal communication. For more **information** about specific skills areas, turn to the relevant chapters.

Stage 1 Relating

Understanding the internal frame of reference
My good skills
My poor skills
Showing attention and interest
My good skills
My poor skills
Reflecting feelings
My good skills
My poor skills
Starting the counselling and helping process
My good skills
My poor skills
*Managing **resistances** and making referrals*
My good skills
My poor skills

Stage 2 Understanding

Assessing feelings and physical reactions
My good skills
My poor skills
Assessing thinking
My good skills
My poor skills

Activity 29.1 Monitoring my counselling and helping skills – cont'd

Assessing communication and actions
My good skills
My poor skills
Providing challenges
My good skills
My poor skills
Providing feedback
My good skills
My poor skills
Self-disclosing
My good skills
My poor skills
Summarizing a client's problem situation and identifying skills
My good skills
My poor skills

Stage 3 Changing

Coaching skills: speaking, demonstrating and rehearsing
My good skills
My poor skills
Improving communication and actions
My good skills
My poor skills
Improving thinking
My good skills
My poor skills
Negotiating homework
My good skills
My poor skills
Conducting middle sessions
My good skills
My poor skills
Terminating counselling and helping
My good skills
My poor skills

1 What are your main counselling and helping skills strengths?
2 What are the main counselling and helping skills areas on which you still need to work?
3 Refer back to the relevant chapters for suggestions on how to improve specific skills and develop and implement a plan to improve your counselling and helping skills.

Becoming more skilled

Introductory counselling skills training courses differ in length, format, content and context. In addition, students on introductory courses come from a **diversity** of backgrounds and plan many different futures. Consequently, any suggestions for becoming more skilled need to be taken in the context of the evaluation of your current counselling skills and also of your personal agendas and career aspirations.

What are some of the things that you can do on your own to maintain and develop your counselling skills? You can observe and listen to demonstrations of skilled counsellors. For instance, cassettes of interviews conducted by leading counsellors and psychotherapists are available for purchase in Britain and Australia. In addition, you can purchase or hire videotapes. In Britain, films and videotapes may be hired from the British Association for Counselling and Psychotherapy. Furthermore, you may learn from written demonstrations of counselling skills. Transcripts of interviews by leading counsellors are available, sometimes accompanying cassettes. Another way you can learn from demonstration is to become clients of skilled counsellors, though probably this should not be the primary motivation for seeking counselling help.

While a whole interview approach to observing, **listening** to and reading transcripts is valuable, this is not the only way to approach the material. One option is to focus on smaller segments of interviews, say five minutes, and look out for how specific counselling skills are used. In addition to verbal communication, remember to focus on **vocal communication** and, if observing videos, on **bodily communication** as well. Furthermore, look out for the **communication patterns** between counsellors and clients as well as to how counsellors respond to single client statements.

Another option is to turn the audio or video recorder off after each client statement, form a response, and then see how the counsellor actually responded. Alternatively, when working with transcripts of a session by someone like Carl Rogers, go down the page, covering up Rogers' responses, form a response, and then check Rogers' responses. Remember that personal responses will not necessarily be inferior to those of the more famous counsellors.

Co-counselling is a form of peer activity whereby in a given time period, say an hour, each person will have a turn at being both counsellor and client. You can practise counselling skills with a colleague, possibly someone who is or was on your introductory skills training course, on a co-counselling basis using audio and video feedback where appropriate. In addition, you may be able to form or become part of a peer learning skills group in which you work with, comment on and support each other as you develop counselling skills.

Whether in informal helping contacts or in more formal counselling sessions, some of you are already using counselling skills as part of your jobs. In some settings, you may be able to monitor yourself by recording and playing back sessions, possibly in the presence of a supervisor or peers. In addition, you can be sensitive to feedback from clients. Some of this feedback will come in how clients respond to the use of counselling skills through their verbal, vocal and bodily communication. Furthermore, where appropriate, clients can be asked for feedback on how they experienced individual sessions and about their overall helping contact. Client feedback may also be gained from questionnaires.

Training paths

Where do introductory counselling skills students go next to gain more training in counselling skills? Given the diversity of introductory counselling skills courses and the different backgrounds and goals of students on them, this is a hard question to answer simply. Many of you may be in professions other than counselling, for example social work, where there may be opportunities for further training both within existing undergraduate or postgraduate courses and on in-service training courses or workshops run by professional associations and by members of them. Others of you may be working in voluntary organizations that may offer their own more advanced counselling skills training courses geared to the populations that they serve.

Those of you wishing to become counsellors or counselling psychologists should look out for accredited and/or well-regarded courses. In Britain, the British Association for Counselling and Psychotherapy annually publishes *The Training in Counselling and Psychotherapy Directory*. An Australian source of information about training opportunities is the Psychotherapy and Counselling Federation of Australia. In both Australia and Britain, the main route to becoming a counselling psychologist now is through undergraduate work in **psychology** followed by a Masters in Counselling Psychology. You can contact the relevant psychological professional associations for details of accredited courses.

Box 29.1 Professional associations in counselling and counselling psychology

Britain

Counselling and psychotherapy
British Association for Counselling and Psychotherapy
BACP House
15 St John's Business Park
Lutterworth
Leicestershire LE17 4HB
Tel: 0870 443 5252
Fax: 0870 443 5160
e-mail: bacp@bacp.co.uk
Website: www.bacp.co.uk

Counselling psychology
British Psychological Society
St Andrews House
48 Princess Road East
Leicester LE1 7DR
Tel: 0116 254 9568
Fax: 0116 247 0787
e-mail: mail@bps.org.uk
Website: www.bps.org.uk

(Continued)

Box 29.1 Professional associations in counselling and counselling psychology – cont'd

UKCP
2nd floor
Edward House
2 Wakley Street
London
EC1V 7LT
Tel:020 7014 9955
Fax: 020 7014 9977
e-mail: info@psychotherapy.org.uk
Website: www.psychotherapy.org.uk

Australia

Counselling and psychotherapy
Psychotherapy and Counselling Federation of Australia
290 Park Street
Fitzroy North
Melbourne
Victoria 3068
Tel: 03 9486 3077
Fax: 03 9486 93933
e-mail: admin@pacfa.org.au
Website: www.pacfa.org.au

Counselling psychology
College of Counselling Psychologists
Australian Psychological Society
PO Box 38
Flinders Lane Post Office
Melbourne
Victoria 8009
Tel: 03 8662 3300
Fax: 03 9663 6177
e-mail: contactus@psychology.org.au
Website: www.psychology.org.au

America
Counselling
American Counseling Association
5999 Stevenson Avenue
Alexandria
VA 22304
Tel: 800 347 6647
Fax: 800 473 2329
Website: www.counseling.org

Box 29.1 Professional associations in counselling and counselling psychology – cont'd

Counselling psychology
Society of Counselling Psychology
American Psychological Association
750 First Street
NE Washington DC 20002-4242
Tel: 800 374 2721 or 202 336 5500
Website: www.apa.org

Graduation from a counselling or counselling psychology course does not in itself mean that former students then become accredited practitioners. To obtain accreditation, you are required to accumulate a set number of hours of supervised counselling practice. Afterwards, to maintain accreditation, you may be required to have ongoing **supervision** (as with the British Association for Counselling and Psychotherapy) or regularly accumulate continuing professional development points by attending conferences, workshops and training courses (as with the Australian Psychological Society).

A distinction exists between accreditation by a professional association and mandatory registration or licensing by either a national registration board or, as in Australia, by a state registration board. In some states in Australia people cannot call themselves counselling psychologists unless certified as such by the relevant state registration board. In both Britain and Australia, the trend is towards tightening up the licensing of counsellors and counselling psychologists. The development of the United Kingdom Register of Counsellors is an important milestone on the British landscape. Since requirements are constantly updated, at an appropriate time readers should check the licensing requirements where they intend to practice that are either in force or in the pipeline.

Attending conferences, short courses and workshops can provide informal training paths whereby both counselling skills students and more experienced helpers can improve knowledge and skills. In Britain details of short courses, workshops and conferences can be found in BACP's journal *Therapy Today* and in the BPS's *The Psychologist*. In Australia, similar information can be found in the APS's journal *InPsych* and in the Society's state branch newsletters. In both countries information about short courses, workshops and conferences can be found in the newsletters and journals of other professional associations and of voluntary agencies, such as *Relate News* in Britain.

If interested in developing skills in a particular counselling approach, enquire whether there is a training centre within reasonable distance. Most major counselling approaches have international networks for training and practice. For example, agencies for specialized training in **person-centred therapy** exist in Britain and for **rational emotive behaviour therapy** in both Britain and Australia.

Books and journals

Books

There is a large theoretical literature that underpins the use of counselling skills. This can be divided into primary sources, books and articles written by the leading theorists themselves, and secondary sources, books and articles written about the different theoretical approaches by people other than their originators. Ultimately, there is no substitute for reading primary sources. However, it can be a daunting task for a beginner to know where to start and how to cover the ground. Perhaps it is better to start with a secondary source book which overviews many of the main approaches and lists primary sources that may be followed up. In the previous chapter my introductory theory textbook (2006) and those edited by Corsini and Wedding (2008) and by Dryden (2007) were recommended for this purpose. These books are readily available in Australia and New Zealand.

The bibliography at the end of this book contains many suggestions for books and articles about counselling skills. Books that cover more advanced counselling skills include my *Practical Counselling and Helping Skills* (2005) and Egan's *The Skilled Helper: A Problem Management and Opportunity-Development Approach to Helping (2007)*.

Journals

Journals provide an excellent means of keeping abreast of the counselling skills literature. Some of you are in fields such as nursing, social work and human resource management, whose professional journals may contain some articles about the use of counselling skills.

Box 29.2 provides a list of some of the main counselling and counselling psychology journals. These journals may be of interest not only to counsellors and counselling psychologists, but to those using counselling skills either as part of other jobs or on a voluntary basis. These journals mainly offer a mixture of applied practice and research articles, with the exception of the *Counselling and Psychotherapy Research* and the *Journal of Counseling Psychology*, which focus more on research.

Box 29.2 Some leading counselling and counselling psychology journals

Counselling
Australian Journal of Guidance and Counselling
British Journal of Guidance and Counselling
Counselling and Psychotherapy Journal (British Association for Counselling and Psychotherapy)
Counselling and Psychotherapy Research (British Association for Counselling and Psychotherapy)
Journal of Counseling & Development (American Association for Counseling)
International Journal for the Advancement of Counselling

Box 29.2 Some leading counselling and counselling psychology journals – cont'd

Counselling psychology
Australian Journal of Counselling Psychology (Australian Psychological Society)
Counselling Psychology Review (British Psychological Society)
Journal of Counseling Psychology (American Psychological Association)
The Counseling Psychologist (American Psychological Association)

Becoming more human

Counselling skills students face the double challenge of assuming responsibility for becoming and staying not only more skilled, but more human as well. A major theme of this book is that you cannot separate your level of functioning as a human being from how you deliver counselling skills.

Being your own client

Love begins at home. So does being a humane and **compassionate** counsellor or helper. All counselling skills students need to assume responsibility for being your own most important client. Following are some suggestions for how as a student you can help yourself to become more human and humane. You should clearly realize that using counselling skills requires both heart and head. In relating to clients it is necessary to steer a middle course between over- and under-involvement as a person.

Once committed to developing as humane counsellors and helpers, students can draw upon experiences in counselling skills training. For instance, when practising counselling skills you can attempt to come over to clients as genuinely caring. In addition, you can ask trainers, supervisors and fellow students to look out for ways in which you either strengthen or weaken the human quality of your interviewing.

Virtually all counselling skills students take time to develop the confidence and skills required for comfortable interviewing styles. If you undergo further skills training in which you gain more experience with clients, you may find yourself letting some fears go and releasing more of your potential for genuine concern and care. However, if you do not practise and are poor at reflecting on what you do, the chances are that you will remain stuck both as a human being and when using counselling skills.

When you identify ways in which you appear wooden or uncaring, you can use these as signals for exploring what is going on either within you or between you and clients that holds you back from expressing your humanity. Experienced trainers and supervisors can help you to pinpoint roadblocks and work through fears and doubts. In addition, students sometimes show excellent skills in offering each other feedback, sharing experiences and giving encouragement.

When reflecting upon the experiences of your daily life, you can also treat yourself as a client. For example, when faced with a problem situation, you can use the RUC counselling and helping process model. You can clear a space so that you can relate to yourself calmly and lovingly. Next, you can clarify and expand your understanding of what is going on in the situation and identify unhelpful thoughts and communications. Then, you can set goals, plan and implement a plan for changing unhelpful into helpful behaviours.

Personal counselling

Without becoming dependent, counselling skills students can use external resources to develop their humanity. Legg (1999) cites three reasons for counselling students undergoing therapy: personal growth, gaining empathic understanding of the client's position, and extending their experience of types of therapy. All three reasons are valid. Personal counselling can be very beneficial in **working through** blocks to being a happier, more fulfilled and humane person. It is difficult to use any counselling approach properly unless skilled at applying it to yourself. Often this is best achieved by first working as a client with a competent practitioner of the approach. Students can also consider **group counselling**, coaching and **life skills** training approaches to becoming stronger and more skilled human beings.

Counselling skills students with the experience of being a client should gain a better understanding of the client role. However, to gain genuine understanding of the process from the client's viewpoint, seeking counselling should not simply be a training experience, but grounded in other motivations based on life experience, hopes and suffering. The better that students understand the client's role, the more humanely you may be able to respond to clients' inevitable ambivalence about being in counselling and helping. You may also experience different aspects of your humanity by working with counsellors from different theoretical orientations. However, it is probably best to start with a firm grounding in one approach rather than act like a magpie hopping from one approach to another.

Staying human

It is one thing to become more human and another to stay human. There is a vast literature on **stress** and **burnout** in the counselling and helping professions. Counselling can be immensely interesting and rewarding. However, many practitioners get emotionally, mentally and physically exhausted. Feeling scarcely human themselves, they are not in a strong position to relate to clients as strong, compassionate and caring human beings. All practitioners require skills of self-care and of monitoring your fitness to practice competently and compassionately. Skills for avoiding tiredness and burnout include managing time well, assertively setting limits, developing **support networks**, and using recreational outlets that nourish and re-energize. Issues of tiredness and burnout can be addressed in supervision and, if necessary, by personal counselling.

Many factors in the modern world make it hard to hold on to being fully human. The rate of technological change is staggering. In addition, Western societies tend to be very materialistic and people may find themselves being measured by the size of their pocket books rather than the size of their hearts. Furthermore, the organizations in which some counsellors and helpers work can be big and impersonal. In addition, academic institutions with their research cultures can compartmentalize knowledge at the expense of a more balanced approach that also **values** the study of whole persons and the teaching of applied skills. Counselling skills students, counsellors and helpers require **inner strength** and the support of like-minded people to hold on to humanistic values in the face of such pressures. This is a challenge that is likely to continue into the foreseeable future.

Activity 29.2 Becoming more human

1 Which of the following potentially harmful motives for learning counselling skills apply to you? How important is each motive?
- unresolved emotional pain
- wanting to dominate and control
- seeking intimacy
- seeking sex
- possessing a victim mentality
- others not mentioned above.
2 How does your level of personal development influence how well or poorly you learn counselling skills?
3 What, if anything, do you intend to do to improve your level of personal development as you learn counselling skills?

Glossary

Acceptance Unconditional affirmation by counsellors and helpers of clients as persons.

Action skills Areas of externally observable actions in which people can make good choices, poor choices, or a mixture of both.

Active listening Accurately understanding clients' communications from their internal frames of reference and then communicating back this understanding in a language and manner attuned to their needs. More colloquially, being a good listener and then responding with understanding.

Advising Telling others how they might feel, think, communicate and act rather than letting them come to their own conclusions.

Anxiety Feelings of fear and apprehension that may be either general or associated with specific people and situations. Anxiety may be realistic and proportionate to the threat as well as unrealistic and disproportionate.

Assertive communication The ability to communicate, if necessary backed up by actions, either positive or oppositional thoughts and feelings in appropriate ways that are neither aggressive nor submissive.

Assessment Collecting and analyzing information about clients to make decisions about counselling interventions, monitor progress and to evaluate changes.

Attending behaviour Body message skills for showing attention and interest to clients.

Avoidance Thinking and acting in ways that avoid dealing directly with the realities of life, for instance by withdrawing.

Awareness Consciousness of and sensitivity to oneself, others, and the environment.

Behaviour therapy An approach that views counselling and therapy in learning terms and focuses on reducing anxiety and on altering specific behaviours.

Between session activities Activities negotiated between counsellor or helper and client designed to support and consolidate learnings taking place during sessions or contact. See *Homework skills, Monitoring*.

Bodily communication Messages that people send with their bodies: for instance, through gaze, eye contact, facial expressions, posture and gestures.

Burnout Depletion of motivation, interest, energy, resilience and, often, of effectiveness on the part of counsellors and helpers.

Careers counselling Using counselling skills to assist clients with career choice, career development and career transition decisions and issues.

Challenging Expanding clients' awareness by reflections and questions focused on actual and potential inconsistent and illogical ways of thinking and communicating. Clients can also challenge themselves.

Clarifying understanding Assisting clients to bring out into the open and become clearer about material from their internal frames of reference.

Client An inclusive term to describe all people with whom counsellors and helpers use counselling skills either in counselling sessions or in informal helping contacts.

Client-centred coaching An approach to coaching that allows clients to retain ownership of their problems, values their contributions, and draws out and builds upon their abilities to change for the better.

Client-centred counselling See *Person-centred therapy*.

Cohesive group A group in which the members are well disposed to one another and stay together to attain common goals.

Cognitive therapy An approach to counselling and therapy originated by Aaron Beck which focuses on improving clients' ability to test the accuracy and reality of their perceptions.

Communication Sending and receiving information by means of verbal, vocal, bodily, touch and/or taking action messages.

Communication patterns Ways of communication in which the counsellor or helper's and the client's verbal, vocal and bodily communication mutually influence one another to produce a degree of stability: for example, talkative counsellor – quiet client.

Communication skills Areas of externally observable communication in which people can make good, or poor choices, or a mixture of both.

Compassionate Being aware of others' suffering and acting with benevolence and care towards them.

Competence Without seeking perfection, striving for and attaining high standards of performance and of service.

Confidentiality Keeping trust with clients and fellow students by not divulging personal information about them unless granted permission. Confidentiality relates to the storage of written records and audiovisual recordings as well as to the spoken word.

Confrontation See *Challenging*.

Congruence Genuineness and lack of facade arising from awareness of one's internal processes. Communicating and acting consistently with one's thoughts and feelings.

Conscious thinking A state of possessing a present awareness of some material in the mind.

Contracting Making agreements with clients and others that may be either implicit, or verbal, or written and countersigned.

Coping Dealing with situations by managing them adequately without necessarily mastering them completely.

Coping self-talk Dimensions of coping self-talk include creating alerting, calming, coaching and affirming statements. See *Self-talk, Visualized rehearsal.*

Core conditions In the person-centred approach, in particular, but also in other approaches to counselling and helping, the core conditions of relationships with clients are empathy, unconditional positive regard, and congruence.

Core values Competence and compassion are the core values underlying ethical helping practice.

Counselling A relationship in which counsellors or helpers assist clients to understand themselves and their problems better. Where appropriate, they then use various interventions to enable clients to feel, think, communicate and act more effectively. Approaches to counselling practice differ according to theoretical orientation.

Counselling and helping process models Simplified step-by-step representations of different goals and activities at progressive stages of counselling and helping.

Counselling relationships The human connections between counsellors and clients both face to face and in one another's minds.

Counselling research Research focusing on the processes and outcomes of counselling.

Counselling schools Three major theoretical groups or counselling schools are the psychodynamic, the humanistic and the cognitive behavioural. Each school is represented by a number of different theoretical positions, though there is also overlap.

Counselling skills Counsellor- or helper-offered communication skills, accompanied by appropriate mental processes, for developing relationships with clients, clarifying and expanding their understanding, and, where appropriate, assisting them to develop and implement strategies for changing how they think, act and feel so that they can attain life-affirming goals.

Counsellor A suitably trained and qualified person who uses counselling skills in exercising the profession of counselling.

Counter-transference Negative and positive thoughts and feelings, based on unresolved areas in their own lives, which arise in counsellors and helpers towards clients.

Couples counselling Counselling two partners in a relationship either together or separately and jointly at different stages.

Crises Situations of excessive stress in which people feel that their coping resources are severely stretched or inadequate to meet the demands being made upon them.

Cross-cultural counselling/helping A counselling or helping relationship in which counsellor and client come from different cultures.

Cross-cultural sensitivity Awareness of actual and potential differences with clients from other cultures and responding carefully and respectfully where differences either are or might be concerned.

Defensive thinking See *Self-protective thinking*.

Demonstration skills Counsellor and helper skills for showing clients what to do and how to think. Demonstrations may be live, recorded, visualized or written.

Denial A self-protective process by which individuals defend themselves from unpleasant, and sometimes pleasing, aspects of themselves and of external reality by avoiding becoming aware of them.

Dependency Clients who are dependent maintain themselves by relying on support from others, for example counsellors or helpers, or from drugs rather than by relying on self-support.

Disclosing skills Counsellor and helper skills of showing involvement and sharing personal experiences. See *Self-disclosure*.

Distortion A self-protective process involving altering unpleasant or discrepant aspects of reality in order to make them less threatening and more consistent with one's existing self-concept.

Diversity Counsellors, helpers and clients may differ on numerous characteristics such as culture, race, social class and biological sex.

Dream interpretation Providing interpretations of the manifest and latent content of clients' dreams. Used in counselling approaches such as psychoanalysis and gestalt therapy.

Dual relationships In addition to their formal counselling or helping relationship, counsellors or helpers may either already be in, or consider entering in, or enter other kinds of relationships with clients: for instance, friend, lover, colleague, or trainer.

Eclecticism Basing one's counselling or helping practice on ideas and interventions drawn from more than one theoretical position.

Empathy Without losing perspective as a counsellor or helper, the capacity to experience and to comprehend accurately the client's internal frame of reference and to sensitively communicate back this understanding.

Empowering mind Developing mind skills that allow the individual to create life-affirming rather than self-defeating thoughts.

Ethical codes Rules of conduct and guidelines for counselling practice. In addition to focusing on counsellors, ethical codes can focus on training, supervision, and use of counselling skills by people who are not qualified counsellors.

Ethical dilemmas Situations requiring counsellors and helpers to make their own decisions because the ethical standards for correct conduct either conflict or are otherwise unclear.

Ethical issues Issues in counselling and helping where there are important consider-ations regarding rules of conduct, moral standards and right and wrong behaviour for different situations.

Existential therapy An approach to counselling and therapy emphasizing helping clients to take responsibility for affirming and defining their existence within the parameters of death, suffering, freedom and meaninglessness.

Expanding understanding Using questions and challenges to assist clients to understand problems more fully and to gain new perspectives on them.

Experiments Counsellors and helpers can work with clients to design and implement experiments to test the reality of expectations about changing specific communications/actions and/or thoughts.

Explanations The reasons people create for what happens in their own and in other people's lives and in their external environments.

Expectations Anticipations and predictions that people create about their futures.

External frame of reference The external viewpoints of other people, such as significant others, counsellors and helpers, rather than the subjective perceptions and experiences of clients themselves.

Facilitation Using active listening and other supportive skills to make it easy for clients to talk and to experience and explore themselves.

Family counselling Approaches to counselling and therapy that focus on relationships within families.

Feedback skills Usually refers to skills of providing feedback or information from the giver's external perspective to another person. However, the term can also refer to the skills of receiving information from another's external perspective about oneself.

Feelings Emotional processes, accompanied by physical sensations, at varying levels of awareness. People can experience, express and manage feelings.

Feminist counselling Approaches to counselling and therapy that address women's issues in the context of gender power imbalances in society.

Gay A colloquial word for people, especially males, who are homosexually oriented. People of varying degrees of bisexuality are much more common than exclusively homosexual people. See *Lesbian and gay counselling*.

Genuineness Absence of facade and of insincerity. Showing consistency between verbal, vocal, bodily, touch and/or action communications.

Gestalt therapy An approach to counselling and therapy consisting of the applica-tion of a number of techniques focused on making clients aware of how they are blocking making good contact or strong gestalts with their senses and with the environment.

Goals Implicit or explicit objectives of counselling or helping relationships and of specific interventions and client plans. Goals can relate to changing specific communications and thoughts as well as to the desired outcomes from solving problems. See *Setting progressive tasks skills*.

Group counselling The relationships, activities and skills involved in counselling three or more people at the same time.

Guilt Feelings of distress, involving self-devaluation and anxiety that result from having transgressed a code of behaviour to which one subscribes.

Habit A learned tendency to respond in a fixed way to a person or situation.

Helper An inclusive term to describe people who use counselling skills either as part of other roles or informally.

Helper's aides People in clients' home environments enlisted to support them in attaining their goals.

Helping relationships The human connections between helpers and clients both face to face and in one another's minds.

Homework skills Skills and formats for negotiating and helping clients to complete homework assignments.

Inhibition Inadequately acknowledging and/or weakening and restraining demonstrating one's feelings, thoughts, communications and actions.

'I' statements Owning and directly stating what one feels and thinks, starting with the words 'I feel ... ' or 'I think ... '.

Immediacy Counsellor or helper and, possibly, client comments that focus on the 'here and now' of their relationship, perhaps by focusing on what either is or has previously been left unsaid. Sometimes expressed as 'you–me' talk.

Information Material relevant to clients' concerns and decisions either that they may seek out for themselves or which may be provided by counsellors or helpers: for example, careers information.

Inner strength Mental development and toughness involving a high level of competence in the different mind skills and a capacity to deal with reality honestly.

Internal frame of reference The subjective perceptions and experiences of an individual rather than an external viewpoint of other people.

Interpretation Explanations from counsellors' or helpers' internal frames of reference of clients' feelings, thoughts, dreams and communications.

Lesbian and gay counselling Using counselling skills to address problems and issues attached to clients being lesbian or gay.

Life skills Sequences of choices that people make in specific skills areas necessary for effective living, for instance the various mind skills and communication skills required for relating well to others.

Listening Attentively hearing and showing speakers that they have been accurately understood. Not only receiving sounds, but accurately understanding their meaning from vocal and bodily as well as verbal communication.

Medication Medically prescribed drugs used independently or in conjunction with helping.

Men's counselling Counselling focused on developing the human potential of men by freeing them from gender-stereotyped feeling, thinking and communication.

Mental development Entails acquiring, maintaining and developing mind skills for the purposes of inner strength and of communicating and acting effectively.

Mental relaxation A counselling and helping as well as a self-help intervention whereby clients are helped to relax by imagining one or more scenes conducive to relaxation.

Micro-skills approach An approach to training in which single communication skills of the counselling process are identified and taught first separately and then together.

Middle session skills Counsellor and helper skills for the starting, working and ending phases of middle sessions.

Mind The psychological manifestation of the human brain. The seat of awareness and thought that is capable of thinking about thinking.

Mind skills Areas for mental processing in which people can make good choices, poor choices, or a mixture of both.

Mindfulness of breathing A meditative practice in which the client concentrates on the natural flow of the breath to establish concentrated awareness.

Modelling Demonstrating specific communications, thoughts and mental processes so that clients may learn from observation.

Monitoring Counsellors, helpers and clients observing and possibly recording the occurrence of clients' feelings, thoughts and/or communications either inside of or outside of sessions. In addition, counsellors and helpers can monitor their own skills.

Open-ended questions Questions that allow clients freedom of choice in how to respond rather than curtail their options.

Opening statements Counsellor or helper statements at the start of initial and subsequent sessions. When starting counselling or helping, brief opening remarks that give clients permission to talk and tell why they have come.

Paraphrasing Expressing the same meaning of another's statements or series of statements in different words.

Partner skills The mind skills and communication skills required for creating happiness in close personal relationships.

Perceptions Thoughts, of varying degrees of accuracy, which the mind creates about oneself, others and the environment.

Person-centred therapy An approach to counselling and therapy formulated by Carl Rogers that lays great stress on the primacy of clients' subjective experiences and on helping them to release their unique actualizing tendencies. Rogers considered a warm, respectful, empathic and genuine helping relationship necessary and sufficient for therapeutic change to occur.

Personal responsibility The process of making the choices that maximize one's happiness and fulfilment. Assuming responsibility for the authorship of one's life and for dealing with problems and problem situations.

Physical reactions Bodily changes that accompany feelings.

Plan A step-by-step outline, either verbal or written, of the specific actions necessary to attain a client's or one's own goals.

Preconscious thinking Thoughts that can be brought into awareness relatively easily.

Preferential rules Rules, beliefs or self-standards based on rational and emotional preferences rather than on rigid and childish demands.

Problem ownership The degree to which clients and/or counsellors/helpers assume responsibility for resolving clients' problems and problem situations.

Problem situations Problem situations are specific situations, often within larger problems, where people experience difficulty in coping and in reaching satisfactory solutions.

Problematic skills Poor mind skills and poor communication/action skills that create and sustain problems and problem situations.

Progressive muscular relaxation A counselling/helping intervention in which clients are taught to relax by sequentially tensing and relaxing various muscle groupings. Sometimes also combined with mental relaxation involving imagining restful scenes.

Psychiatry The branch of medicine dealing with understanding, treating and preventing mental disorders.

Psychoanalysis An approach to counselling and therapy originated by Sigmund Freud that emphasizes making clients' unconscious thinking conscious, for instance by interpreting dreams.

Psychodrama A primarily group approach to counselling and therapy that involves clients participating in dramatic enactments of scenes for which the relevance to their lives and problems is then discussed.

Psychology The science and study of human behaviour.

Psychosis Severe mental disorder involving loss of contact with reality and usually characterized by delusions and/or hallucinations.

Psychotherapy Often used interchangeably with counselling. May have connotations of moderately to severely disturbed clients seen in medical setting, but not necessarily so. It is more accurate to speak of the psychotherapies since there are many theoretical and practical approaches to psychotherapy.

Questions Sentences worded or expressed to seek information: for instance, about specific details of problems or problem situations, personal meanings, and about client strengths.

Rational emotive behaviour therapy An approach to counselling and therapy originated by Albert Ellis in which counsellors and helpers assist clients to dispute demanding beliefs and to replace them with preferential beliefs.

Reality-testing perceptions Testing how closely perceptions based on inference accord to available facts and whether there are more accurate ways of viewing oneself, other people, problems and problem situations.

Reality therapy A form of counselling and therapy originated by William Glasser that sees people as control systems who need to acknowledge reality as a basis for responsible behaviour that will enable them to fulfil their needs for love and worth and thus attain a success identity.

Records Counsellors and helpers may keep records focused on initial assessment, progress during helping, and termination details. Clients may also keep records of their progress both in general and in terms of specific thoughts and behaviours.

Referral skills Counsellor and helper skills for referring clients to other people who may be in a better position to assist them. Referral skills include both knowing when not to refer and when to refer the client's problem for discussion with an appropriate person rather than the client.

Reflecting feelings Feeling and accurately understanding the flow of another's emotions and experiencing and sensitively communicating this understanding back to them.

Reflective practitioner A counsellor or helper who monitors, evaluates and reflects deeply about her/his counselling work, often with the assistance of supervisors and trusted colleagues.

Regard Non-possessive liking or prizing of another, for example the client. Unconditional acceptance of another as a person. See *Unconditional positive regard*.

Rehearsing skills Counsellor and helper skills, such as role playing, for rehearsing clients in changing specific communications and thoughts. Clients can also use rehearsing skills on their own. See *Visualized rehearsal*.

Relating–Understanding–Changing (RUC) model A three stage Relating–Understanding–Changing counselling and helping process model for managing problem situations and problems better.

Relaxation Either a restful state or one of numerous approaches to gaining that state: for instance imagining restful scenes. See *Progressive muscular relaxation*.

Reluctance Either unwillingness or disinclination on the part of potential or actual clients to enter into the counselling/helping process.

Resistance Any feelings, thoughts and communications on the part of clients that frustrate and prevent them from participating effectively in the counselling/helping process. Behaviour that impedes, slows down or stops the counselling/helping process.

Reward skills Counsellor, helper and client skills include identifying suitable rewards. Client skills include self-administering both external and internal rewards.

Role playing Engaging in simulated enactments for understanding clients' problems and problem situations better and for rehearsing changed communications and thoughts. See *Rehearsing skills, Visualized rehearsal.*

Rules The standards people have for themselves, others and the environment. Rules vary in how demanding or how preferential they are.

Schizophrenia A psychosis characterized by the disintegration of personality, emotional withdrawal and disorders of feelings, perception and communication.

Self-acceptance Accepting oneself as a person while remaining aware of one's strengths and limitations.

Self-awareness Being aware of one's significant thoughts, feelings and experiences and of the impact that one makes on others.

Self-concept The ways in which people see themselves and to which they attach terms like 'I' or 'me'.

Self-disclosure Revealing feelings and sharing personal information, especially by intentional verbal communication.

Self-helping The ultimate aim of all counselling and helping is to assist clients to develop thoughts and communications whereby they can help themselves.

Self-protective thinking The processes by which people deny and distort information at variance with their conceptions of self when this information threatens their feelings of adequacy and worth.

Self-talk What people say to themselves before, during or after specific situations.

Self-worth Sense of adequacy, positive or negative evaluation of oneself as a person.

Session agendas Agreements between counsellors or helpers and clients, usually near the beginning of sessions, on what tasks will be addressed during them and in what order. Session agendas can be developed or amended during sessions.

Setting progressive tasks skills Counsellor and helper skills for assisting clients to break situations down and set themselves progressively more difficult goals and tasks as steps towards attaining their ultimate goal.

Skills Skills can be defined by area, level or competence, and by the sequences of choices they entail.

Small verbal rewards Brief expressions of interest designed to encourage another to continue talking.

Social rules The implicit and explicit rules of conduct that vary according to the social contexts in which communication takes place.

Speaking skills When coaching, these skills include counsellors and helpers preparing clear content and then communicating it by using good vocal and body delivery.

STC framework A Situation–Thoughts–Consequences framework for analyzing the relationships between how people think, feel, physically react and communicate/act. The framework can be used to analyze the effect of mind skills as well as thoughts.

Strengths Areas of thinking and communication/actions in which clients possess good skills. See *Inner strength*.

Stress Perceived demands on one's energy and coping abilities.

Stress tolerance The level of stress or cumulative amount of stressors that an individual can tolerate before experiencing distinct physiological and psychological distress.

Structuring The verbal, vocal and bodily communications used by counsellors and helpers to explain to clients what is going on and what their respective roles are at the start of, during and at the end of the overall counselling or helping process.

Study skills Skills for learning efficiently and for getting the most out of studying: for example, reading skills, report-writing skills, and test-taking skills.

Summarizing Pulling together, clarifying and reflecting back in more succinct form a series of client statements either during a discussion unit, at the end of a discussion unit, or at either the beginning or end of counselling/helping sessions. Sometimes clients are asked to summarize.

Supervision Counselling and helping supervisions can differ regarding goals, formats and how material gets presented, for example either by videotape or by role playing.

Support networks Networks of people available to provide strength and encouragement to one another, especially when in difficulty.

Supportive counselling and helping Offering clients a relationship in which they get understood and affirmed when they feel that some extra support might assist them through an awkward phase in their lives or help them make a difficult decision better.

Supports In clients' home environments people who can support their efforts to attain communication, action and thinking goals.

Taking action communication Messages people send when not face to face with one another through their actions, for instance sending flowers or tidying the house.

Telephone counselling Counselling and helping clients on the phone, often used in helping clients in crisis, for instance the work of the Samaritans.

Tension Feeling mentally and physically stretched and under strain.

Termination The ending of counselling or helping sessions and relationships.

Tests Psychological tests are ways of gathering information about people by taking objective and standardized measures of samples of their behaviour. Tests can also be used to explore subjective reality.

Thinking difficulties Ways of thinking that cause clients to have negative emotions and to communicate and act less effectively than they might otherwise do.

Threat A perception of either real or imagined danger.

Timetabling skills Include client skills for timetabling daily activities, minimum goals, personal space, and keeping contracts.

Timing The 'when' of making counsellor, helper and client responses and of implementing interventions.

Touch communication Messages that people send by touching one another.

Transactional analysis An approach to counselling and therapy, originated by Eric Berne, based on the analysis of 'Parent', 'Adult' and 'Child' ego states in interpersonal transactions.

Transference The process by which clients transfer feelings, perceptions and communications applicable to previous relationships on to their counsellors and helpers: emphasized in psychoanalysis.

Transition statements Counsellor or helper statements that move or suggest moving the content of a session from one topic area to another or from one phase of the session to another.

Transitions Changes that people undergo during the course of their lives: for example, the birth of a first child or retirement.

Tunnel vision A narrowing of perception under threat so that the individual focuses only on certain factors in a situation and excludes others which may be important.

Unconditional positive regard Consists of two dimensions: first, prizing and feeling positively towards clients and, second, non-judgmental acceptance of clients' experiencing and disclosures as their subjective reality.

Unconscious thinking Thinking that is beneath the level of conscious awareness and frequently inadmissible to consciousness because of the anxiety it generates.

Unfinished business Unexpressed and, possibly, insufficiently acknowledged and worked through thoughts and feelings that can negatively affect current functioning.

Unrealistic standards Standards for behaviour and self-evaluation which are dysfunctional in helping individuals to cope with their lives and meet their physiological and psychological needs. Usually in counselling and helping, but not always, clients' standards are too high rather than too low.

Values The underlying beliefs or philosophies by which people lead their lives.

Visual images The pictures that people create in their minds.

Visualized rehearsal Rehearsing desired communications and actions in imagination prior to enacting them. This usually also involves rehearsing accompanying coping self-talk.

Vocal communication Messages that people send through the voice: for instance, volume, articulation, pitch, emphasis and speech rate.

Voluntary counselling Use of counselling skills by counsellors and helpers in unpaid capacities, frequently under the auspices of primarily voluntary and non-profit agencies, such as Relate in Britain or Relationships Australia.

Vulnerability Being psychologically at risk, especially when faced with negative occurrences and feedback. A tendency to contribute to, if not cause, one's own difficulties.

Withdrawal Mentally, emotionally and/or physically retreating or pulling back from situations and experiences.

Working alliance Collaboration between counsellor or helper and client to achieve the goals of counselling and helping.

Working through Facing up to a feeling, problem or decision and mentally working on it until a satisfactory resolution is reached.

References

American Psychiatric Association (2000) *Quick Reference to the Diagnostic Criteria from DSM-IV-TR.* Washington, DC: APA.

Argyle, M. (1999) *The Psychology of Interpersonal Behaviour,* 5th edn. London: Penguin Books.

Australian Bureau of Statistics (2006) *Australian Demographic Statistics, June 2006.* Canberra: Australian Bureau of Statistics.

Bandura, A. (1986) *Social Foundations of Thought and Action: A Social Cognitive Theory.* Englewood Cliffs, NJ: Prentice Hall.

Barrett-Lennard, G. T. (1998) *Carl Rogers' Helping System: Journey and Substance.* London: Sage.

Beck, A.T. (1976) *Cognitive Therapy and the Emotional Disorders.* New York: New American Library.

Beck, A.T. (1988) *Love is Never Enough: How Couples Can Overcome Misunderstandings, Resolve Conflicts, and Solve Relationship Problems Through Cognitive Therapy.* New York: Harper and Row.

Beck, A.T., Rush, A. J., Shaw, B. F. and Emery, G. (1979) *Cognitive Therapy of Depression.* New York: John Wiley.

Beck, A. T. and Weishaar, M. E. (2008) 'Cognitive therapy', in R. J. Corsini and D. Wedding (eds), *Current Psychotherapies,* 8th edn. Belmont, CA: Thomson Brooks/Cole. pp. 263–94.

Blatner, A. (2005) 'Psychodrama', in R. J. Corsini and D. Wedding (eds), *Current Psychotherapies,* 7th edn. Belmont, CA: Thomson Brooks/Cole. pp. 405–38.

Bond, T. (2000) *Standards and Ethics for Counselling in Practice,* 2nd edn. London: Sage.

Bond, T. (2006) 'Ethical codes and guidelines', in C. Feltham and I. Horton (eds), *The Sage Handbook of Counselling and Psychotherapy.* London: Sage. pp.177–83.

Burns, D. D. and Spangler, D. L. (2000) 'Does psychotherapy homework lead to improvements in depression in cognitive-behavioral therapy or does improvement lead to homework compliance?', *Journal of Consulting and Clinical Psychology,* 68: 46–56.

Corey, M. S. and Corey, G. (2003) *Becoming a Helper,* 4th edn. Belmont, CA: Wadsworth.

Cormier, S. and Nurius, P. S. (2002) *Interviewing and Change Strategies for Helpers: Fundamental Skills and Cognitive Behavioral Interventions,* 5th edn. Belmont, CA: Thomson Brooks/Cole.

Corsini, R. J. and Wedding, D. (eds) (2008) *Current Psychotherapies,* 8th edn. Belmont, CA: Thomson Brooks/Cole.

Department of Health (2001) *Treatment Choice in Psychological Therapies and Counselling: Evidence Based Clinical Practice Guideline. Brief Version.* London: Crown Copyright.

Department of Immigration and Multicultural Affairs (1997) *Australia's Population Trends and Prospects 1996.* Canberra: Department of Immigration and Multicultural Affairs.

Division 44/Committee of Lesbian, Gay, and Bisexual Concerns Joint Task Force (2000) 'Guidelines for psychotherapy with lesbian, gay, and bisexual clients', *American Psychologist*, 55: 1440–51.

Dryden, W. (1991) *A Dialogue with Arnold Lazarus: 'It Depends'.* Milton Keynes: Open University Press.

Dryden, W. (ed.) (2007) *Dryden's Handbook of Individual Therapy*, 5th edn. London: Sage.

Dryden, W. and Feltham, C. (1992) *Brief Counselling: A Practical Guide for Beginning Practitioners.* Buckingham: Open University Press.

Dryden, W., Horton, I. and Mearns, D. (1995) *Issues in Professional Counsellor Training.* London: Cassell.

Dryden, W., Mearns, D. and Thorne, B. (2000) 'Counselling in the United Kingdom: past, present and future', *British Journal of Guidance & Counselling*, 28: 467–83.

Egan, G. (2007) *The Skilled Helper: A Problem-Management and Opportunity-Development Approach to Helping*, 8th edn. Belmont, CA: Thomson Brooks/Cole.

Ekman, P., Friesen, W. V. and Ellsworth, P. (1972) *Emotions in the Human Face.* New York: Pergamon Press.

Elliott, R. (1985) 'Helpful and nonhelpful events in brief counseling interviews: an empirical taxonomy', *Journal of Counseling Psychology*, 32: 307–22.

Ellis, A. (2001) *Feeling Better, Getting Better, Staying Better: Profound Self-Help Therapy For Your Emotions.* Atascadero, CA: Impact Publishers.

Ellis, A. (2003) *Ask Albert Ellis? Straight Answers and Sound Advice from America's Best-Known Psychologist.* Atascadero, CA: Impact Publishers.

Ellis, A. (2008) 'Rational emotive behaviour therapy', in R. J. Corsini and D. Wedding (eds), *Current Psychotherapies*, 8th edn. Belmont, CA: Thomson Brooks/Cole. pp. 187–222.

Fischer, R. L. (1972) *Speak to Communicate: An Introduction to Speech.* Encino, CA: Dickenson Publishing Company.

Fortune, L. and Watts, M. (2000) 'Examining supervision: comparing the beliefs of those who deliver and those who receive', *Counselling Psychology Review*, 15(3): 5–15.

Gask, K. (2006) 'Population review of 2004 and 2005: England and Wales', *Population Trends,* Winter: 8–15.

Geldard, D. and Geldard, K. (2005) *Basic Personal Counselling: a Training Manual for Counsellors*, 5th edn. Frenchs Forest, NSW: Pearson Education Australia.

Goldfried, M. R. (2001) 'Integrating gay, lesbian and bisexual issues into mainstream psychology', *American Psychologist*, 56: 977–88.

Goss, S. and Anthony, K. (eds) (2003) *Technology in Counselling and Psychotherapy: A Practitioner's Guide.* Basingstoke: Palgrave Macmillan.

Greenberger, D. and Padesky, C. A. (1995) *Mind Over Mood: Change How You Feel by Changing the Way You Think.* New York: Guilford.

Harris, A. H. S., Thoresen, C. E. and Lopez, S. L. (2007) 'Integrating positive psychology into counseling: why and (when appropriate) how', *Journal of Counseling & Development*, 85: 3–13.

Haskey, J. (2002) 'One parent families – and the dependent children living in them – in Great Britain', *Population Trends*, 109: 46–57.

Horton, I. (2006) 'Structuring work with clients', in C. Feltham and I. Horton (eds), *The Sage Handbook of Counselling and Psychotherapy*, 2nd edn. London: Sage. pp. 118–25.

Kazdin, A. E. (1994) *Behavior Modification in Applied Settings*, 5th edn. Pacific Grove, CA: Brooks/Cole.

Kelly, E. W. (1995) 'Counselor values: a national survey', *Journal of Counseling & Development*, 73: 648–53.

King, M. (1963) *Strength to Love*. Philadelphia, PA: Fortress Press.

Kocet, M. M. (2006) 'Ethical challenges in a complex world: highlights of the 2005 ACA Code of Ethics', *Journal of Counseling & Development*, 84: 228–34.

Ladany, N., Constantine, M. G., Miller, K., Erickson, C. D. and Muse-Burke, J. L. (2000) 'Supervisor countertransference: a qualitative investigation into its identification and description', *Journal of Counseling Psychology*, 47: 102–15.

Lazarus, A. A. (1993) 'Tailoring the therapeutic relationship, or being an authentic chameleon', *Psychotherapy*, 3: 404–7.

Lazarus, A. A. (2008) 'Multimodal therapy', in R. J. Corsini and D. Wedding (eds), *Current Psychotherapies*, 8th edn. Belmont, CA: Thomson Brooks/Cole: pp. 368–401.

Legg, C. (1999) 'Getting the most out of personal therapy', in R. Bor and M. Watts (eds), *The Trainee Handbook: A Guide for Counselling and Therapy Trainees*. London: Sage. pp. 131–45.

Lewinsohn, P. M., Munoz, R. F., Youngren, M. A. and Zeiss, A. M. (1986) *Control Your Depression* (rev. edn). New York: Prentice Hall Press.

Lindsay, G. and Clarkson, P. (1999) 'Ethical dilemmas of psychotherapists', *The Psychologist*, 12: 182–5.

Locke, E. A. and Latham, G. P. (2002) 'Building a practically useful theory of goal setting and task motivation: a 35-year odyssey', *American Psychologist*, 57: 705–17.

MacPhillamy, D. J. and Lewinsohn, P. M. (1982) 'The Pleasant Events Schedule: studies on reliability, validity and scale intercorrelation', *Journal of Consulting and Clinical Psychology*, 50: 363–80.

Mahrer, A. R., Fairweather, D. R., Passey, S., Gingras, N. and Boulet, D. B. (1999) 'The promotion and use of strong feelings in psychotherapy', *Journal of Humanistic Psychology*, 39: 189–202.

McLeod, J. (2003) *Doing Counselling Research*, 2nd edn. London: Sage.

Mearns, D. (2003) *Developing Person-Centred Counselling*. London: Sage.

Mearns, D. and Cooper, M. (2005) *Working at Relationship Depth in Counselling and Psychotherapy*. London: Sage.

Mearns, D. and Thorne, B. (2007) *Person-Centred Counselling in Action*, 3rd edn. London: Sage.

Montgomery, B. (2006) 'The keys to successful behaviour change', *InPsych*, 28(6): 18–19.

Moodley, R. (2007) '(Re)placing multiculturalism in counselling and psychotherapy', *British Journal of Guidance & Counselling*, 35: 1–21.

Nelson-Jones, R. (2001) 'Counsellors, psychotherapists and research', *Counselling and Psychotherapy Journal*, 12(2): 6–9.

Nelson-Jones, R. (2003) 'Skilling the client: an important concept for counselling psychologists', *Counselling Psychology Review*, 18(2): 3–11.

Nelson-Jones, R. (2005) *Practical Counselling and Helping Skills*, 5th edn. London: Sage.

Nelson-Jones, R. (2006) *The Theory and Practice of Counselling and Therapy*, 4th edn. London: Sage.

Nelson-Jones, R. (2008) *Basic Counselling Skills: A Helper's Manual,* 2nd edn. London: Sage.

Office for National Statistics (2002) 'Annual update: marriages and divorces during 2000, and adoptions in 2001: England and Wales', *Population Trends*, 109: 100–4.

Padesky, C. A. and Greenberger, D. (1995) *Clinician's Guide to Mind Over Mood*. New York: Guilford Press.

Persons, J. B., Roberts, N. A and Zalecki, C. A. (2003) 'Anxiety and depression change together during treatment,' *Behavior Therapy*, 34: 149–63.

Pointon, C. (2006) 'Positive psychology', *Therapy*, 17(5): 4–7.

Poon, D., Nelson-Jones, R. and Caputi, P. (1993) 'Asian students' perceptions of culture-sensitive and culture-neutral counselling', *The Australian Counselling Psychologist*, 9: 3–16.

Price, C. A. (2000) *Australians: Who on Earth are We?* Deakin, ACT: Charles Price.

Psychotherapy & Counselling Federation of Australia (2006) *Professional Standards 2006*. Melbourne: PACFA.

Raskin, N.J., Rogers, C. R. and Witty, M. C. (2008) 'Client-centered therapy', in R. J. Corsini and D. Wedding (eds), *Current Psychotherapies*, 8th edn. Belmont, CA: Thomson Brooks/Cole. pp. 141–86.

Rogers, C. R. (1957) 'The necessary and sufficient conditions of therapeutic personality change', *Journal of Consulting Psychology,* 21: 95–103.

Rogers, C. R. (1961) *On Becoming a Person*. Boston: Houghton Mifflin.

Rogers, C. R. (1965) 'Client-centred therapy' (16 mm film of interview with 'Gloria'), in E. Shostrom (ed.), *Three Approaches to Psychotherapy*. Santa Ana, CA: Psychological Films Inc.

Rogers C. R. (1975) 'Empathic: an unappreciated way of being', *The Counseling Psychologist*, 5: 2–10.

Rokeach, M. (1967) *Value Survey*. Palo Alto, CA: Consulting Psychologists Press.

Rokeach, M. and Ball-Rokeach, S. J. (1989) 'Stability and change in American value priorities, 1968–81', *American Psychologist*, 44: 775–84.

Schwartz, S. Z. (1992) 'Universals in the content and structure of values: theoretical advances and empirical tests in 20 countries', *Advances in Experimental Psychology*, 25: 1–65.

Schwartz, S. H. and Bilsky, W. (1990) 'Toward a theory of the universal structure and content of human values: extensions and cross-cultural replications', *Journal of Personality and Social Psychology*, 53: 550–62.

Seligman, M. (2002) *Authentic Happiness: Using the New Positive Psychology to Realize Your Potential for Lasting Fulfillment*. New York: Free Press.

Selye, H. (1974) *Stress Without Distress*. Sevenoaks: Hodder & Stoughton.

Sexton, J. and Legg, C. (1999) 'Psychopharmacology: a primer', in R. Bor and M. Watts (eds), *The Trainee Handbook: A Guide for Counselling and Psychotherapy Trainees*. London: Sage. pp. 201–18.

Sichel, J. and Ellis, A. (1984) *RET Self-Help Form*. New York: Institute for Rational-Emotive Therapy.

Strong, S. R. (1968) 'Counseling: an interpersonal influence process', *Journal of Counseling Psychology*, 15: 215–224.

Strong, S. R., Welsh, J. A., Cocoran, J. L. and Hoyt, W. T. (1992) 'Social psychology and counseling psychology: the history, products, and promise of an interface', *Journal of Counseling Psychology*, 39: 139–157.

Strong, S. R., Yoder, B. and Cocoran, J. (1995) 'Counseling: a social process for constructing personal powers', *The Counseling Psychologist*, 23: 374–384.

Sue, D. W. and Sue, D. (2003) *Counselling the Culturally Diverse: Theory and Practice*, 4th edn. New York: John Wiley & Sons.

Thitavanno, P. (2002) *A Buddhist Way of Mental Training*. Bangkok: Chuan Printing Press.

Thurman, I (2006) 'Population estimates mid-2005', *Population Trends*, Winter, 3.

Tyrrell, K. (ed.) (2001) *Annual Abstract of Statistics: 2001 Edition United Kingdom*. London: the Stationary Office.

US Census Bureau (2001/2002) *Census News Releases*. www.census.gov

Wallace, B. A and Shapiro, S. L. (2006), 'Mental balance and well-being: building bridges between Buddhism and western psychology', *American Psychologist*, 61: 690–701.

Walsh, R. W. and Shapiro, S. L. (2006) 'The meeting of meditative disciplines and western psychology: a mutually enriching dialogue', *American Psychologist*, 61: 227–39.

Wampold, B. E., Lichtenberg, J. W. and Waehler, C. A. (2002) 'Principles of empirically supported interventions in counseling psychology', *The Counseling Psychologist*, 30: 197–217.

Watkins, C. E. (1990) 'The effects of counselor self-disclosure: a research review', *The Counseling Psychologist*, 18: 477–500.

Westbrook, D. and Kirk, J. (2005). 'The clinical effectiveness of cognitive behaviour therapy: outcome for a large sample of adults treated in routine practice', *Behaviour Research and Therapy*, 43: 1243–61.

Weston, R., Qu, L. and Soriano, G. (2001) 'Ageing yet diverse: the changing shape of Australia's population', *Australian Family Briefing No. 10*. Melbourne: Australian Institute of Family Studies.

Wolpe, J. (1990) *The Practice of Behavior Therapy*, 4th edn. Oxford: Pergamon.

Name Index

Subject Index

The Qualitative Research Kit

Edited by Uwe Flick

Read sample chapters online now!

Doing Ethnographic and Observational Research — Michael Angrosino

Using Visual Data in Qualitative Research — Marcus Banks

Doing Focus Groups — Rosaline Barbour

Designing Qualitative Research — Uwe Flick

Managing Quality in Qualitative Research — Uwe Flick

Analyzing Qualitative Data — Graham Gibbs

Doing Interviews — Steinar Kvale

Doing Conversation, Discourse and Document Analysis — Tim Rapley

The SAGE Qualitative Research Kit
Edited by Uwe Flick

www.sagepub.co.uk